CAMBRIDGE TEXTS IN
HISTORY OF PHILOSO

D0721057

═══

ARISTOTLE
Nicomachean Ethics

CAMBRIDGE TEXTS IN THE
HISTORY OF PHILOSOPHY

Series editors

KARL AMERIKS
Professor of Philosophy at the University of Notre Dame

DESMOND M. CLARKE
Professor of Philosophy at University College Cork

The main objective of Cambridge Texts in the History of Philosophy is to expand the range, variety and quality of texts in the history of philosophy which are available in English. The series includes texts by familiar names (such as Descartes and Kant) and also by less well-known authors. Wherever possible, texts are published in complete and unabridged form, and translations are specially commissioned for the series. Each volume contains a critical introduction together with a guide to further reading and any necessary glossaries and textual apparatus. The volumes are designed for student use at undergraduate and postgraduate level and will be of interest not only to students of philosophy, but also to a wider audience of readers in the history of science, the history of theology and the history of ideas.

For a list of titles published in the series, please see end of book.

ARISTOTLE

Nicomachean Ethics

TRANSLATED AND EDITED BY

ROGER CRISP

St Anne's College, Oxford

CAMBRIDGE
UNIVERSITY PRESS

CAMBRIDGE UNIVERSITY PRESS
Cambridge, New York, Melbourne, Madrid, Cape Town, Singapore, São Paulo

Cambridge University Press
The Edinburgh Building, Cambridge CB2 8RU, UK

Published in the United States of America by Cambridge University Press, New York

www.cambridge.org
Information on this title: www.cambridge.org/9780521632218

First published 2000
Ninth printing 2006

Printed in the United Kingdom at the University Press, Cambridge

A catalogue record for this publication is available from the British Library

Library of Congress Cataloguing in Publication data
Aristotle.
[Nicomachean ethics. English]
Nicomachean ethics / Aristotle: translated and edited by Roger Crisp.
p.   cm. - (Cambridge texts in the history of philosophy)
Includes index.
ISBN 0 521 63221 8
I. Ethics.   I. Crisp, Roger, 1961– .   II. Title.   III. Series.
B430.A5C7513   2000
171'.3-dc21   99-36947   CIP

ISBN-13 978-0-521-63221-8 hardback
ISBN-10 0-521-63221-8 hardback
ISBN-13 978-0-521-63546-2 paperback
ISBN-10 0-521-63546-2 paperback

Contents

Acknowledgements

Several friends and colleagues have offered helpful advice and comments on parts of this translation. I wish here to thank the following: Elizabeth Ashford, Lesley Brown, Troels Engberg-Pedersen, R. M. Hare, Rosalind Hursthouse, Christopher Kirwan, Christopher Megone, Dominic Scott, Robert Wardy, and David Wiggins. Errors that remain are, of course, my own responsibility, and I would be grateful to be informed of them. I am obliged also to Will Allan for help with literary references, and to Desmond Clarke for his encouragement and for his comments on the penultimate draft of the translation. First drafts were completed during a British Academy Postdoctoral Research Fellowship held at University College, Oxford, 1989–91. I am grateful to both institutions for their support.

someone who is performing just actions is *already* just?' Aristotle resolves this puzzle by pointing out that if an agent is virtuous he will perform virtuous actions in the correct way: knowing what he is doing, choosing them for their own sake, and doing them from a well-grounded disposition (II.4, 1105a).

The second condition provides a link between Aristotle's view and that of the German philosopher Immanuel Kant (1724–1804). According to Kant, in his *Groundwork of the Metaphysics of Morals*, moral worth attaches to an action only to the extent that it is motivated by respect for the moral law. Some have taken exception to this claim, suggesting not only that moral worth can lie in other motivations, such as love, but that pure respect for duty is itself sometimes out of place. Aristotle here tells us that a virtuous person will choose virtuous actions for their own sake. Elsewhere, he says that he will choose them for the sake of 'the noble', and we can plausibly see choosing an action for its own sake as equivalent to choosing it for the sake of the noble. Again, as with Kant, there is no reference to love of others. But we should not forget Aristotle's account of friendship, which does allow for the concern one person may have for another (see below).

Virtues, then, are dispositions engendered in us through practice or habituation. The notions of excess and deficiency, which play such an important part in Aristotle's account of the virtues, are first introduced in connection with the notion of habituation (II.2, 1104a). In the case of healthy eating, for example, getting into the habit of eating too much or of eating too little will ruin one's health. Aristotle compares someone who is afraid of everything to someone who is afraid of nothing, and this kind of comparison has led some commentators to think he is offering us a quantitative account, according to which virtue is to be captured in, for example, being afraid of a middling number of things. But Aristotle's thinking is clearly prescriptive or normative: the brave person is the one who stands firm against terrifying situations, when he should, for the right reasons, and so on.

We should bear this in mind also when seeking to understand the notion that, in the case of virtue, the relevant mean is relative to us. Some have been tempted to think that Aristotle is here allowing the character we already have to influence what virtue requires of us. If I am a highly irascible person, for instance, the mean relative to me, when you are slightly late for an unimportant meeting with me, might be merely to hurl a book in your direction, an action in between glowering at you and physically assaulting you, both of which I have been known to do in similar situations. But this cannot be the correct interpretation of Aristotle, since the right action in any situation is that which the virtuous person would do. What Aristotle means is that what is morally required is what the virtuous person would do in our circumstances – if he, for example, was as rich as we were, since what is generous in any case depends on the resources one possesses (IV.1, 1120b).

What, then, is the 'doctrine of the mean'? In II.6, 1106b, Aristotle says that we can feel fear, for example, either too much or too little, but that having fear at the right time, of the right things, and so on is 'the mean and best'. But how are we to understand feeling fear at the right time as in a mean? Again we have to remember the normative nature of the doctrine. No one should be fearless, since there are some things one should fear. Likewise, there are things one should not fear. There are, then, two directions in which we may go wrong: feeling fear at the right time is in between not feeling fear at the right time, and feeling fear at the wrong time.

This analysis helps us to see how the doctrine of the mean works with actions. Generosity, for example, involves giving away money at the right time, and to the right people, and one may fail to live up to its requirements both by failing to give away money when one should (which is stinginess) and giving away money when one should not (which is wastefulness). We can also see how one's character may consist partly in two 'opposite' vices, and Aristotle explicitly says (IV.1, 1121a–b) that some of the characteristics of wastefulness (such as spending money when one should not) are commonly found with certain characteristics of stinginess (such as taking money from the wrong sources). Aristotle's doctrine is therefore not one of moderation. Sometimes, for example, one will be required to be very angry, and sometimes to give away only a tiny amount of money. It depends on the circumstances, and moderation has nothing in itself to be said for it.

The doctrine of the mean works when we have a single morally neutral action or feeling that it is possible to do or feel at the right time, fail to do or feel at the right time, and do or feel at the wrong time. It is not surprising, therefore, that Aristotle runs into trouble with courage by including both feeling fear and assessing probabilities within its remit. Likewise, appropriate indignation cannot be a mean between both envy and spite, since these two vices concern different things, viz., pain at others' doing well and pleasure at their doing badly. And there are certainly problems with justice, which we shall consider below. But the doctrine rests on an important insight: there are spheres of human action and feeling, and virtue consists in success within these spheres.

It has been claimed by some that the doctrine is empty, and Aristotle himself appears to move in the direction of saying this in VI.1, 1138b: my telling you to perform the mean action is like my telling you, when you are ill, to take the medicines the doctor would prescribe. But Aristotle does use the doctrine to offer advice in II.9, 1109a–b: you should, for instance, take care to avoid the extreme to which you are most tempted (if you are a bit stingy, do what seems to you somewhat extravagant, and you will end up closer to getting it right). Taken on its own, the doctrine would be pretty useless. But combined with 'first principles' (I.7, 1098b), i.e., basic ethical beliefs, it can help one to assess one's own character and direct its formation.

In recent years, there has been a revival of interest in the virtues, and in the ethics of virtue. This revival began with an article of G. E. M. Anscombe's, in which she recommended dropping the modern language of 'obligation', with its connotations of a divine lawgiver whose existence is no longer widely accepted, and seeking an understanding of human psychology as a possible grounding of an ethics of virtue.[5]

The two main modern competitors to virtue ethics are utilitarianism and Kantianism. It is important to recognize that these three theories may largely converge in their practical conclusions. They may all, for instance, recommend that one be generous, or just. But the reasons that the theories offer differ greatly. According to utilitarianism, what makes actions right is their producing the largest amount of well-being overall. According to Kantianism, what makes actions right is their being in accordance with the law of reason. We might understand Aristotle, and a pure virtue ethics, as claiming that what makes actions right is their being virtuous.

There are differences between Aristotle and modern writers on the virtues. The virtue of kindness or beneficence, for example, is almost entirely absent from Aristotle's account, though he does allow that human beings do feel some common bonds with one another on the

---

[5] G. E. M. Anscombe, 'Modern Moral Philosophy', *Philosophy* 33 (1958); repr. in R. Crisp and M. Slote (eds.), *Virtue Ethics* (Oxford: Oxford University Press, 1997).

basis of their shared humanity (VIII.1, 1155a). And the crown of the virtues for Aristotle is a distinctly unmodern and pre-Christian disposition, greatness of soul (IV.3), which consists in thinking oneself worthy of great things and being concerned almost entirely with honour. The great-souled person is unlikely to stir himself to help the vulnerable.

Aristotle's discussions may be tabulated as follows:

Virtue	*Sphere*	*Discussion in NE*
Courage	Fear and confidence	III.6–9
Temperance	Bodily pleasure and pain	III.10–12
Generosity	Giving and retaining money	IV.1
Magnificence	Giving and retaining money on a large scale	IV.2
Greatness of soul	Honour on a large scale	IV.3
[Nameless]	Honour on a small scale	IV.4
Even temper	Anger	IV.5
Friendliness	Social relations	IV.6
Truthfulness	Honesty about oneself	IV.7
Wit	Conversation	IV.8
Justice	Distribution	V
Friendship	Personal relations	VIII–IX

Aristotle also briefly discusses shame, which he says is not really a virtue, and appropriate indignation.

Another difference between Aristotle and modern theorists of the virtues is his objective notion of happiness. The idea that there is some universal account of well-being, especially one grounded in human nature, is denied by most important modern writers who otherwise see themselves as returning to Aristotle. Likewise, none of them goes as far as to identify happiness with the exercise of the virtues.

It is also important to remember the context in which Aristotle composed his lectures. He was writing two and a half millennia ago, for noblemen in a city-state of tens of thousands. He believed such a city to be the best form of human society, and might well have thought it absurd even to attempt carrying across his conclusions about happiness in such a polity to what he would have seen as highly degenerate nation-states. It is not, in other words, a good idea to claim Aristotle as an ally in a modern debate the very assumptions of which he might have questioned. Rather, he should be read, carefully and sensitively, with an understanding of historical, social, and political context, as one of the best sources of insight into the human ethical condition available to us.

Voluntariness and responsibility

Though the *Ethics* forms separate books, the themes of the books are closely connected. We have already seen that Aristotle identifies happiness with virtuous activity. He recognizes next that virtuous actions are praised, and vicious actions blamed, only when they are voluntary. So the discussion of voluntariness in III.1–5 should not be seen as a general disquisition on free will. We should also remember Aristotle's audience, many of whom might have hoped for careers in legislation. For them, Aristotle thought, it was important to understand what is, and what is not, to be rewarded and punished.

Aristotle begins by identifying two excusing conditions, ignorance and force, which have remained central in philosophical and legal accounts of responsibility (III.1, 1110a–b). Here he was himself influenced by the Athenian legal system already in operation. In a case of force, the 'first principle' or source of the action is external to the agent. Thus, I might say that I am going to Egypt, even when being carried there against my will by the wind. An obvious question here is whether this account of force is too narrow, and whether there may not be cases of inner compulsion. It is partly reflecting upon this question that leads Aristotle into a discussion of what he calls 'mixed actions'. An example is a captain's throwing cargo overboard to stop his ship going down: he might well claim, in mitigation, that he had no choice. Aristotle here sticks to his guns. The source of the action is internal, and so it is voluntary. But he does allow that in a sense such actions are, understood 'without qualification', involuntary: they are the sorts of thing no one would choose voluntarily in themselves. This is really a new sense of involuntariness, but no confusion need arise if we take Aristotle to be saying merely that throwing cargo overboard is not the sort of thing that someone chooses in itself. He does, however, go on to soften the force criterion a little: there are some things that are too much for a human being, such as severe torture, where pardon rather than blame is called for.

Besides voluntariness and involuntariness, Aristotle suggests a third category: the non-voluntary. Imagine that I finish with the brush I am using to paint an upstairs window frame, and drop it to the ground below. Unbeknownst to me, my neighbour is passing at the time, and the brush lands squarely on her head. Here, we might have expected my ignorance to cause my action to be involuntary, but Aristotle claims that, if I do not regret my action, then it is non-voluntary, not involuntary. This distinction may perhaps arise out of Aristotle's concern with praise and blame, for if I am not sorry for what I did, there may be said to be a case for blaming me (even if it is true that I would not have done what I did had I known of my neighbour's presence).

Further reflection on ignorance and responsibility leads Aristotle to further refinement. There is a distinction between acting in ignorance and acting through ignorance. A drunk acts merely in ignorance, and he is responsible not only for getting himself into that state but for what he does while in it. Further, it is only ignorance of particular circumstances and not of moral principles themselves which can excuse.

Aristotle's central interest in virtue also drives his argument in later chapters of book III. Rational choice and deliberation are discussed in III.2–3 because the virtuous person is the one who deliberates and rationally chooses correctly. As often, Aristotle begins by telling us what the object of his inquiry is not: rational choice is not appetite, spirit, wish, or belief. It involves deliberation, the sphere of which is what is 'up to us', and we rationally choose to do what we have judged to be right as the result of deliberation. So rational choice is deliberative desire, and is the point at which the thought of the virtuous person emerges in the world in his actions.

In III.5, an important chapter, Aristotle begins by repeating that virtuous and vicious actions are up to us, and suggesting that therefore the Socratic view that no one is willingly bad must be rejected. Aristotle imagines someone's objecting that a vicious person's character *makes him* act wrongly, so that he cannot be held responsible. Aristotle responds that such a person is himself responsible for having that character. If someone is unjust, he has become unjust through performing unjust actions, which at the time he must have known would lead to his developing an unjust character. An unjust person is like someone who has become ill by ignoring his or her doctor's advice.

Aristotle courageously continues to face up to the objector, who he now imagines claiming that the end we aim at in our actions is natural, and so never something for which any vicious person could be held responsible at any time. Among Aristotle's responses is the suggestion that what a person pursues in their actions is at least partly up to them. This response strikes many people as plausible. Although Aristotle does not explicitly allow for unusual cases, such as brainwashing or fully deterministic genetic propensities, his account makes good sense of the everyday assumptions that underlie our ascriptions of responsibility in the courts and in ordinary life.

He makes no room for moral luck. The virtuous person deserves praise, even if, as it happened, it was easy for him to become virtuous, since, perhaps, he was brought up in a prosperous household, given a solid education, and surrounded by attractive role-models. Likewise, the vicious person is to be blamed even if it would in fact have been quite hard for him to be virtuous. Aristotle's concern is not the modern, Kant-inspired, one of awarding moral responsibility solely in proportion to what the agent is solely and ultimately responsible for (if indeed there is such a thing), but of praising and blaming people for what they voluntarily do.

Justice

The subject of Plato's *Republic* is what in Greek is called *dikaiosunē*. This word is usually translated 'justice', but in a recent translation the word 'morality' is used.[6] This choice reflects an ambiguity in the Greek, itself implicit in Aristotle's distinction between general and particular justice in the first two chapters of book v.

Aristotle uses the notion of general justice to take an angle, or rather several angles, on virtue as a whole. He first distinguishes virtue as exercised in relation to oneself – temperance, for example – from virtue exercised in relation to others. The person with general justice has both. He also exercises both, and so general justice will be a quality found only within a community in which the virtuous person can find people to serve as objects of his virtuous actions. It is complete.

Aristotle ties this conception of complete virtue to the law, his thought being that the law (ideally speaking) aims ultimately at the

---

[6] Plato, *Republic*, trans. R. Waterfield (Oxford: Oxford University Press, 1998).

instantiation of all the virtues in the citizens it governs. So what is generally just is what is lawful. Because Aristotle is thinking of the law in an ideal sense (though it has to be admitted that he does not say this explicitly), he cannot be accused plausibly of holding that whatever the law prescribes within any jurisdiction is what is virtuous there. Aristotle is, as we have seen, an ethical objectivist, and he was perfectly aware of the possibility of bad laws. Nevertheless, he does extend the boundaries of legal concern too widely. The law cannot plausibly be said to be aiming at inculcating virtues such as generosity or wit in its citizens, other than highly indirectly. Here, however, we must face up to the possibility that Aristotle may have thought that the law should concern itself with such issues, a possibility that seems not unlikely in the light of his enthusiasm at the end of the *Politics* for detailed legislation concerning the playing of flutes.

Particular justice is another individual virtue, to be set alongside even temper, generosity, courage, and so on, as part of general justice. The doctrine of the mean requires Aristotle to find a special feeling or action to characterize it, and he chooses greed (v.2, 1130a). His line of thought is clear enough: the unjust person will give himself more than his fair share, which is what the greedy person does. But what is the feeling of which greed is the excess? The right concern for one's own rights or property? But then what is the deficiency? An unwillingness to exert one's rights is not any kind of injustice. Aristotle's problem is that there seems to be no central feeling or action in the case of justice. It is a quality applied primarily to outcomes or states of affairs, and actions and characters are then characterized as just or unjust on the basis of whether they bring about, or demonstrate a proper concern for, such outcomes. Aristotle sees this: his influential discussion of justice in book v is largely a discussion of such outcomes and states of affairs, and not 'the just person'. It is only when Aristotle seeks to force justice into the mould of the doctrine of the mean that he goes wrong.

He has another attempt in his discussion of distributive justice (v.3, 1131a), stretching the doctrine of the mean by bringing in the notion of what is equal as the mean. Again, this is not what we have in the case of the other virtues: a characteristic feeling or action. In v.7, 1134b, he focuses on the distinction between 'too much' and 'too little', noting that 'having too much' may constitute doing injustice, and 'having too little' may constitute suffering it. Justice is then said to be a mean between doing injustice and suffering it. But as Aristotle himself admits, suffering injustice cannot be said to be a vice, and indeed many just people exemplify their justice in their being treated unjustly by others.

Aristotle should, then, have been readier to accept that the doctrine of the mean had its limits. But his discussion of justice itself has been highly influential. Consider, for example, his analysis of distributive justice in v.3, which classifies theories of distributive justice according to the criterion that they advocate as the basis of distributions (according to a democratic theory, for example, all citizens fall within the scope of justice). Another chapter, v.5, contains Aristotle's seminal account of money, as designed to achieve proportionate reciprocity in exchange. Consider also his distinction between natural and legal justice (v.7, 1134b). In this chapter, Aristotle claims that there is, as regards certain aspects of any society, a 'naturally best' way for them to be, while other aspects may be grounded only in the traditions and customs of that particular society. Here we see the root of the natural law tradition, according to which certain claims about right and wrong can be based upon a general account of human good and evil, arrived at by rational reflection. This tradition was continued by Aquinas, and today can be found in the writings of John Finnis and others.[7]

Aristotle's discussion of 'equity' in v.10 begins to move us in the direction of discussing practical wisdom, the key intellectual virtue in ethics. Equity is the virtue of a judge which allows him to 'fill in the gaps' left by the law. Human life is of such unpredictability and complexity that any law, however skilfully drafted, will leave room for 'hard cases', which call for legal discretion. A classic case is the skateboarder in the park, on the railings of which hangs a sign forbidding the use of vehicles in the park. Is a skateboard a vehicle? A judge may have to decide, and he will make his decision by careful attention to the salient features of the situation in question, including the law and the intentions of those who originally framed it. This quasi-perceptual, non–rule-governed capacity has much in common with practical wisdom, as we shall now see.

[7] See, e.g., J. Finnis, *Natural Law and Natural Rights* (Oxford: Clarendon Press, 1980).

Practical wisdom

Having read Aristotle's detailed discussions of the various individual virtues of character in books II–V, one might be forgiven for thinking that he had completed his account of the nature of virtuous action. But there remains an important gap, to be filled by practical wisdom. Virtue, as we have seen, is a matter of getting it right within particular spheres of human life. Virtue of character rests partly on the development of dispositions towards virtuous action through habituation. This habituation will be guided by, for example, one's parents or teachers. But the virtuous person is able to get it right in each sphere without guidance from others, and his capacity to do that is what centrally constitutes practical wisdom.

The mean is what one should be aiming at because it is 'determined by the reason by reference to which the practically wise person would determine it' (II.6, 1107a). Some have read book VI in the hope that Aristotle would provide us with an explicit rule or principle that we might apply to determine the mean in particular situations. Their hope has been disappointed, since no such rule is forthcoming. Nor should we expect one. Aristotle frequently says that ethics is not capturable in a set of explicit principles (e.g., I.3, 1094b), and VI.8, 1142a, makes it clear that practical wisdom is less a capacity to apply rules than an ability to see situations correctly. This perception is rational; hence Aristotle's use of the word 'reason' in his account of the determination of the mean.

As we have seen, virtues of character correspond to one particular part of the soul – that part which is not strictly rational, but is obedient to reason. In book VI, Aristotle divides the rational part of the soul into two, and postulates two classes of intellectual virtue corresponding, respectively, to each part. He does this because he believes both that objects of reasoning can themselves be divided into two – the invariable (e.g., mathematics) and the variable (e.g., human action) – and that parts of the soul have kinship with their objects. Book VI concerns primarily the practical side of reason, but the last sentence of VI.1 makes it clear that he is also interested in the scientific part of the soul that corresponds to the invariable. This makes sense, as happiness consists in the exercise of any virtue of the soul, and this part of the soul has its own virtues, as becomes clear in X.7.

Aristotle claims that there are five states of the soul that grasp the truth 'by affirmation or denial' (VI.3, 1139b). One is practical wisdom, while the others are:

(i)   science, or scientific knowledge: grasps what is necessary and eternal, such as mathematics;

(ii) skill: concerned with the variable, and with production rather than action (i.e., with instrumental activities rather than ends-in-themselves);

(iii) intellect: concerned with non-demonstrable first principles, it grasps the minor premise in practical syllogisms (see below), so is related to practical wisdom;

(iv) wisdom: not really a separate virtue, since it consists in (i) and (iii) when they concern what is 'most honourable', i.e., philosophy.

We know from III.2–3 that being virtuous involves deliberating well, and Aristotle expands upon this in VI.5. Here we find that the person of practical wisdom can deliberate about what advances living well, that is, about what is virtuous. Good deliberation, like virtue in itself, involves getting it right (VI.9, 1142b), that is, achieving something good by using the right steps in one's reasoning. Deliberation, then, is itself a part of being practically wise.

Again, we see Aristotle's objectivism emerging. Practical wisdom is a grasp of 'practical truth', independent of what we think (VI.2, 1139a). But, as we have seen, it is not something to be learned or articulated in explicit principles. Human action is variable and complex, and so practical wisdom concerns matters that are inexact. Its acquisition requires experience, and consists in one's becoming able to see what matters in certain circumstances, and why. It is closely related to common sense, except that its sphere is that of the virtues as a whole. It is important also to remember that it consists not merely in the ability to see or to understand, but in a capacity to give orders (VI.10, 1143a). Unlike judgement, practical wisdom involves the virtuous person's commanding himself to perform what is called for in the circumstances.

So we can already see how both practical wisdom and the habituated dispositions of the virtues of character work together. Towards the end of book VI, Aristotle returns to this question, and claims that virtue makes the aim right, and practical wisdom the 'things towards it' (VI.12, 1144a). One might understand this to mean that virtue is primary in the virtuous person's acting, the role of practical wisdom being merely to work out the means to ends set independently of it. Even if it is a capacity to see what constitutes various ends, the setting of those ends in itself may seem not to concern it. But a better way to understand the relation here is as follows. Practical wisdom requires virtue of character, in the sense that it cannot develop or operate unless one has been brought up in the correct habits. Practical wisdom is in fact what 'gets the goal right' in action, while virtue is what enables one to get it right (i.e., it 'makes the goal right'). Imagine that you see someone in need of money. As a virtuous person, you might think as follows: 'Since the highest good is virtuous activity [and you would not be thinking this unless you had been brought up properly to the point that you developed the practical wisdom to think it with], and since this is a case where generosity is called for, and since generosity here will call for giving roughly two *minae*, then I had better deliberate about how best to get hold of the money...'.

In VI.13, 1144b–1145a, we also find that practical wisdom comes only in a package along with all the virtues of character. One cannot be, say, courageous but stingy, or even-tempered but unjust. The reason for this is that practical wisdom is the capacity to succeed in action through giving oneself the correct orders. If you have a vice, this will damage your capacity to see situations correctly, and you will not be 'good without qualification' (Aristotle is of course aware that many will fall short of this ideal to a greater or lesser degree).

We should remember that, despite the perceptual nature of practical wisdom, moral rules can play a part in ethics. Such rules will of course be inexact, such as, 'You should return favours rather than do favours for your companions; but if your father needs ransoming from pirates, you should not pay back the person who ransomed you' (see IX.2, 1164b–1165a). This is inexact, because it would not decide, for example, the following case: one group of pirates has your villainous father on their ship, while another group has your mother and virtuous twin brother; you have enough only to satisfy one group. Moral rules always run out, as we saw happen with legal rules in our discussion of equity. And here judgement 'lies in perception' (II.9, 1109b).

Incontinence

From the beginning of the *Ethics*, we see that Aristotle understands human lives in terms of nested goals. Each of us aims at our own happiness, and we each have our own conception of what that is. If I think that happiness consists in honour, then I shall pursue happiness by pursuing honour. And if I think honour is best achieved in politics, I shall pursue honour by seeking a political career. And so on.

But one apparently common human phenomenon seems to throw doubt on Aristotle's position: incontinence, or weakness. Incontinent people seem to have a particular conception of what their own happiness will consist in, but, when being incontinent, they seem not to pursue it at all. An example. Larry is overweight, and strongly wishes to lose weight so that he can return to his favourite activity, waterskiing. But Larry also likes chocolate, and can rarely resist eating a piece when he gets the chance. He says that he knows he really should not be eating the chocolate, but goes ahead and does it anyway.

Aristotle is particularly concerned with the question of what kind of knowledge the incontinent person has. This is partly because of the role of that issue in the Socratic philosophical tradition he was continuing. As Aristotle points out, Socrates had denied that incontinence was possible, and explained apparent incontinence as mere ignorance of what is best. Socrates denied that knowledge could be overcome by desire, and Aristotle notes that this is inconsistent with what people ordinarily think. Aristotle has also his own reason to be concerned about the power of knowledge. He has stressed the practicality of ethics, but if people can know what the right thing to do is, but fail to do it, it will be harder to make ethics practical.

So what is Aristotle's explanation of incontinence? He offers it in an important chapter: VII.3. He notes first that one can distinguish between two ways of knowing something. Imagine that I know that eating corned beef is dangerous, and you catch me eating a corned beef sandwich. I may just have failed to make use of my knowledge, and stop eating the sandwich once you remind me. So we can know without using our knowledge, and, as Aristotle says, there is nothing particularly strange about that. What would be strange would be my eating the sandwich while attending to, or 'using', the knowledge.

In the non-puzzling case, you can actualize my dispositional knowledge about corned beef merely by pointing out to me what I am eating. But there is a second way in which knowledge can be dispositional, viz., if I am asleep, mad, or drunk. Merely telling me what I eating if I am in one of these states will be insufficient to actualize my knowledge. Rather, you will have first to wake me, make me sane, or sober me up. This kind of dispositional knowledge is what incontinent people have, Aristotle suggests, and this gives him an answer to a question Socrates failed to address: if an incontinent person is ignorant of what is best, how is it that he often says, at the very time he is being incontinent, that he knows? Aristotle sees the words of the incontinent as like the words of a drunk: in a sense, they do not know what they are saying.

Aristotle expands his explanation using his notion of the practical syllogism. The practical syllogism is Aristotle's attempt to provide a framework for explaining, fully and without remainder, all human action. In a theoretical syllogism, the conclusion follows of necessity:

> All men are mortal.
> Socrates is a man.
> Therefore, Socrates is mortal.

Aristotle wishes to explain how an action follows with a similar degree of necessity when two practical premises come together. For example:

> Sweet things are to be tasted.
> This is a sweet thing.
> Therefore, this must be tasted. [Sometimes, the conclusion is itself
>   understood as the action of tasting.]

In an ordinary case of eating something sweet, the above syllogism might be all that is required to explain what is going on. But in the case of incontinence, there is another syllogism which deters the agent from tasting. What is this syllogism? Some commentators have thought that its first, or major, premise is:

> Sweet things are not to be tasted.

But this is impossible, since we know that we have the minor premise:

> This is a sweet thing.

With these two premises in place, a non-tasting must follow by necessity, and of course it does not in the case of incontinence. Rather, the major premise here must be something like:

Fattening things should not be tasted.

To return to the case of Larry, what then happens is that his desire interferes with his practical reasoning and loosens his grip on the relevant minor premise:

This is a fattening thing.

He may well say that he knows that this chocolate is fattening (and of course that he should not eat it), but desire, like alcohol, has led him to speak without fully understanding the import of what he says.

It is in this way that Aristotle seeks to retain both the Socratic view that knowledge cannot be overridden, alongside the view of common sense that it can. For Larry's understanding that fattening things should not be eaten is left untouched, while his awareness of the salient feature of the particular case at hand is dimmed by desire.

Aristotle's account has struck many as unacceptable, in that the knowledge we have when incontinent often appears to be, in itself, unaffected by our desire. Its only defect is its failure to issue in the appropriate action. But we should take care to distinguish between mere propositional knowledge, and the kind of evaluative or practical understanding Aristotle appears to have in mind here. This kind of understanding, if you have it, will issue in action, and lack of action is a clear sign of lack of knowledge. But here it may begin to seem as if Aristotle wins only by changing the terms of the debate, since many will continue to think that the knowledge of the incontinent is the same as that of the continent and of the virtuous. It is merely that the incontinent's knowledge does not issue in action.

Friendship

Some have thought that Aristotle's discussion of friendship in books VIII and IX, which do indeed appear to have been composed as a separate entity, was mistakenly tacked on to the *Ethics* by a later editor. But there seems no reason to think that Aristotle himself did not include it in his own composition of the *Ethics*, since it fits perfectly well into his overall project.

Aristotle's conception of friendship is broad. It includes parents' relation to their children (including animals' relations to their offspring), the natural kinship felt by one human being with another, and the amicable relations of business partners. In VIII.2, 1155b, Aristotle tells us that friendship involves goodwill – the wishing of goods for the sake of the other – which is reciprocated, and of which each party is aware. We then find that goodwill is really found only in friendships between virtuous people (VIII.3, 1156a). In the case of friendships for utility and for pleasure, Aristotle suggests, the people seem to have goodwill towards themselves, rather than one another (IX.5, 1167a). It is worth noting that, if the virtue mentioned in IV.6, 1126b, is roughly the same as that discussed in books VIII–IX, then Aristotelian friendship does involve people's actually liking one another.

Is friendship a virtue? The first sentence of VIII.1 might be taken to suggest that Aristotle is not sure: 'it is a virtue or involves virtue'. Aristotle would not have hesitated over such an important matter, however, and we must take the sentence to mean that friendship both is a virtue, and involves the exercise of virtues. Given that it is a virtue, what is its relation to happiness? As a virtue, it will involve feeling goodwill to the right people, in the right way, and so on, and exercising this virtue will be a constituent of happiness. But friendship is also an 'instrumental good' (see I.8, 1099a–b), since friends may serve, for example, as beneficiaries of one's virtuous action. Further, virtuous activity itself involves the pleasure of contemplating one's own virtuous actions. The virtuous actions of a virtuous friend are, in a sense, one's own, so one can enjoy contemplating them (IX.9, 1169b). Relatedly, just as the virtuous person's own being or life is worth choosing, so is that of the friend, for the friend is 'another self' (IX.9, 1170b).

We saw how at the beginning of book VI Aristotle appeared to doubt his own doctrine of the mean. It might seem as if, at the beginning of book VIII, he is hesitating about the stress he has placed on justice earlier in the work. He says that friendship is, in a sense, more important than justice: legislators aim at concord, and if people are friends, they do not need justice. Aristotle's point here is that justice provides external arbitration on matters which are potentially disputable. If people are friends, such disputes will not arise, since friends wish good to one another. But we should not take Aristotle to be rejecting justice entirely, since there are bound in any city to be some areas of social life which require the governance of justice. Indeed, in VIII.9, 1159b, Aristotle seems to suggest that the boundaries of friendship are also the boundaries of justice. So parents, for example, who are friends to their children, will also thereby be just. But, importantly, their motivation will be concern for the other person, not a concern for justice. And without some degree of this kind of concern, no community is possible (VIII.11, 1161a–b). There are hints here of issues that have arisen recently in the debate in political theory between liberals, who advocate rights, and communitarians, who propose modelling the state on the relations of trust and concern found in the family.[8] As often, Aristotle had the answer long before this debate began: the city is not a family, and it would be absurd to try to make it such; one should seek to encourage concern of citizens for one another, but justice will be required to regulate certain spheres in society.

Friendship involves 'being friendly towards', or loving. Aristotle thinks that certain things are worth loving, i.e., loveable. These fall into three categories (VIII.2, 1155b): the good, the pleasant, and the useful. Corresponding to these three objects are three species of friendship. We have already noted that friendships for pleasure and for utility do not involve real goodwill for another. So complete (or perfect) friendship is found only between virtuous people, fond of one another in so far as each is who he is – that is, virtuous people love one another for their characters. The other two kinds of friendship count as such only because of their resemblance to complete friendship, good people being both pleasant and useful to one another.

Here a problem arises. Is there a genuine conceptual difference between loving another because I find him pleasant, and loving another because I find him virtuous? Understanding Aristotle's position here will require us to return to the *ergon* argument of 1.7, 1098a, where we saw that exercising virtue is doing what is characteristic of humanity, i.e., essential to humanity as a species. Since I am a human being, what makes me most fully a human being, what makes me what I am, is exercising the virtues. Further, human beings are to be identified with their reason, not their contingent desires, or emotions. Reason is the source of the virtues, but it is not the source of what I find useful or pleasing in another. Here an objector is likely to claim both that Aristotle's biology has been excessively moralized, and that his view of personal identity is excessively rationalistic.

In the end, most will not accept Aristotle's view that only the virtuous

---

[8] See e.g. M. Sandel (ed.), *Liberalism and its Critics* (Oxford: Blackwell, 1984).

can have genuine friendships. Indeed, it seems that many vicious people – members of criminal fraternities, for example – may have close bonds of loyalty and concern with one another of a kind indistinguishable from those in the friendships of the virtuous. Certainly, Aristotle's view contradicts 'the way things appear to people' (VII.2, 1145b). But it is important to see that rejecting it requires understanding of, and objecting to, carefully argued Aristotelian views concerning personal identity, metaphysics, biology, and the theory of value.

Pleasure

Pleasure plays a central role in Aristotle's account of ethics. Virtue involves pleasure and pain both in its exercise, and in its acquisition. The virtue of temperance focuses on the bodily pleasures, while the virtuous person enjoys the exercise of any virtue, even courage. What people enjoy or dislike has a strong influence on what they do, so that pleasure and pain are very important aspects of any moral education. Hence pleasure is part of happiness itself.

What is pleasure, according to Aristotle? He addresses this question most straightforwardly in X.4. Here, we learn that pleasure is not a process, that is, something that takes time, and has a beginning, a middle, and an end (such as, for example, walking into town). There is a grammatical test to distinguish processes from non-processes or activities: if 'I am ϕ-ing' implies 'I have ϕ-ed', then ϕ-ing is not a process. Consider, for example, seeing. Once I see, then I have seen.

There might appear to be a problem here, in that it is also true that once I walk, then I have walked. But Aristotle's point is closely related to the 'form' of the item in question, what makes ϕ-ing, in this case, what it is. Take the initial instant of seeing or of pleasure. These will be full-blooded cases of seeing and of pleasure, and will require nothing else to complete them. But the initial instant of walking will require further movement for this to be a case of walking.

We may recall here an earlier distinction Aristotle drew, between action and production (VI.4). Building is production, since it aims at an end beyond itself. Pleasure is a candidate for being an end in itself, since it is in this respect unlike building. Thus, those arguments that seek to downgrade its claims as a value by characterizing it as a process are mistaken.

In VII.12, 1153a, while considering the argument that pleasure is a process – a 'coming-to-be' – and therefore not an end in itself, Aristotle says that it is not a coming-to-be but an unimpeded activity of one's natural state. This gives rise to a notorious problem, since we are told in X.4, 1174b, that pleasure 'completes' activities. Because books VII and X appear to be from different periods of Aristotle's development, some have said that we have here a straightforward example of Aristotle's changing his mind. But this is to give up too easily: we should seek a unified account of the *Ethics* as far as we can. First, note what VII.12 and X.4 agree on: pleasure is not a process. In VII.12, it can be argued that all that Aristotle means by calling pleasure 'activity' is that it is a non-process, and he says the same in X.4. So why does he in X.4 go on to say that it completes activity? In a famous paper, G. E. L. Owen provides the answer.[9] We may distinguish two senses of 'pleasure'. I may say, 'Dining is one of my pleasures', or, 'Dining gives me pleasure'. In the first sense, a pleasure is an activity, while in the second pleasure is a mental state, consequent upon an activity. Owen plausibly suggests that by the time of book X Aristotle had noticed this distinction, through thinking about the process/non-process distinction. He had seen that I may say, for example, 'I enjoy dining quickly', but not, 'I quickly enjoy dining', and that the activity and the pleasure can therefore be distinguished.

What does Aristotle mean by 'completion'? Here we may refer back to book I, and its discussion of completeness. Pleasure may be said to complete an activity – Aristotle has in mind particularly the best activities – by adding to their value to the point that they are, in a sense, 'lacking in nothing' (I.7, 1097b). This brings us to another closely related question considered by Aristotle: are pleasures good? His answer is that some are good without qualification, that is, always worth choosing. If I am in a fever, I may enjoy a bitter medicine. This is not a pleasure that is good without qualification, since I find the medicine pleasurable only because of some quirk or defect in my gustatory capacity, though we may say that it is good for me. The things I should be really interested in are those that are good without qualification, because these are the things which will be genuinely and truly good for me.

[9] G.E.L. Owen, 'Aristotelian Pleasures', *Proceedings of the Aristotelian Society* 72 (1971–2); repr. in his *Logic, Science and Dialectic* (London: Duckworth, 1986).

Why should we think that pleasure is a good? Answers Aristotle takes very seriously are that people think that the happy life is pleasant (VII.13, 1153b), and that all animals seek pleasure (X.2, 1172b–1173a): 'what seems so to all we say is so'. Aristotle's views about the goodness of pleasure are soundly based in his philosophical methodology, with its respect for common sense, and in the biological principle on which his ethics is founded, that all things aim at the good.

So which pleasures are good? Those which have good sources (X.3, 1173b–1174a). Which are these? Bodily pleasures? Bodily pleasures are good up to a point (VII.14, 1154a), that is, when their enjoyment is part of, or constrained by, temperance. There is a question, however, about what Aristotle means by, say, enjoying a meal 'in the right way'. VII.12, 1153a, may be read as suggesting that the temperate person will not seek the pleasure of a delicious meal as an end in itself. Rather he avoids bodily pleasures *qua* bodily pleasures, and seeks only painlessness (i.e., freedom from hunger). His pleasure in eating must then consist in his awareness of, or reflection upon, his temperance, its nobility, and its value for his happiness. Ultimately, as have seen, Aristotle believes happiness to consist only in virtuous activities, and it will be only those pleasures, those activities, that are really good and worth pursuing.

Is Aristotle a hedonist? Only in the sense that he believes happiness to consist in certain pleasures. These are good not solely because of their being pleasurable, which is what a full hedonist must accept. Aristotle further distances himself from most hedonists in claiming that many of the experiences commonly thought to be pleasant are not pleasant at all. The only real pleasures, Aristotle suggests, are those of the virtuous person. Pleasantness, then, can be understood on an analogy with colours, such as redness:

> x is red = x is such as to look red to a standard observer in normal
> conditions;
> y is pleasant = y is such as to be enjoyed by the virtuous person.

Surely, however, whatever pleasantness is, it is a quality of experience rather than of its object? In other words, what is really pleasant is what is really enjoyed. We might accept that virtuous activity is the only pleasure worth having, or the only proper pleasure, but it is hard to see it as the only real pleasure. Here we have another example of Aristotle's being willing to allow his ethics too much influence over other areas of his thought, in this case, his psychology. We find the implications also in his metaphysics. In the *Metaphysics*, Aristotle says of the prime mover, the first principle behind everything in the universe (i.e. God): 'Its course of life is such as the best we can have only for a short time. For it is always in this state, which we cannot be, since its actuality is also pleasure.'[10] Perhaps it should be no surprise, then, to find Aristotle claiming towards the end of the *Ethics* (X.8, 1177b) that 'we ought to take on immortality as much as possible, and do all that we can to live in accordance with the highest element within us; for even if its bulk is small, in its power and value it far exceeds everything'. The pleasures of philosophy, according to Aristotle, are the pleasures of God.

Aristotle's *Ethics* was written a very long time ago, by someone with a world view quite different from that of any modern writer. But on nearly all of those topics central to modern moral philosophy, Aristotle's position cannot be ignored: moral epistemology, realism and objectivism, ethical methodology, rationality, agency, reasons for action, the relation between morality and self-interest, moral motivation, the criterion of right action, the nature and importance of the virtues, justice and equality, well-being, love and friendship, the emotions, moral perception, and a multitude of other issues. Aristotle's enduring importance in ethics is assured for at least two reasons. First, he addresses questions concerning how best to live which will always be asked in any society where rational reflection upon human aims is possible. Secondly, his answers to these questions, based on the recognition that any civilized human life will centre around spheres in which there are right and wrong ways to feel and to act, and on a conception of the human good grounded in an understanding of human nature, will be a perennial source of insight and inspiration.

---

[10] *Metaphysics* XII.7, 1072b14–16.

Chronology

All dates are BCE

384 Aristotle born in Stagira in Chalcidice, the peninsula projecting from Macedonia. His father, Nicomachus, was physician at the court of Amyntas II, king of Macedonia. Aristotle may have spent some of his childhood at the court

367 Travelled to Athens. Joined Plato's Academy

347 On the death of Plato, left Athens, probably because of difficulties arising from his links with Macedonia. At the invitation of the Platonist Hermias, travelled to Assos, of which Hermias was ruler. Married Hermias' adoptive daughter, Pythias

345 Travelled to Mytilene, and continued biological research begun at Assos

342 At the invitation of Philip II of Macedon, travelled to Pella and became tutor to Philip's son, Alexander the Great

335 After a brief period in Stagira, returned to Athens. Established his own school, the Lyceum. Pythias died, having borne Aristotle one daughter. Aristotle lived for the remainder of his life with a slave, Herpyllis, who bore him a son, Nicomachus

323 On the death of Alexander, Aristotle was charged by anti-Macedonians with impiety on the ground that a poem he wrote for

Hermias befitted a god, not a human being. This led Aristotle to leave Athens for Chalcis

322 Death of Aristotle from a digestive illness

Further reading

Aristotle's Greek is compressed, and his meaning frequently indeterminate. For this reason, a reader of Aristotle in translation is well advised to consult more than one translation, especially of important passages. Perhaps the most useful is that of T. H. Irwin (Indianapolis: Hackett, 1985), which contains analyses of the argument, as well as notes and a substantial glossary. An elegant translation is provided by Harris Rackham (Ware: Wordsworth, 1996). The 'World's Classics' translation by W. D. Ross, revised by J. L. Ackrill and J. O. Urmson (Oxford: Oxford University Press, 1980), and that by M. Ostwald (Indianapolis: Bobbs-Merrill, 1962), are also deservedly popular.

The revised Oxford translation of the *Complete Works of Aristotle* is available in two volumes edited by Jonathan Barnes (Princeton, NJ: Princeton University Press, 1984). Other works by Aristotle particularly relevant to the reader of the *Nicomachean Ethics* are *On the Soul*, *Eudemian Ethics*, *Politics*, and *Rhetoric*. An overview is provided in W. D. Ross, *Aristotle* (London: Methuen, 1923).

There are several good commentaries on the *Ethics*. The best is R. Gauthier and J. Jolif, *Aristote: l'Ethique à Nicomaque* (Louvain: Publications Universitaires de Louvain, 2nd edn, 4 vols., 1970). Also useful are A. Grant, *The Ethics of Aristotle* (London: Longmans, Green, and Co., 1885), J. Stewart, *Notes on the Nicomachean Ethics of Aristotle* (Oxford: Clarendon Press, 1982), J. Burnet, *The Ethics of Aristotle* (London: Methuen, 1900), and H. Joachim, *The Nicomachean Ethics* (Oxford: Clarendon Press, 1951). All of these commentaries contain material of use to readers without Greek, though, of course, the Gauthier-Jolif requires French.

For an introductory essay on Aristotle, see T. H. Irwin, 'Aristotle', in E. Craig (ed.), *Routledge Encyclopedia of Philosophy* (London: Routledge, 1998). This includes an annotated bibliography. An outstanding and brief introduction to Aristotle is Jonathan Barnes, *Aristotle* (Oxford: Oxford University Press, 1982). J. L. Ackrill, *Aristotle the Philosopher* (Oxford: Oxford University Press, 1981) is clear, and contains helpful quotations from Aristotle. Longer volumes useful to someone with some philosophical expertise are J. Lear, *Aristotle: The Desire to Understand* (Cambridge: Cambridge University Press, 1988) and T. H. Irwin, *Aristotle's First Principles* (Oxford: Clarendon Press, 1988). Jonathan Barnes (ed.), *The Cambridge Companion to Aristotle* (Cambridge: Cambridge University Press, 1995) contains essays on central areas of Aristotle's thought, including a chapter on his ethics by D. S. Hutchinson, as well as a full bibliography.

A brief introduction to Aristotle's ethics is J. Urmson, *Aristotle's Ethics* (Oxford: Blackwell, 1988). A fuller handbook is W. Hardie, *Aristotle's Ethical Theory* (Oxford: Clarendon Press, 2nd edn, 1980). S. Broadie, *Ethics with Aristotle* (New York: Oxford University Press, 1991) is a suggestive discussion of various central topics in the *Ethics*, including happiness and the virtues.

Several important essays are collected in A. Rorty (ed.), *Essays on Aristotle's Ethics* (Berkeley, CA: University of California Press, 1980). See also J. Barnes, M. Schofield, and R. Sorabji (eds.), *Articles on Aristotle*, vol. 2 (London: Duckworth, 1977); and J. Anton and A. Preus (eds.), *Aristotle's Ethics: Essays in Ancient Greek Philosophy*, vol. 4 (Albany: State University of New York Press, 1991).

Other helpful books include Julia Annas, *The Morality of Happiness* (New York: Oxford University Press, 1993) (on ancient views of happiness, including that of Aristotle); David Charles, *Aristotle's Philosophy of Action* (London: Duckworth, 1984); John Cooper, *Reason and Human Good in Aristotle* (Cambridge, Mass.: Harvard University Press, 1975); Norman Dahl, *Practical Reason, Aristotle, and Weakness of Will* (Minneapolis: University of Minnesota Press, 1984); Troels Engberg-Pedersen, *Aristotle's Theory of Moral Insight* (Oxford: Clarendon Press, 1983); J. Gosling and C. Taylor, *The Greeks on Pleasure* (Oxford:

Clarendon Press, 1982); D. S. Hutchinson, *The Virtues of Aristotle* (London: Routledge and Kegan Paul, 1986); Anthony Kenny, *Aristotle's Theory of the Will* (London: Duckworth, 1979); Richard Kraut, *Aristotle on the Human Good* (Princeton: Princeton University Press, 1989); S. Sauvé Meyer, *Aristotle on Responsibility* (Oxford: Blackwell, 1993); Martha Nussbaum, *The Fragility of Goodness* (Cambridge: Cambridge University Press, 1986) (on the relation of fortune to happiness and virtue in ancient writers, including Aristotle); Anthony Price, *Love and Friendship in Plato and Aristotle* (Oxford: Clarendon Press, 1989); Nancy Sherman, *The Fabric of Character* (Oxford: Clarendon Press, 1989); R. Sorabji, *Necessity, Cause and Blame* (London: Duckworth, 1979); Stephen White, *Sovereign Virtue* (Stanford: Stanford University Press, 1992).

Note on the text

The numbers followed by letters (e.g., 1094a) in the margins are those of the pages and columns of Immanuel Bekker's Greek text of 1831. They are standardly used in making reference to Aristotle's text.

I have translated the Oxford Classical Text (ed. J. Bywater, Oxford: Clarendon Press, 1894), emended in the following ways:

1096a9: καὶ for καίτοι
1098a12 16: delete square brackets
1098b12: delete τἀληθές
1102b9: εἴ πῃ for εἰ μὴ
1107b11: ἑαυτοῖς for ἐν αὐταῖς
1107b27: insert μικρᾶς before τιμῆς
1108b9–10: delete ὁμοίως … ἀρετῶν
1111a9: delete αὐτούς
1116a7–9: insert καὶ οἱ … ἡσύχιοι. after ὑπομένουσιν., 1115b33
1120b9: delete δίδωσιν
1124b27: μέλειν for ἀμελεῖν; close bracket after φοβουμένου
1124b28: delete bracket after δόξης
1127a13–14: delete καὶ εἰρωνείας
1127b12–13: delete ὡς ὁ ἀλαζών,
1127b20: ἰατρον ἤ μάντιν σοφόν for μάντιν … ἰατρόν
1128b25: διὰ for καὶ
1132a29–30: insert τὸ δ' ἴσον … ἀναλογίαν. after δικαστής., 1132a32
1132b11–20: insert ἐλήλυθε … ὕστερον. after κέρδους., 1132a19
1133a23–4: delete ἢ τροφήν
1133b9: insert οὐκ after οὐ

1134a17–23: insert ἐπεὶ ... τῶν ἄλλων. after βλάβη·, 1135b24

1134a35: νόμον for λόγον

1137b4–5: delete οὐ δίκαιον

1139b28: ἀρχῆς for ἀρχή

1140a11: delete καὶ

1142a28: delete square brackets

1142b19: δεῖν for ἰδεῖν

1143b28: χρήσιμον for φρόνιμον

1143b30: οὖσιν for ἔχουσιν

1144a28: insert τοὺς after καὶ

1146b18–19: delete ἔπειτ᾽ ... οὔ.

1148a23–6: delete round brackets; insert dashes before τῶν γὰρ and after πρότερον; continue sentence after τιμή

1149b32: τι for τινι

1150a19–20: delete ἢ καθ᾽ ... ἢ

1154a10: comma for full stop

1155b15–16: delete εἴρηται ... ἔμπροσθεν.

1158a13: πολλοῖς for πολλοὺς

1158a14: ἀγαθὸν for ἀγαθοὺς

1160a19–20: delete square brackets

1160a22: full stop for asterisks

1161a35: delete καὶ ... δοῦλον

1163a2: delete square brackets

1172a8: ὡς οἷον τε for οἷς οἴονται συζῆν

1173a4: delete φυσικὸν ἀγαθὸν

1173a31: κινησις for κίνησιν

1174b10: τῆς ἡδονῆς for τὴν ἡδονήν

1178b12: delete asterisks

1180a32: insert καὶ δρᾶν αὐτὸ δύνασθαι in place of asterisks

Nicomachean Ethics

Book I

Chapter 1

Every skill and every inquiry, and similarly every action and rational 1094a
choice, is thought to aim at some good; and so the good has been aptly
described as that at which everything aims. But it is clear that there is
some difference between ends: some ends are activities, while others are
products which are additional to the activities. In cases where there are
ends additional to the actions, the products are by their nature better
than the activities.

Since there are many actions, skills, and sciences, it happens that
there are many ends as well: the end of medicine is health, that of
shipbuilding, a ship, that of military science, victory, and that of
domestic economy, wealth. But when any of these actions, skills, or
sciences comes under some single faculty – as bridlemaking and other
sciences concerned with equine equipment come under the science of
horsemanship, and horsemanship itself and every action in warfare
come under military science, and others similarly come under others –
then in all these cases the end of the master science is more worthy of
choice than the ends of the subordinate sciences, since these latter
ends are pursued also for the sake of the former. And it makes no
difference whether the ends of the actions are the activities themselves, or something else additional to them, as in the sciences just
mentioned.

3

Chapter 2

So if what is done has some end that we want for its own sake, and everything else we want is for the sake of this end; and if we do not choose everything for the sake of something else (because this would lead to an infinite progression, making our desire fruitless and vain), then clearly this will be the good, indeed the chief good. Surely, then, knowledge of the good must be very important for our lives? And if, like archers, we have a target, are we not more likely to hit the right mark? If so, we must try at least roughly to comprehend what it is and which science or faculty is concerned with it.

Knowledge of the good would seem to be the concern of the most authoritative science, the highest master science. And this is obviously the science of politics, because it lays down which of the sciences there 1094b should be in cities, and which each class of person should learn and up to what level. And we see that even the most honourable of faculties, such as military science, domestic economy, and rhetoric, come under it. Since political science employs the other sciences, and also lays down laws about what we should do and refrain from, its end will include the ends of the others, and will therefore be the human good. For even if the good is the same for an individual as for a city, that of the city is obviously a greater and more complete thing to obtain and preserve. For while the good of an individual is a desirable thing, what is good for a people or for cities is a nobler and more godlike thing. Our enquiry, then, is a kind of political science, since these are the ends it is aiming at.

Chapter 3

Our account will be adequate if its clarity is in line with the subject-matter, because the same degree of precision is not to be sought in all discussions, any more than in works of craftsmanship. The spheres of what is noble and what is just, which political science examines, admit of a good deal of diversity and variation, so that they seem to exist only by convention and not by nature. Goods vary in this way as well, since it happens that, for many, good things have harmful consequences: some people have been ruined by wealth, and others by courage. So we should be content, since we are discussing things like these in such a way, to demonstrate the truth sketchily and in outline, and, because we are making generalizations on the basis of generalizations, to draw conclusions along the same lines. Indeed, the details of our claims, then, should be looked at in the same way, since it is a mark of an educated person to look in each area for only that degree of accuracy that the nature of the subject permits. Accepting from a mathematician claims that are mere probabilities seems rather like demanding logical proofs from a rhetorician.

Each person judges well what he knows, and is a good judge of this. So, in any subject, the person educated in it is a good judge of that subject, 1095a and the person educated in all subjects is a good judge without qualification. This is why a young person is not fitted to hear lectures on political science, since our discussions begin from and concern the actions of life, and of these he has no experience. Again, because of his tendency to follow his feelings, his studies will be useless and to no purpose, since the end of the study is not knowledge but action. It makes no difference whether he is young in years or juvenile in character, since the deficiency is not related to age, but occurs because of his living and engaging in each of his pursuits according to his feelings. For knowledge is a waste of time for people like this, just as it is for those without self-restraint. But knowledge of the matters that concern political science will prove very beneficial to those who follow reason both in shaping their desires and in acting.

Let these comments – about the student, how our statements are to be taken, and the task we have set ourselves – serve as our preamble.

Chapter 4

Let us continue with the argument, and, since all knowledge and rational choice seek some good, let us say what we claim to be the aim of political science – that is, of all the good things to be done, what is the highest. Most people, I should think, agree about what it is called, since both the masses and sophisticated people call it happiness, understanding being happy as equivalent to living well and acting well. They disagree about substantive conceptions of happiness, the masses giving an account which differs from that of the philosophers. For the masses think it is something straightforward and obvious, like pleasure, wealth, or honour, some thinking it to be one thing, others another. Often the same person can give different accounts: when he is ill, it is health; when he is poor, it is wealth. And when people are aware of their ignorance, they marvel at those who say it is some grand thing quite beyond them. Certain thinkers used to believe that beyond these many good things there is something else good in itself, which makes all these good things good. Examining all the views offered would presumably be rather a waste of time, and it is enough to look at the most prevalent ones or those that seem to have something to be said for them.

Let us not forget, however, that there is a difference between arguments from first principles and arguments to first principles. For Plato rightly used to wonder about this, raising the question whether 1095b the way to go is from first principles or to first principles, as in the racecourse whether it is from the judges to the post or back again as well. For while we should begin from things known, they are known in two senses: known by us, and known without qualification. Presumably we have to begin from things known by us. This is why anyone who is going to be a competent student in the spheres of what is noble and what is just – in a word, politics – must be brought up well in his habits. For the first principle is the belief *that* something is the case, and if this is sufficiently clear, he will not need the reason *why* as well. Such a person is in possession of the first principles, or could easily grasp them. Anyone with neither of these possibilities open to him should listen to Hesiod:

> This person who understands everything for himself is the best of all,
> And noble is that one who heeds good advice.
> But he who neither understands it for himself nor takes to heart
> What he hears from another is a worthless man.[1]

Chapter 5

But let us begin from where we digressed. For people seem, not unreasonably, to base their conception of the good – happiness, that is – on their own lives. The masses, the coarsest people, see it as pleasure, and so they like the life of enjoyment. There are three especially prominent types of life: that just mentioned, the life of politics, and thirdly the life of contemplation. The masses appear quite slavish by

---

[1] Hesiod, *Works and Days*, 293, 295–7.

rationally choosing a life fit only for cattle; but they are worthy of consideration because many of those in power feel the same as Sardanapallus.[2]

Sophisticated people, men of action, see happiness as honour, since honour is pretty much the end of the political life. Honour, however, seems too shallow to be an object of our inquiry, since honour appears to depend more on those who honour than on the person honoured, whereas we surmise the good to be something of one's own that cannot easily be taken away. Again, they seem to pursue honour in order to convince themselves of their goodness; at least, they seek to be honoured by people with practical wisdom, among those who are familiar with them, and for their virtue. So it is clear that, to these people at least, virtue is superior.

One might, perhaps, suppose virtue rather than honour to be the end of the political life. But even virtue seems, in itself, to be lacking something, since apparently one can possess virtue even when one is asleep, or inactive throughout one's life, and also when one is suffering 1096a terribly or experiencing the greatest misfortunes; and no one would call a person living this kind of life happy, unless he were closely defending a thesis. But enough of this, because these issues have been sufficiently dealt with in our everyday discussions.

The third kind of life is that of contemplation, which we shall examine in what follows.

The life of making money is a life people are, as it were, forced into, and wealth is clearly not the good we are seeking, since it is merely useful, for getting something else. One would be better off seeing as ends the things mentioned before, because they are valued for themselves. But they do not appear to be ends either, and many arguments have been offered against them. So let us put them to one side.

Chapter 6

It would perhaps be quite a good idea to examine the notion of the universal and go through any problems there are in the way it is employed, despite the fact that such an inquiry turns out to be difficult going because those who introduced the Forms[3] are friends. It will

---

[2] A mythical king of Assyria.   [3] I.e., Plato and his followers.

presumably be thought better, indeed one's duty, to do away with even what is close to one's heart in order to preserve the truth, especially when one is a philosopher. For one might love both, but it is nevertheless a sacred duty to prefer the truth to one's friends.

Those who introduced this idea did not set up Forms for series in which they spoke of priority and posteriority, and this is why they did not postulate a Form of numbers. But the good is spoken of in the categories of substance, of quality and of relation; and that which exists in itself, namely, substance, is naturally prior to what is relative (since this seems like an offshoot and attribute of what is). So there could not be some common Form over and above these goods.

Again, good is spoken of in as many senses as is being: it is used in the category of substance, as for instance god and intellect, in that of quality – the virtues, in that of quantity – the right amount, in that of relation – the useful, in that of time – the right moment, and in that of place – the right locality, and so on. So it is clear that there could not be one common universal, because it would be spoken of not in all the categories, but in only one.

Again, since there is a single science for the things answering to each individual Form, there should have been some single science for all the goods. But as it happens there are many sciences, even of the things in one category. For example, the right moment: in war, it is military science, in illness, medicine; or the right amount: in diet, it is medicine, in exercise, gymnastics.

One might also be puzzled about what on earth they mean by speaking 1096b of a 'thing-in-itself', since the definition of humanity is one and the same in humanity-in-itself and human being. Inasmuch as they are human, they will not differ. And if this is so, the same will be true of good.

Nor will a thing be any the more good by being eternal, since a longlasting white thing is no whiter than a short-lived one.

The Pythagoreans[4] seem to give a more plausible account of the good, when they place the one in their column of goods; and Speusippus[5] seems to have followed them in this. But let this be the topic of another discussion.

An objection to what we have said might be that they did not speak

---

[4] Followers in Southern Italy of Pythagoras of Samos, who flourished around 530 BCE.
[5] Nephew of Plato, and head of Plato's Academy from 407–339 BCE.

about every good, and that things which are pursued and valued for their own sake are called good by reference to a single Form, while those that tend to be instrumental to these things or in some way to preserve them or prevent their contraries are called good for the sake of these – in a different way, in other words. Clearly, then, things should be called good in two senses: things good in themselves, and things good for the sake of things good in themselves. So let us distinguish things good in themselves from those that are means to them and see whether the former are called good with reference to a single Form. What sort of things should one put in the class of things good in themselves? Those that are sought even on their own, such as understanding, sight, certain types of pleasure, and honours? For even if we do seek these for the sake of something else, one would nevertheless put them in the class of things good in themselves. Perhaps nothing but the Form? Then the Form would be useless. But if those other things are in the class of things good in themselves, the same definition of the good will have to be exemplified in all of them, as is that of whiteness in snow and white lead. But the definitions of honour, practical wisdom and pleasure are distinct, and differ with respect to their being good. There is therefore no common good answering to a single Form.

But how, then, are things called good? For they do not seem like items that have the same name by chance. Is it through their all deriving from one good, or their all contributing to one good, or is it rather by analogy? For as sight is good in the body, so intellect is in the soul, and so on in other cases. But perhaps we should put these questions aside for the time being, since seeking precision in these matters would be more appropriate to another area of philosophy.

But the same is true of the Form. For even if there is some one good predicated across categories, or a good that is separate, itself in itself, clearly it could not be an object of action nor something attainable by a human being, which is the sort of thing we are looking for.

Perhaps someone might think that it would be better to understand it 1097a with an eye to those goods that are attainable and objects of action. For with this as a sort of paradigm we shall know better the goods that are goods for us, and if we know them, we shall attain them. This argument has some plausibility, but seems to be inconsistent with the sciences: they all aim at some good and seek to remedy any lack of the good, but they leave to one side understanding the universal good. And if there were such an important aid available, it is surely not reasonable to think that all practitioners of skills would be ignorant of it and fail even to look for it.

There is also a difficulty in seeing how a weaver or carpenter will be helped in practising his skill by knowing this good-in-itself, or how someone who has contemplated the Form itself will be a better doctor or general. For apparently it is not just health that the doctor attends to, but human health, or perhaps rather the health of a particular person, given that he treats each person individually.

That is enough on these issues.

Chapter 7

But let us return again to the good we are looking for, to see what it might be, since it appears to vary between different actions and skills: it is one thing in medicine, another in military science, and so on in all other cases. What then is the good in each case? Surely it is that for the sake of which other things are done? In medicine it is health, in military science, victory, in housebuilding, a house, and in other cases something else; in every action and rational choice the end is the good, since it is for the sake of the end that everyone does everything else. So if everything that is done has some end, this will be the good among things done, and if there are several ends, these will be the goods.

Our argument, then, has arrived at the same point by a different route, but we should try to make it still clearer. Since there appear to be several ends, and some of these, such as wealth, flutes, and implements generally, we choose as means to other ends, it is clear that not all ends are complete. But the chief good manifestly is something complete. So if there is only one end that is complete, this will be what we are looking for, and if there are several of them, the most complete. We speak of that which is worth pursuing for its own sake as more complete than that which is worth pursuing only for the sake of something else, and that which is never worth choosing for the sake of something else as more complete than things that are worth choosing both in themselves and for the sake of this end. And so that which is always worth choosing in itself and never for the sake of something else we call complete without qualification.

Happiness in particular is believed to be complete without qualifica-

tion, since we always choose it for itself and never for the sake of 1097b
anything else. Honour, pleasure, intellect, and every virtue we do indeed
choose for themselves (since we would choose each of them even if they
had no good effects), but we choose them also for the sake of happiness,
on the assumption that through them we shall live a life of happiness;
whereas happiness no one chooses for the sake of any of these nor
indeed for the sake of anything else.

The same conclusion seems to follow from considering self-
sufficiency, since the complete good is thought to be self-sufficient. We
are applying the term 'self-sufficient' not to a person on his own, living
a solitary life, but to a person living alongside his parents, children,
wife, and friends and fellow-citizens generally, since a human being is
by nature a social being. We must, however, set some limit on these,
since if we stretch things so far as to include ancestors and descendants
and friends of friends we shall end up with an infinite series. But we
must think about this later. For now, we take what is self-sufficient to be
that which on its own makes life worthy of choice and lacking in
nothing. We think happiness to be such, and indeed the thing most of all
worth choosing, not counted as just one thing among others. Counted as
just one thing among others it would clearly be more worthy of choice
with even the least good added to it. For the good added would cause an
increase in goodness, and the greater good is always more worthy of
choice. Happiness, then, is obviously something complete and self-
sufficient, in that it is the end of what is done.

But perhaps saying that happiness is the chief good sounds rather
platitudinous, and one might want its nature to be specified still more
clearly. It is possible that we might achieve that if we grasp the
characteristic activity of a human being. For just as the good – the doing
well – of a flute-player, a sculptor or any practitioner of a skill, or
generally whatever has some characteristic activity or action, is thought
to lie in its characteristic activity, so the same would seem to be true of a
human being, if indeed he has a characteristic activity.

Well, do the carpenter and the tanner have characteristic activities and
actions, and a human being none? Has nature left him without a
characteristic activity to perform? Or, as there seem to be characteristic
activities of the eye, the hand, the foot, and generally of each part of the
body, should one assume that a human being has some characteristic
activity over and above all these? What sort of thing might it be, then?

For living is obviously shared even by plants, while what we are looking
1098a for is something special to a human being. We should therefore rule out
the life of nourishment and growth. Next would be some sort of sentient
life, but this again is clearly shared by the horse, the ox, indeed by every
animal. What remains is a life, concerned in some way with action, of
the element that possesses reason. (Of this element, one part has reason
in being obedient to reason, the other in possessing it and engaging in
thought.) As this kind of life can be spoken of in two ways, let us assume
that we are talking about the life concerned with action in the sense of
activity, because this seems to be the more proper use of the phrase.

If the characteristic activity of a human being is an activity of the soul
in accordance with reason or at least not entirely lacking it; and if we say
that the characteristic activity of anything is the same in kind as that of a
good thing of the same type, as in the case of a lyre-player and a good
lyre-player, and so on, without qualification, in the same way in every
case, the superiority of the good one in virtue being an addition to the
characteristic activity (for the characteristic activity of the lyre-player is
to play the lyre, that of the good lyre-player to play it well); then if this
is so, and we take the characteristic activity of a human being to be a
certain kind of life; and if we take this kind of life to be activity of the
soul and actions in accordance with reason, and the characteristic
activity of the good person to be to carry this out well and nobly, and a
characteristic activity to be accomplished well when it is accomplished
in accordance with the appropriate virtue; then if this is so, the human
good turns out to be activity of the soul in accordance with virtue, and if
there are several virtues, in accordance with the best and most complete.
Again, this must be over a complete life. For one swallow does not make
a summer, nor one day. Neither does one day or a short time make
someone blessed and happy.

So let this serve as an outline of the good, since perhaps we have first
to make a rough sketch, and then fill it in later. One would think that
anyone with a good outline can carry on and complete the details, and
that in this task time will bring much to light or else offer useful
assistance. This is how skills have come to advance, because anyone can
fill in the gaps. But we must bear in mind what we said above, and not
look for the same precision in everything, but in each case whatever is in
line with the subject-matter, and the degree appropriate to the inquiry.
A carpenter and a geometrician approach the right-angle in different

ways: the carpenter in so far as it is useful for his work, while the geometrician seeks to know what it is, or what sort of thing it is, in that he aims to contemplate the truth. We should therefore do the same in every other case, so that side-issues do not dominate the tasks in hand. Nor should we demand an explanation in the same way in all cases. A 1098b sound proof that something *is* the case will suffice in some instances, as with first principles, where the fact itself is a starting-point, that is, a first principle. Some first principles we see by induction, some by perception, some by a kind of habituation, and others in other ways. We must try to investigate each type in the way appropriate to its nature, and take pains to define each of them well, because they are very important in what follows. The first principle seems to be more than half the whole thing, and to clarify many of the issues we are inquiring into.

Chapter 8

But we must consider the first principle in the light not only of our conclusion and premises, but of the things that people say about it. For all the data harmonize with the truth, but soon clash with falsity.

Goods have been classifed into three groups: those called external goods, goods of the soul, and goods of the body. Goods of the soul are the ones we call most strictly and most especially good, and the actions and activities of the soul we may attribute to the soul. Our conception of happiness, then, is plausible in so far as it is accords with this view, a venerable one that has been accepted by philosophers.

Our account is right also in that we are claiming that the end consists in certain actions and activities. For the end thus turns out to be a good of the soul and not an external good.

Another belief that harmonizes with our account is that the happy person lives well and acts well, for we have claimed that happiness is pretty much a kind of living well and acting well.

Again, all the things that people look for in happiness appear to have been included in our account. Some think that happiness is virtue, some practical wisdom, others a kind of wisdom; while others think it is a combination of these or one of these along with more or less pleasure. Yet others include external prosperity as well. Some of these views are popular and of long standing, while others are those of a few distinguished men. It is not likely that either group is utterly mistaken, but rather that at least one component of their view is on the right track, perhaps even most of them.

Our account of happiness is in harmony with those who say that happiness is virtue or some particular virtue, since activity in accordance with virtue is characteristic of virtue. Presumably, though, it makes a great difference whether we conceive of the chief good as consisting in possession or in use, that is to say, in a state or in an 1099a activity. For while a state can exist without producing any good consequences, as it does in the case of a person sleeping or lying idle for some other reason, this is impossible for an activity: it will necessarily engage in action, and do so well. As in the Olympic Games it is not the most attractive and the strongest who are crowned, but those who compete (since it is from this group that winners come), so in life it is those who act rightly who will attain what is noble and good.

It is also the case that the life of these people is pleasurable in itself. For experiencing pleasure is an aspect of the soul, and each person finds pleasure in that of which he is said to be fond, as a horse-lover finds it in a horse, and someone who likes wonderful sights finds it in a wonderful sight. In the same way, a lover of justice finds it in the sphere of justice and in general a person with virtue finds pleasure in what accords with virtue. The pleasures of the masses, because they are not pleasant by nature, conflict with one another, but the pleasures of those who are fond of noble things are pleasant by nature. Actions in accordance with virtue are like this, so that they are pleasant to these people as well as in themselves. Their life therefore has no need of pleasure as some kind of lucky ornament, but contains its pleasure in itself, because, in addition to what we have already said, the person who does not enjoy noble actions is not good. For no one would call a person just if he did not enjoy acting justly, or generous if he did not enjoy generous actions; and the same goes for the other virtues. If this is so, it follows that actions in accordance with virtue are pleasant in themselves. But they are also good and noble as well as pleasant; indeed, since the good person is a good judge of goodness and nobility, actions in accordance with virtue have them to a degree greater than anything else; and here he judges in accordance with our views.

Happiness, then, is the best, the noblest and the pleasantest thing, and these qualities are not separate as in the inscription at Delos:

Noblest is that which is the most just, and best is being healthy.
But most pleasant is obtaining what one longs for.

This is because the best activities have all of these qualities. And we say that happiness consists in them, or one of them – the best.

Nevertheless, as we suggested, happiness obviously needs the presence of external goods as well, since it is impossible, or at least no easy matter, to perform noble actions without resources. For in many actions, we employ, as if they were instruments at our disposal, friends, wealth, 1099b and political power. Again, being deprived of some things – such as high birth, noble children, beauty – spoils our blessedness. For the person who is terribly ugly, of low birth, or solitary and childless is not really the sort to be happy, still less perhaps if he has children or friends who are thoroughly bad, or good but dead. As we have said, then, there seems to be an additional need for some sort of prosperity like this. For this reason, some identify happiness with good fortune, while others identify it with virtue.

Chapter 9

Hence the problem also arises of whether happiness is to be acquired by learning, habituation, or some other training, or whether it comes by virtue of some divine dispensation or even by chance.

If there is anything that the gods give to men, it is reasonable that happiness should be god-given, especially since it is so much the best thing in the human world. But this question would perhaps be more suited to another inquiry. Even if it is not sent by the gods, however, but arises through virtue and some sort of learning or training, it is evidently one of the most divine things. For that which is the prize and end of virtue is clearly the chief good, something both divine and blessed.

It would also be something widely shared, since everyone who was not incapacitated with regard to virtue could attain it through some kind of learning and personal effort. And if it is better to be happy in this way than by chance, it is reasonable that happiness should be attained like this. For what is in accordance with nature is by nature as noble as it can be, and so is what is in accordance with skill and every other cause, especially that in accordance with the best cause. To entrust what is greatest and most noble to chance would be quite inappropriate.

The answer to our question is also manifest from our account of happiness, since we said that it was a certain kind of activity of the soul in accordance with virtue; and of the other goods, some are necessary conditions of happiness, and others are naturally helpful and serve as useful means to it.

And this agrees with what we said at the beginning. We took the end of political science to be the chief good, and political science is concerned most of all with producing citizens of a certain kind, namely, those who are both good and the sort to perform noble actions.

It is with good reason, then, that we do not call an ox, a horse or any 1100a other animal happy, because none of them can share in such activity. And for this same reason, a child is not happy either, since his age makes him incapable of doing such actions. If he is called blessed, he is being described as such on account of the potential he has, since, as we have said, happiness requires complete virtue and a complete life. For there are many vicissitudes in life, all sorts of chance things happen, and even the most successful can meet with great misfortunes in old age, as the story goes of Priam[6] in Trojan times. No one calls someone happy who meets with misfortunes like these and comes to a wretched end.

Chapter 10

Should we then call no one happy while they are alive, but rather, as Solon advises, wait to see the end?[7] Even if we must assume this to be right, is it really the case that he is happy when he is dead? Or is this not quite ridiculous, especially for us, claiming as we do that happiness is some kind of activity?

But if it is not that we call the dead person happy, and Solon meant not this, but that we can at that stage safely call a person blessed in so far as he is now beyond the reach of evils and misfortunes, even this claim is open to dispute. For both good and evil are thought to happen to a dead person, since they can happen to a person who is alive but not aware of them. Take, for example, honours and dishonours, and the good and bad fortunes of his children or his descendants generally. But this view also gives rise to a problem. Though a person may have lived a blessed

---

[6] King of Troy at the time of its destruction by Agamemnon.
[7] See Herodotus, *Histories* 1.30–2. Solon was an Athenian lawgiver in the early sixth century, thought to be the founder of democracy.

life into his old age and died accordingly, many reverses may happen in connection with his descendants. Some of them may be good and meet with the life they deserve, others the contrary; and clearly the relation to their ancestors can vary to any degree. It would indeed be odd if the dead person also were to share in these vicissitudes, and be sometimes happy, sometimes wretched. But it would also be odd if the fortunes of descendants had no effect on their ancestors for any time at all.

But we should return to the original question, since considering it might shed light on the one now under discussion. If we must wait to see the end and only then call a person blessed, not as such but as having been so before, surely it is odd that – because we do not wish to 1100b call the living happy on account of possible changes in their fortunes, and because happiness is understood as something permanent and not at all liable to change, while the living experience many turns of the wheel – when he is happy, he will not be truly described as such? For clearly, if we were to follow his fortunes, we should often call the same person happy and then wretched, representing the happy person as a kind of chameleon, or as having an unsound foundation. Or is following a person's fortunes the wrong thing to do? For they are not what doing well or badly depend on, though, as we said, they are required as complementary to a fully human life. What really matter for happiness are activities in accordance with virtue, and for the contrary of happiness the contrary kind of activities.

The question we have been discussing is further confirmation of our account, since nothing in the sphere of human achievement has more permanence than activities in accordance with virtue. They are thought to be more lasting even than the sciences, and the most honourable to be the more lasting, because the blessed spend their lives engaged, quite continually, in them above all (which seems to be why there is no forgetting in connection with these activities).

The quality in question, then, will belong to the happy person, and he will be happy throughout his life. For he will spend all, or most, of his time engaged in action and contemplation in accordance with virtue. And he will bear changes in fortune in a particularly noble way and altogether gracefully, as one who is 'genuinely good' and 'foursquare without a flaw'.[8]

---

[8] Simonides; see Plato, *Protagoras* 339b. Simonides (*c.* 556–468) was a Greek poet from Ceos.

Many things, however, both large and small, happen by chance. Small pieces of good fortune or its contrary clearly do not affect the balance of life. But many great events, if they are good, will make a life more blessed, since they will themselves naturally embellish it, and the way a person deals with them can be noble and good. But if they turn out the other way, they will oppress and spoil what is blessed, since they bring distress with them and hinder many activities. Nevertheless, even in their midst what is noble shines through, when a person calmly bears many great misfortunes, not through insensibility, but by being well bred and great-souled.

If activities are, as we have said, what really matter in life, no one blessed could become wretched, since he will never do hateful and petty 1101a actions. For the truly good and wise person, we believe, bears all the fortunes of life with dignity and always does the noblest thing in the circumstances, as a good general does the most strategically appropriate thing with the army at his disposal, and a shoemaker makes the noblest shoe out of the leather he is given, and so on with other practitioners of skills. If this is so, the happy person could never become wretched, though he will not be blessed if he meets with luck like that of Priam. Nor indeed will he be unstable and changeable. He will not be shifted easily from happiness, and not by ordinary misfortunes, but by many grave ones. He would not recover from these to become happy again in a short space of time. If he does recover, it will be after a long and complete period of great and noble accomplishments.

What is to prevent us, then, from concluding that the happy person is the one who, adequately furnished with external goods, engages in activities in accordance with complete virtue, not for just any period of time but over a complete life? Or should we add that he will live like this in the future and die accordingly? The future is obscure to us, and we say that happiness is an end and altogether quite complete. This being so, we shall call blessed those of the living who have and will continue to have the things mentioned, but blessed only in human terms.

So much for the distinctions we draw in these areas.

Chapter 11

Nevertheless, the idea that the fortunes of a person's descendants and all his friends have no effect on him seems excessively heartless and contrary to what people think. But, given that the things that happen are many and various, some affecting us more and others less, it looks as if it would be a long – even interminable – job to distinguish them in detail. It will be enough, perhaps, to give a general outline.

If, then, as some of a person's misfortunes have a certain weight and influence on his life, while others seem lighter, so too there are similar differences between the fortunes of all his friends; and if it makes a difference whether each of these misfortunes happens to people when they are alive or when they are dead (a greater difference even than whether the dreadful crimes in tragedies happened before the play or are perpetrated on the stage); then this difference must be taken into account in our reasoning, or rather, perhaps, the fact that there is a puzzle about whether the dead can partake of any good or evil. For it 1101b does seem, from what we have said, that if anything good or bad does actually affect them, it will be pretty unimportant and insignificant, either in itself or in relation to them; or if not, it must at least be of such an extent and kind as not to make happy those who are not happy already nor to deprive those who are happy of their being blessed. So when friends do well, and likewise when they do badly, it does seem to have some effect on the dead. But it is of such a nature and degree as neither to make not happy those who are happy, nor anything like that.

Chapter 12

Now that these matters have been sorted out, let us consider whether happiness is a thing to be praised or instead something to be honoured. For it is clearly not just a capacity.

Anything that is praised seems to be praised for its being of a certain kind and its standing in a certain relation to something else: the just person, the brave person, and the good person and virtue in general we praise for their actions and what they bring about. And we praise the strong person, the fast runner, and each of the others, because he is naturally of a certain kind and stands in some sort of relation to something good and excellent. This is clear also from praise of the gods. For it seems absurd that they should be judged by reference to us, but this happens because, as we have said, praise involves reference to something else. But if praise applies only to things standing in relations, clearly it is not praise that applies to the best things, but something greater and better. This is in fact obvious, since the gods and the most godlike of people we call blessed and happy. The same goes for things that are good, since we never praise happiness as we might justice, but rather call it blessed, as something better and more divine.

And Eudoxus[9] seems to have been right in pressing the claims of pleasure to supremacy. He believed that the fact that it is not praised despite its being a good indicates that it is better than things that are praised; and he thought that god and the good are like this, because it is by reference to these that other goods are praised. For praise is indeed appropriate to virtue, since it makes us the kind of people to perform noble actions; eulogies, however, are bestowed on what is achieved in the spheres of the body and of the soul alike. But perhaps clarity here is more the job of those who have gone into the subject of encomiums. For 1102a us, anyway, it is clear from what has been said that happiness is something honourable and complete.

And that it is so seems to follow as well from its being a first principle. It is for the sake of this this we all do all the rest of our actions, and the first principle and cause of goods we take to be something honourable and divine.

Chapter 13

Since happiness is a certain kind of activity of the soul in accordance with complete virtue, we ought to look at virtue. For perhaps then we might be in a better position to consider happiness.

Besides, the true politician is thought to have taken special pains over this, since he wants to make citizens good and obedient to the laws. As an example, we have the lawgivers of the Cretans and the Spartans, and any others of that ilk. If this inquiry is a part of political science, pursuing it will clearly accord with our original purpose.

Clearly, it is human virtue we must consider, since we were looking for human good and human happiness. By human virtue, we mean that of the soul, not that of the body; and happiness we speak of as an activity of the soul. If this is right, the politician clearly must have some understanding of the sphere of the soul, as the person who is to attend to eyes must have some understanding of the whole body; more so,

---

[9] c. 390–c. 340 BCE. Outstanding mathematician and pupil of Plato.

indeed, in that political science is superior to medicine, and held in higher esteem, and even among doctors, the sophisticated ones go to a great deal of effort to understand the body. The politician, then, must consider the soul, and consider it with a view to understanding virtue, just to the extent that is required by the inquiry, because attaining a higher degree of precision is perhaps too much trouble for his current purpose.

Some aspects of the soul have been dealt with competently in our popular works as well, and we should make use of these. It is said, for example, that one element of the soul has reason, while another lacks it. It does not matter for the moment whether these elements are separate like the parts of the body or anything else that can be physically divided, or whether they are naturally inseparable but differentiated in thought, like the convex and concave aspects of a curved surface.

Of the element without reason, one part seems to be common: the vegetative, the cause of nutrition and growth. For one should assume such a capacity of the soul to exist in everything that takes in nutrition, 1102b even embryos, and to be the same in fully grown beings, since this is more reasonable than assuming that they have a different capacity.

The virtue of this element is clearly something shared and not specific to human beings. For this part and its capacity are thought more than others to be active during sleep, and the good and bad person to be hardest to distinguish when they are asleep (hence the saying that the happy are no different from the wretched for half of their lives – which makes sense, since sleep is a time when the soul is not engaged in the things that lead to its being called good or bad), except that in some way certain movements on a small scale reach the soul, and make the dreams of good people better than those of ordinary people. But enough of this. Let us leave the nutritive capacity aside, since by nature it plays no role in human virtue.

But there does seem to be another natural element in the soul, lacking reason, but nevertheless, as it were, partaking in it. For we praise the reason of the self-controlled and of the incontinent, that is, the part of their soul with reason, because it urges them in the right direction, towards what is best; but clearly there is within them another natural element besides reason, which conflicts with and resists it. For just as paralysed limbs, when one rationally chooses to move them to the right, are carried off in the opposite direction to the left, so also in the soul:

the impulses of incontinent people carry them off in the opposite direction. In the body we do indeed see the lack of control, while in the soul we do not see it; but I think that we should nevertheless hold that there is some element in the soul besides reason, opposing and running counter to it. In what way it is distinct from the other elements does not matter. But it does seem to partake in reason, as we said. The element in the soul of the self-controlled person, at least, obeys reason and presumably in the temperate and the brave person it is still more ready to listen, since in their case it is in total harmony with reason.

So the element without reason seems itself to have two parts. For the vegetative part has no share at all in reason, while the part consisting in appetite and desire in general does share in it in a way, in so far as it listens to and obeys it. So it has reason in the sense that a person who listens to the reason of his father and his friends is said to have reason, not reason in the mathematical sense. That the element without reason is in some way persuaded by reason is indicated as well by the offering 1103a of advice, and all kinds of criticism and encouragement. And if we must say that this element possesses reason, then the element with reason will also have two parts, one, in the strict sense, possessing it in itself, the other ready to listen to reason as one is ready to listen to the reason of one's father.

Virtue is distinguished along the same lines. Some virtues we say are intellectual, such as wisdom, judgement and practical wisdom, while others are virtues of character, such as generosity and temperance. For when we are talking about a person's character, we do not say that he is wise or has judgement, but that he is even-tempered or temperate. Yet we do praise the wise person for his state, and the states worthy of praise we call virtues.

Book II

Chapter 1

Virtue, then, is of two kinds: that of the intellect and that of character. Intellectual virtue owes its origin and development mainly to teaching, for which reason its attainment requires experience and time; virtue of character (*ēthos*) is a result of habituation (*ethos*), for which reason it has acquired its name through a small variation on '*ethos*'. From this it is clear that none of the virtues of character arises in us by nature. For nothing natural can be made to behave differently by habituation. For example, a stone that naturally falls downwards could not be made by habituation to rise upwards, not even if one tried to habituate it by throwing it up ten thousand times; nor can fire be habituated to burn downwards, nor anything else that naturally behaves in one way be habituated to behave differently. So virtues arise in us neither by nature nor contrary to nature, but nature gives us the capacity to acquire them, and completion comes through habituation.

Again, in all the cases where something arises in us by nature, we first acquire the capacities and later exhibit the activities. This is clear in the case of the senses, since we did not acquire them by seeing often or hearing often; we had them before we used them, and did not acquire them by using them. Virtues, however, we acquire by first exercising them. The same is true with skills, since what we need to learn before doing, we learn by doing; for example, we become builders by building, and lyre-players by playing the lyre. So too we become just by doing 1103b just actions, temperate by temperate actions, and courageous by courageous actions. What happens in cities bears this out as well, because legislators make the citizens good by habituating them, and this is what every legislator intends. Those who do not do it well miss their target; and it is in this respect that a good political system differs from a bad one.

Again, as in the case of a skill, the origin and means of the development of each virtue are the same as those of its corruption: it is from playing the lyre that people become good and bad lyre-players. And it is analogous in the case of builders and all the rest, since from building well, people will be good builders, from building badly, bad builders. If this were not so, there would have been no need of a person to teach them, but they would all have been born good or bad at their skill.

It is the same, then, with the virtues. For by acting as we do in our dealings with other men, some of us become just, others unjust; and by acting as we do in the face of danger, and by becoming habituated to feeling fear or confidence, some of us become courageous, others cowardly. The same goes for cases of appetites and anger; by conducting themselves in one way or the other in such circumstances, some become temperate and even-tempered, others intemperate and bad-tempered. In a word, then, like states arise from like activities. This is why we must give a certain character to our activities, since it is on the differences between them that the resulting states depend. So it is not unimportant how we are habituated from our early days; indeed it makes a huge difference – or rather all the difference.

Chapter 2

The branch of philosophy we are dealing with at present is not purely theoretical like the others, because it is not in order to acquire knowledge that we are considering what virtue is, but to become good people – otherwise there would be no point in it. So we must consider the matter of our actions, and in particular how they should be performed, since, as we have said, they are responsible for our states developing in one way or another.

The idea of acting in accordance with right reason is a generally accepted one. Let us here take it for granted – we shall discuss it later, both what right reason is and how it is related to the other virtues. But
1104a this we must agree on before we begin: that the whole account of what is to be done ought to be given roughly and in outline. As we said at the

start, the accounts we demand should be appropriate to their subject-matter; and the spheres of actions and of what is good for us, like those of health, have nothing fixed about them.

Since the general account lacks precision, the account at the level of particulars is even less precise. For they do not come under any skill or set of rules: agents must always look at what is appropriate in each case as it happens, as do doctors and navigators. But, though our present account is like this, we should still try to offer some help.

First, then, let us consider this – the fact that states like this are naturally corrupted by deficiency and excess, as we see in the cases of strength and health (we must use clear examples to illustrate the unclear); for both too much exercise and too little ruin one's strength, and likewise too much food and drink and too little ruin one's health, while the right amount produces, increases and preserves it. The same goes, then, for temperance, courage and the other virtues: the person who avoids and fears everything, never standing his ground, becomes cowardly, while he who fears nothing, but confronts every danger, becomes rash. In the same way, the person who enjoys every pleasure and never restrains himself becomes intemperate, while he who avoids all pleasure – as boors do – becomes, as it were, insensible. Temperance and courage, then, are ruined by excess and deficiency, and preserved by the mean.

Not only are virtues produced and developed from the same origins and by the same means as those from which and by which they are corrupted, but the activities that flow from them will consist in the same things. For this is also true in other more obvious cases, like that of strength. It is produced by eating a great deal and going through a great deal of strenuous exercise, and it is the strong person who will be most able to do these very things. The same applies to virtues. By abstaining from pleasures we become temperate, and having become so we are most able to abstain from them. Similarly with courage: by becoming habitu- 1104b ated to make light of what is fearful and to face up to it, we become courageous; and when we are, we shall be most able to face up to it.

Chapter 3

We must take as an indication of a person's states the pleasure or pain consequent on what he does, because the person who abstains from bodily pleasures and finds his enjoyment in doing just this is temperate, while the person who finds doing it oppressive is intemperate; and the person who enjoys facing up to danger, or at least does not find it painful to do so, is courageous, while he who does find it painful is a coward. For virtue of character is concerned with pleasures and pains: it is because of pleasure that we do bad actions, and pain that we abstain from noble ones. It is for this reason that we need to have been brought up in a particular way from our early days, as Plato says,[10] so we might find enjoyment or pain in the right things; for the right education is just this.

Again, if the virtues are to do with actions and situations of being affected, and pleasure and pain follow from every action and situation of being affected, then this is another reason why virtue will be concerned with pleasures and pains.

The fact that punishment is based on pleasure and pain is further evidence of their relevance; for punishment is a kind of cure, and cures by their nature are effected by contraries.

Again, as we said recently, every state of the soul is naturally related to, and concerned with, the kind of things by which it is naturally made better or worse. It is because of pleasures and pains that people become bad – through pursuing or avoiding the wrong ones, or at the wrong time, or in the wrong manner, or in any other of the various ways distinguished by reason. This is why some have classified virtues as forms of insensibility or states of rest; but this is wrong, because they speak without qualification, without saying 'in the right way' and 'in the wrong way', 'at the right time' and 'at the wrong time', and the other things one can add.

We assume, then, that virtue will be the sort of state to do the best actions in connection with pleasures and pains, and vice the contrary. The following considerations should also make it plain to us that virtue and vice are concerned with the same things.

There are three objects of choice – the noble, the useful, and the pleasant – and three of avoidance – their contraries, the shameful, the harmful, and the painful. In respect of all of these, especially pleasure, the good person tends to go right, and the bad person to go wrong. For pleasure is shared with animals, and accompanies all objects of

10 Plato, *Republic* 401e–402a; *Laws* 653a–c.

choice, because what is noble and what is useful appear pleasant as 1105a
well.

Again, pleasure has grown up with all of us since infancy and is consequently a feeling difficult to eradicate, ingrained as it is in our lives. And, to a greater or lesser extent, we regulate our actions by pleasure and pain. Our whole inquiry, then, must be concerned with them, because whether we feel enjoyment and pain in a good or bad way has great influence on our actions.

Again, as Heraclitus says, it is harder to fight against pleasure than against spirit.[11] But both skill and virtue are always concerned with what is harder, because success in what is harder is superior. So this is another reason why the whole concern of virtue and political science is pleasures and pains: the person who manages them well will be good, while he who does so badly will be bad.

Let it be taken as established, then, that virtue is to do with pleasures and pains; that the actions which produce it also increase it, or, if they assume a different character, corrupt it; and that the sphere of its activity is the actions that themselves gave rise to it.

Chapter 4

Someone might, however, wonder what we mean by saying that becoming just requires doing just actions first, and becoming temperate, temperate actions. For if we do just and temperate actions, we are already just and temperate; similarly, if we do what is literate or musical, we must be literate or musical.

But surely this is not true even of the skills? For one can produce something literate by chance or under instruction from another. Someone will be literate, then, only when he produces something literate and does so in a literate way, that is, in accordance with his own literacy.

Again, the case of the skills is anyway not the same as that of the virtues. For the products of the skills have their worth within themselves, so it is enough for them to be turned out with a certain quality. But actions done in accordance with virtues are done in a just or temperate way not merely by having some quality of their own, but

---

[11] Heraclitus, 22 B 85 DK. *fl. c.* 500 BCE. Important Ionian philosopher.

rather if the agent acts in a certain state, namely, first, with knowledge, secondly, from rational choice, and rational choice of the actions for their own sake, and, thirdly, from a firm and unshakeable character. The 1105b second and third of these are not counted as conditions for the other skills, only the knowledge. With regard to virtues, knowledge has little or no weight, while the other two conditions are not just slightly, but all-important. And these are the ones that result from often doing just and temperate actions. Actions, then, are called just and temperate when they are such as the just and the temperate person would do. But the just and temperate person is not the one who does them merely, but the one who does them as just and temperate people do. So it is correct to say that it is by doing just actions that one becomes just, and by doing temperate actions temperate; without doing them, no one would have even a chance of becoming good.

But the masses do not do them. They take refuge in argument, thinking that they are being philosophers and that this is the way to be good. They are rather like patients who listen carefully to their doctors, but do not do what they are told. Just as such treatment will not make the patients healthy in body, so being this kind of philosopher will not make the masses healthy in soul.

Chapter 5

Next we must consider what virtue is. There are three things to be found in the soul – feelings, capacities, and states – so virtue should be one of these. By feelings, I mean appetite, anger, fear, confidence, envy, joy, love, hate, longing, emulation, pity, and in general things accompanied by pleasure or pain. By capacities, I mean the things on the basis of which we are described as being capable of experiencing these feelings – on the basis of which, for example, we are described as capable of feeling anger, fear or pity. And by states I mean those things in respect of which we are well or badly disposed in relation to feelings. If, for example, in relation to anger, we feel it too much or too little, we are badly disposed; but if we are between the two, then well disposed. And the same goes for the other cases.

Neither the virtues nor the vices are feelings, because we are called good or bad on the basis not of our feelings, but of our virtues and vices; and also because we are neither praised nor blamed on the basis of our feelings (the person who is afraid or angry is not praised, and the person who is angry without qualification is not blamed but rather the person 1106a who is angry in a certain way), but we are praised and blamed on the basis of our virtues and vices. Again, we become angry or afraid without rational choice, while the virtues are rational choices or at any rate involve rational choice. Again, in respect of our feelings, we are said to be moved, while in respect of our virtues and vices we are said not to be moved but to be in a certain state.

For these reasons they are not capacities either. For we are not called either good or bad, nor are we praised or blamed, through being capable of experiencing things, without qualification. Again, while we have this capacity by nature, we do not become good or bad by nature; we spoke about this earlier.

So if the virtues are neither feelings nor capacities, it remains that they are states. We have thus described what virtue is generically.

Chapter 6

But we must say not just that virtue is a state, but what kind of state. We should mention, then, that every virtue causes that of which it is a virtue to be in a good state, and to perform its characteristic activity well. The virtue of the eye, for example, makes it and its characteristic activity good, because it is through the virtue of the eye that we see well. Likewise, the virtue of the horse makes a horse good – good at running, at carrying its rider and at facing the enemy. If this is so in all cases, then the virtue of a human being too will be the state that makes a human being good and makes him perform his characteristic activity well.

We have already said how this will happen, and it will be clear also from what follows, if we consider what the nature of virtue is like.

In everything continuous and divisible, one can take more, less, or an equal amount, and each either in respect of the thing itself or relative to us; and the equal is a sort of mean between excess and deficiency. By the mean in respect of the thing itself I mean that which is equidistant from each of the extremes, this being one single thing and the same for everyone, and by the mean relative to us I mean that which is neither excessive nor deficient – and this is not one single thing, nor is it the same for all. If, for example, ten are many and two are few, six is the mean if one takes it in respect of the thing, because it is by the same amount that it exceeds the one number and is exceeded by the other. This is the mean according to arithmetic progression. The mean relative to us, however, is not to be obtained in this way. For if ten pounds of food is a lot for someone to eat, and two pounds a little, the trainer will not necessarily prescribe six; for this may be a lot or a little for the person about to eat it – for Milo,[12] a little, for a beginner at gymnastics, a lot. The same goes for running and wrestling. In this way every expert in a science avoids excess and deficiency, and aims for the mean and chooses it – the mean, that is, not in the thing itself but relative to us.

If, then, every science does its job well in this way, with its eye on the mean and judging its products by this criterion (which explains both why people are inclined to say of successful products that nothing can be added or taken away from them, implying that excess and deficiency ruin what is good in them, while the mean preserves it, and why those who are good at the skills have their eye on this, as we say, in turning out their product), and if virtue, like nature, is more precise and superior to any skill, it will also be the sort of thing that is able to hit the mean.

I am talking here about virtue of character, since it is this that is concerned with feelings and actions, and it is in these that we find excess, deficiency and the mean. For example, fear, confidence, appetite, anger, pity, and in general pleasure and pain can be experienced too much or too little, and in both ways not well. But to have them at the right time, about the right things, towards the right people, for the right end, and in the right way, is the mean and best; and this is the business of virtue. Similarly, there is an excess, a deficiency and a mean in actions. Virtue is concerned with feelings and actions, in which excess and deficiency constitute misses of the mark, while the mean is praised and on target, both of which are characteristics of virtue. Virtue, then, is a kind of mean, at least in the sense that it is the sort of thing that is able to hit a mean.

Again, one can miss the mark in many ways (since the bad belongs to the unlimited, as the Pythagoreans portrayed it, and the good to the limited), but one can get things right in only one (for which reason one is easy and the other difficult – missing the target easy, hitting it difficult). For these reasons as well, then, excess and deficiency are characteristics of vice, the mean characteristic of virtue:

[12] Famous athlete from Croton of the later sixth century.

For good people are just good, while bad people are bad in all sorts
of ways.[13]

Virtue, then, is a state involving rational choice, consisting in a mean
relative to us and determined by reason – the reason, that is, by 1107a
reference to which the practically wise person would determine it. It is a
mean between two vices, one of excess, the other of deficiency. It is a
mean also in that some vices fall short of what is right in feelings and
actions, and others exceed it, while virtue both attains and chooses the
mean. So, in respect of its essence and the definition of its substance,
virtue is a mean, while with regard to what is best and good it is an
extreme.

But not every action or feeling admits of a mean. For some have
names immediately connected with depravity, such as spite, shameless-
ness, envy, and, among actions, adultery, theft, homicide. All these, and
others like them, are so called because they themselves, and not their
excesses or deficiencies, are bad. In their case, then, one can never hit
the mark, but always misses. Nor is there a good or bad way to go about
such things – committing adultery, say, with the right woman, at the
right time, or in the right way. Rather, doing one of them, without
qualification, is to miss the mark.

It would be equally wrong, therefore, to expect there to be a mean, an
excess and a deficiency in committing injustice, being a coward, and
being intemperate, since then there would be a mean of excess and a
mean of deficiency, an excess of excess and a deficiency of deficiency.
Rather, just as there is no excess and deficiency of temperance and
courage, because the mean is, in a sense, an extreme, so too there is no
mean, excess or deficiency in the cases above. However they are done,
one misses the mark, because, generally speaking, there is neither a
mean of excess or deficiency, nor an excess or deficiency of a mean.

Chapter 7

But this general account on its own is not enough. We must also apply it
to particular cases, because though more general discussions of actions
are of wider application, particular ones are more genuine. This is

---

[13] Unknown.

because actions are to do with particulars, and what we say should accord with particulars. We may take them from our diagram.

1107b   In fear and confidence, courage is the mean. Of those who exceed it, the person who exceeds in fearlessness has no name (many cases lack names), while the one who exceeds in confidence is rash. He who exceeds in being afraid and is deficient in confidence is a coward.

With respect to pleasures and pains – not all of them, and less so with pains – the mean is temperance, the excess intemperance. People deficient with regard to pleasures are not very common, and so do not even have a name; let us call them insensible.

In giving and taking money, the mean is generosity, while the excess and deficiency are wastefulness and stinginess. People with these qualities are excessive and deficient in contrary ways to one another. The wasteful person exceeds in giving away and falls short in taking, while the stingy person exceeds in taking and falls short in giving away. (At present, we can be content with giving a rough and summary account of these things; a more detailed classification will come later.)

There are other dispositions connected with money. One mean is magnificence, for the magnificent person, in so far as he deals with large amounts, differs from the generous one, who deals with small. The excess is tastelessness and vulgarity, the deficiency niggardliness, and they differ from the states opposed to generosity; how they differ will be stated below.

In honour and dishonour, the mean is greatness of soul, while the excess is referred to as a kind of vanity, the deficiency smallness of soul. And just as we said generosity is related to magnificence, differing from it by being concerned with small amounts, so there is a virtue having to do with small honours that corresponds in the same way to greatness of soul, which is to do with great ones. For one can desire small honours in the right way, and in excessive and deficient ways as well. The person who exceeds in his desires is described as a lover of honour, the person who is deficient as not caring about it, while the one in between has no name. Their dispositions are nameless as well, except that of the lover of honour, which is called love of honour. This is why those at the extremes lay claim to the middle ground. We ourselves sometimes refer to the person in the middle as a lover of honour, sometimes as one who
1108a does not care about it; and sometimes we praise the person who loves

honour, sometimes the one who does not care about it. The reason for our doing this will be stated below. For now, let us discuss the remaining virtues and vices in the way laid down.

In anger too there is an excess, a deficiency, and a mean. They are virtually nameless, but since we call the person in between the extremes even-tempered, let us call the mean even temper. Of those at the extremes, let the one who is excessive be quick-tempered, and the vice quick temper, while he who is deficient is, as it were, slow-tempered, and his deficiency slow temper.

There are three other means, having something in common, but also different. For they are all to do with our association with one another in words and actions, but differ in that one is concerned with the truth to be found in them, while the other two are respectively concerned with what is pleasant in amusement and in life as a whole. We should talk about these things as well, then, so that we can better see that in all things the mean is praiseworthy, while the extremes are neither praiseworthy nor correct, but blameworthy. Most of them again have no names, but, for the sake of clarity and intelligibility, we must try, as in the other cases, to produce names ourselves.

With respect to truth, then, let us call the intermediate person truthful and the mean truthfulness, pretence that exaggerates is boastfulness and the person who has this characteristic is a boaster, while that which understates is self-depreciation and the person who has this is self-depreciating. In connection with what is pleasant in amusement, let us call the intermediate person witty, and the disposition wit; the excess clownishness, and the person with that characteristic a clown; and the person who falls short a sort of boor and his state boorishness. With respect to the remaining kind of pleasantness, that found in life in general, let us call the person who is pleasant in the right way friendly and the mean friendliness, while he who goes to excess will be obsequious if there is no reason for it, and a flatterer if he is out for his own ends; someone who falls short and is unpleasant all the time will be a quarrelsome and peevish sort of person.

There are also means in the feelings and in connection with the feelings. Shame, for example, is not a virtue, but praise is also bestowed on the person inclined to feel it. Even in these cases one person is said to be intermediate, and another – the shy person who feels shame at everything – excessive; he who is deficient or is ashamed of nothing at all is called shameless, while the person in the middle is properly disposed to feel shame.

1108b   Appropriate indignation is a mean between envy and spite; these three are concerned with pain and pleasure felt at the fortunes of those around us. The sort of person to experience appropriate indignation is pained by those who do well undeservedly; the envious person goes beyond him and is pained by anybody's doing well; while the spiteful person, far from being pained at the misfortunes of others, actually feels enjoyment.

There will also be an opportunity elsewhere to discuss means like these.

As for justice, since it is a term used in more than one way, we shall distinguish its two varieties after discussing the other virtues, and say how each variety is a mean.

Chapter 8

Of these three dispositions, then, two are vices – one of excess, the other of deficiency – and the third, the mean, is virtue. Each is in a way opposed to each of the others, because the extremes are contrary to the mean and to one another, and the mean to the extremes. For as the equal is greater in relation to the less, but less in relation to the greater, so the mean states are excessive in relation to the deficiencies, but deficient in relation to the excesses; this is so in both feelings and actions. For the courageous person seems rash in relation to the coward, and a coward in relation to the rash person. Similarly, the temperate seems intemperate in relation to the insensible, but insensible in relation to the intemperate, and the generous person wasteful in relation to the stingy person, but stingy in relation to the wasteful. This is why those at one extreme push away the intermediate person to the other, the coward calling the courageous person rash, the rash person calling him a coward, and analogously in other cases.

Since they are set against one another in this way, the greatest opposition is that of the extremes to one another, rather than to the mean. For they are further from each other than from the mean, as the great is further from the small and the small further from the great than either is from the equal. Again, some of the extremes seem rather like the mean, as rashness seems like courage, and wastefulness like gener-

34

osity. The greatest dissimilarity is that between extremes; and the things that are furthest from each other are defined as contraries, so that the further things are apart, the more contrary they will be. In some cases, the deficiency is more opposed to the mean than is the excess, in others the excess is more opposed than the deficiency; for example, it is not rashness, the excess, which is more opposed to courage, but cowardice, the deficiency; while it is not insensibility, the deficiency, but intemperance, the excess, which is more opposed to temperance. There are two reasons for this.

1109a

One derives from the nature of the thing itself. Because one extreme is nearer and more like the mean, we set in opposition to the mean not this but rather its contrary; for example, since rashness is thought to be more like courage and nearer to it, and cowardice less like it, it is cowardice rather than rashness that we set in opposition, because things that are further from the mean are thought more contrary to it. This, then, is one reason, deriving from the nature of the thing itself.

The other derives from our nature. It is the things to which we ourselves are naturally more inclined that appear more contrary to the mean; for example, we are naturally more inclined to pleasures, and are therefore more prone to intemperance than self-discipline. We describe as more contrary to the mean, then, those extremes in the direction of which we tend to go; this is why intemperance, an excess, is more contrary to temperance.

Chapter 9

Enough has been said, then, to show that virtue of character is a mean, and in what sense it is so; that it is a mean between two vices, one of excess and one of deficiency; and that it is such because it is the sort of thing able to hit the mean in feelings and actions. This is why it is hard to be good, because in each case it is hard to find the middle point; for instance, not everyone can find the centre of a circle, but only the person with knowledge. So too anyone can get angry, or give and spend money – these are easy; but doing them in relation to the right person, in the right amount, at the right time, with the right aim in view, and in the right way – that is not something anyone can do, nor is it easy. This is why excellence in these things is rare, praiseworthy and noble.

So the person who is aiming at the mean must first steer away from the extreme that is in greater opposition to it, as Calypso advised:

Beyond this spray and swell keep your ship.[14]

For one of the extremes is a greater missing of the mark, the other less so; and since hitting the mean is extremely hard, we must take the next 1109b best course, as they say, and choose the lesser of two evils. This will be done best in the way we are suggesting.

But we must also consider the things towards which we as individuals are particularly prone. For we each have different natural tendencies, and we can find out what they are by the pain and pleasure that occur in us. And we should drag ourselves in the opposite direction, because we shall arrive at the mean by holding far off from where we would miss the mark, just as people do when straightening warped pieces of wood. In everything, we should be on our guard especially against the pleasant – pleasure, that is – because we are not impartial judges of it. So we should adopt the same attitude to it as the elders did towards Helen, and utter their words in everything we do;[15] for by dismissing pleasure in this way, we shall miss the mark to a lesser degree.

To sum up, then, it is by doing these things that we shall best be able to hit the mean. Admittedly, however, hitting it is difficult, especially in particular cases, since it is not easy to determine how one should be angry, with whom, for what reasons, and for how long; indeed we sometimes praise those who fall short and call them even-tempered, and sometimes those who flare up, describing them as manly. But the person who is blamed is not the one who deviates a little, either in excess or deficiency, from the right degree, but the one who deviates rather more, because he does not escape our notice. But how far and to what extent someone must deviate before becoming blameworthy it is not easy to determine by reason, because nothing perceived by our senses is easily determined; such things are particulars, and judgement about them lies in perception.

This much, then, is clear – that the mean state is in every case to be praised, but that sometimes we must incline towards the excess, sometimes towards the deficiency, because in this way we shall most easily hit the mean, namely, what is good.

[14] Homer, *Odyssey* xii.219f.   [15] Homer, *Iliad* iii.156–60.

Book III

Chapter 1

Since virtue is to do with feelings and actions, and since voluntary feelings and actions are praised and blamed, while the involuntary ones are pardoned and occasionally even pitied, presumably anyone considering virtue must determine the limits of the voluntary and the involuntary. It will be useful as well for legislators, in connection with honours and punishments.

Things that happen by force or through ignorance are thought to be involuntary. What is forced is what has an external first principle, such that the agent or the person acted upon contributes nothing to it – if a wind, for example, or people with power over him carry him somewhere.

As for things done through fear of greater evils or for the sake of something noble – if a tyrant, for example, had one's parents and children in his power and ordered one to do something shameful, on the condition that one's doing it would save them, while one's not doing it would result in their death – there is some dispute about whether they are involuntary or voluntary. The same sort of thing happens also in the case of people throwing cargo overboard in storms at sea. Without qualification, no one jettisons cargo voluntarily; but for his own safety and that of others any sensible person will do it.

Such actions, then, are mixed, though they seem more like voluntary ones, because at the time they are done they are worthy of choice, and the end of an action depends on the circumstances. So both voluntariness and involuntariness are to be ascribed at the time of the action. In fact, the person acts voluntarily, because in actions like this the first principle

1110a

37

of moving the limbs that serve as instruments lies in him; and where the first principle lies in a person, it is in his power to act or not to act. Such actions are therefore voluntary, but, without qualification, they are presumably involuntary, since no one would choose any of them in itself.

People are sometimes praised for actions like this, when they endure some disgrace or pain in return for great and noble objects; and if they do the contrary, they are blamed, since it is characteristic of a bad person to endure the greatest disgraces for no noble end or for something unimportant.

In some cases, not praise but pardon is given, when a person does wrong because of things that strain human nature to breaking-point and no one would endure. But some things perhaps we cannot be compelled to do, and rather than do them we ought to die after the most terrible suffering; for the things that compelled Euripides' Alcmaeon to kill his mother seem absurd.[16] It is nevertheless hard sometimes to determine what should be chosen at what cost, and what should be endured for what gain; and harder still to stand by our decisions, because the expected consequences are generally painful, and what one is compelled to do is shameful. This is why those who have been compelled or not are praised and blamed.

1110b

What sort of actions, then, should we describe as forced? If we speak without qualification, is it not whenever the cause is in the external circumstances and the agent contributes nothing? On the other hand, actions that in themselves are involuntary, but worth choosing at a certain time and for certain benefits, and have their first principle in the agent, are in themselves involuntary, but at that time and for those benefits voluntary. But they are more like voluntary actions, because actions are in the sphere of particulars, and here the particulars are voluntary. It is not easy, however, to explain what sort of things ought to be chosen in return for what, since there are many differences in particulars.

If someone were to claim that sweet and noble things are forcible (in that they compel us from an external position), he would be committed to all actions' being forced, since it is with those ends in view that everyone does everything. And people who are forced to act and do so involuntarily find it painful, while those who act because of what is

---

[16] The play is now lost. Alcmaeon's father, Amphiaraus of Argos, had been persuaded by his wife to join an expedition against Thebes. Amphiaraus foresaw his own death, and charged his sons to avenge him, by killing his wife.

pleasant or noble do so with pleasure. It is ridiculous to blame external circumstances and not oneself for being an easy prey to such things, and to take responsibility for noble actions oneself, but to make pleasant things responsible for shameful ones. What is forced, then, seems to be what has an external first principle, where the person forced contributes nothing.

Everything done through ignorance is non-voluntary, but what is involuntary also causes pain and regret; for the person who acted through ignorance, and is not upset in the slightest by what he has done, has not acted voluntarily, in that he did not know what he was doing, nor again involuntarily, in that he is not pained. Of those who act through ignorance, then, the one who regrets what he did seems to be an involuntary agent, while the one who shows no regret, since he is a different case, can be thought of as a non-voluntary agent; since he is a separate case, it is better that he should have a name of his own.

Acting through ignorance seems to be different from acting in ignorance, because the drunk or the person in a rage is not thought to act through ignorance, but through drunkenness or anger; he does so, however, not knowingly but in ignorance. In fact, every wicked person is ignorant of what he should do and refrain from doing, and missing the mark in this way makes people unjust and generally bad. An action is not properly called involuntary, however, if the agent is ignorant of what is beneficial, because it is not ignorance in rational choice that causes the involuntariness (that rather causes wickedness), nor ignorance of the universal (since people are blamed for that), but ignorance of 1111a particulars – the circumstances of the action and what it is concerned with. For it is on these that pity and pardon depend, since someone who is ignorant of any of them is acting involuntarily.

Perhaps it would be no bad thing, therefore, to delineate their nature and number. A person may be ignorant of who he is, of what he is doing, of the sphere in which or to what he is doing it, and sometimes also of what it is that he is doing it with (e.g., a tool), of what it is for (e.g., safety), and of the way in which he is doing it (e.g., gently or roughly). No one could be ignorant of all of these unless he were mad, and clearly not of the person doing the action; for how could he be ignorant of himself? But someone could be ignorant of what he is doing: people, for example, who say they are 'flustered while speaking', or 'did not know that it was a secret', as Aeschylus said of the Mysteries, or 'let it off when they wanted to show how it worked', as the person said of the catapult. Again, someone might think his son an enemy, as did Merope,[17] or that a pointed spear had a button on it, or that a stone was a piece of pumice. Or one might kill someone with a drink intended to save him. Or when wanting only to seize a person's hand, as in sparring, one might hurt him. There may be ignorance, then, concerning all of these aspects of the action, and the person who is ignorant of any of them seems to have acted involuntarily, especially in the case of the most important – these seem to be to what the action is being done and what it is for. It is, then, an action called involuntary on the basis of this particular kind of ignorance that must also give rise to pain and regret.

So, since what is involuntary is what is done by force or because of ignorance, what is voluntary would seem to be what has its first principle in the person himself when he knows the particular circumstances of the action.

It is probably a mistake to describe actions done through spirit or appetite as involuntary. For, first, none of the other animals, or children, will act voluntarily; and, secondly, is it meant that none of the actions we do through appetite and spirit is done involuntarily, or that we do the noble ones voluntarily, the disgraceful ones involuntarily? Would this not be absurd, since there is only one cause in play? And it would presumably also be odd to describe as involuntary things that we ought to desire; and there are indeed some things at which we ought to feel angry, and others, like health and learning, that we ought to want. Also, what is involuntary is thought to be painful, but what is in accordance with appetite pleasant. Again, what is the difference, as far as their being involuntary is concerned, between actions that miss the mark on the basis of calculation and those that miss it on the basis of spirit? For both are to be avoided, and the non-rational feelings are thought to be no less part of human nature, so that actions arising from spirit and appetite are also characteristic of a human being. It would be odd, then, to class them as involuntary.

Chapter 2

Now that we have delineated what is voluntary and what involuntary, we should next discuss rational choice; for it is thought to be very

[17] In Euripides' *Cresphontes* (lost). Merope was wife of Cresphontes, king of Messenia.

closely tied to virtue, and a better guide to men's characters than their actions.

Rational choice is obviously a voluntary thing, but it is not the same as what is voluntary, which is a broader notion: children and the other animals share in what is voluntary, but not in rational choice, and we describe actions done spontaneously as voluntary, but not as done in accordance with rational choice.

People who claim it is appetite or spirit or wish or some kind of belief do not seem to be right, since rational choice is not shared by beings who lack reason, while appetite and spirit are shared. Again, the incontinent person acts from appetite, but not from rational choice; while the self-controlled person does the contrary, and acts from rational choice, but not from appetite. Also, appetite can be in opposition to rational choice, but not to appetite. Again, appetite is concerned with what is pleasant and what is painful, rational choice with neither. Still less is it spirit, since actions done from spirit are least of all thought to be in accordance with rational choice.

But, though it does seem closely connected with wish, it is not this either. For there is no rational choice of what is impossible, and someone claiming that he was rationally choosing this would be thought a fool. But there may be wish even for things that are impossible, such as immortality. And wish can also be for things one could never bring about by one's own efforts, such as that some actor or athlete win in a competition. No one, however, rationally chooses things like this, but only things that he thinks might come about through his own efforts. Again, wish is more to do with the end, rational choice with what is conducive to the end; for example, we wish to be healthy, but we rationally choose things that will make us healthy; and we wish to be happy, and say that we do, but to claim that we rationally choose to be so does not sound right. For in general rational choice seems to be concerned with things that are in our power.

Neither could it be belief, because belief seems to be concerned with everything – no less with what is eternal and what is impossible than with what is in our power. Besides, distinctions are made here on grounds of truth and falsity, not badness and goodness, as happens with rational choice.

Now perhaps no one does claim that it is the same as belief in general. 1112a But it is not even the same as any particular species of belief, since our characters arise from our rationally choosing what is good and bad, not from having certain beliefs. And what we rationally choose is to obtain or avoid something good or bad, while we hold beliefs about what that is, whom it benefits, or in what way; we never really believe to obtain or avoid things. And rational choice is praised for its being of what is right rather than for its being correct, while belief is praised for being true. And we rationally choose what we best know to be good, while we hold beliefs about what we do not know at all to be good. And it appears as well that it is not the same people who are best at rationally choosing and at believing: some seem quite good at believing, but through vice choose what they should not. Whether belief is prior to rational choice or accompanies it makes no difference, because it is not this we are considering, but whether it is the same as some species of belief.

Given that it is none of the things we have mentioned, what is it, then, or what sort of thing is it? It is obviously something voluntary, but not everything that is voluntary is an object of rational choice. Well, is it what has been decided by prior deliberation? For rational choice does involve reason and thought, and its name (*prohairesis*) too seems to signify something that is chosen (*haireton*) before (*pro*) other things.

Chapter 3

Do people deliberate about everything, and is everything an object of deliberation, or is there no deliberation about some things? Presumably, we ought to describe as an object of deliberation what a sane person would deliberate about, not some fool or lunatic.

No one deliberates about eternal things, such as the universe, or the fact that the diagonal is incommensurable with the side; nor things that involve movement but always happen in the same way, either from necessity or by nature or through some other cause, such as the solstices or the rising of the stars; nor things that happen now in one way, now in another, such as droughts and rains; nor what happens by chance, such as the finding of treasure. We do not deliberate even about all human affairs; no Spartan, for example, would deliberate about the best form of government for the Scythians. The reason is that we could not bring about any of these things.

Rather, we deliberate about what is in our power, that is, what we can do; this is what remains. For nature, necessity and chance do seem to be causes, but so also do intellect and everything that occurs through human agency. Each group of people deliberates about what they themselves can do.

There is no deliberation about precise and self-sufficient sciences – 1112b letters, for example, because we are in no doubt about how they should be written. Rather, what we deliberate about are things that we bring about, and not always in the same way – questions of medicine and of finance, for example, and of navigation more than of gymnastics, in that navigation has not been developed to such a level of exactness. We deliberate about other fields in the same way, and more about the skills than about the sciences, since we are less certain about the skills.

Deliberation is concerned with what usually happens in a certain way, where the consequences are unclear, and where things are not definite. On important issues, we do not trust our own ability to decide and call in others to help us deliberate.

We deliberate not about ends, but about things that are conducive to ends. For a doctor does not deliberate about whether to cure, nor an orator whether to persuade, nor a politician whether to produce good order; nor does anyone else deliberate about his end. Rather they establish an end and then go on to think about how and by what means it is to be achieved. If it appears that there are several means available, they consider by which it will be achieved in the easiest and most noble way; while if it can be attained by only one means, they consider how this will bring it about, and by what further means this means is itself to be brought about, until they arrive at the first cause, the last thing to be found. For the person who deliberates seems to inquire and analyse in the way described as though he were dealing with a geometrical figure (it seems that not all inquiry is deliberation – mathematics, for example – but that all deliberation is inquiry), and the last step in the analysis seems to be the first that comes to be.

If people meet with an impossibility, they give up: take, for example, the case where they need money, but there is none available. But if it seems possible they will try to do it. What is possible is what can be accomplished by our own efforts; what can be brought about through our friends is in a sense accomplished by our own efforts, in that the first principle is in us. The question is sometimes what tools to use, sometimes what use to make of them. The same goes for other cases:

sometimes the question is the means, sometimes how they are to be used or the means to that use.

It seems, then, as we have said, that a human being is a first principle of actions. Deliberation is about what he can do himself, and actions are done for the sake of other things, because it is not the end but what is conducive to an end that is the object of deliberation. Nor are 1113a particulars the object, such as whether this is bread or has been baked as it should; these are matters of perception, and if we are always deliberating, it will never come to an end.

The objects of deliberation and of rational choice are the same, except that the object of rational choice has already been determined, since it is what has been decided upon as the result of deliberation that is the object of rational choice. For each person stops inquiring how he is to act as soon as he has traced the first principle back to himself, that is, to the part of him that gives commands, because it is this that rationally chooses. There is a good illustration of this in the ancient constitutions depicted by Homer: the kings proclaimed to the people what they had rationally chosen.

Since the object of rational choice is one of the things in our power that is desired after deliberation, rational choice will be deliberative desire for things in our power; for, when we have decided on the basis of deliberation, we desire in accordance with our deliberation.

Let this serve as an outline of rational choice, the nature of its objects, and the fact that it is concerned with what is conducive to ends.

Chapter 4

Wish, we have said, is for the end; but some think that the end here is the good, others the apparent good. Those who claim that the object of wish is the good are committed to the view that what a person wishes if he is choosing incorrectly is not an object of wish (if it were an object of wish, it would also be a good, but it was, perhaps, bad). On the other hand, those who claim the apparent good to be the object of wish must say that nothing is an object of wish by nature, but only what seems so to each person; and different people have different, and perhaps opposing, views.

If these consequences are unsatisfactory, then, should we say that, without qualification and in truth, the object of wish is the good, but for the individual it is the apparent good? Then for the good person the object of wish is that which is truly an object of wish, but for the bad person it is any chance thing. This is like the case of bodies, where things that are truly healthy are healthy for bodies that are in good condition, while for those that are diseased other things are healthy; and the same goes for things that are bitter, sweet, hot, heavy, and so on. The good person judges each case rightly, and in each case the truth is manifest to him. For each state has its own conception of what is noble and pleasant, and one might say that the good person stands out a long way by seeing the truth in each case, being a sort of standard and measure of what is noble and pleasant. In the case of the masses, however, pleasure seems to deceive them, because it looks like a good 1113b when it is not; people therefore choose what is pleasant thinking it to be a good, and avoid pain thinking it to be an evil.

Chapter 5

Since, then, the object of wish is the end, and the object of wish and of rational choice is what conduces to the end, actions concerning what conduces to the end will be in accordance with rational choice and voluntary. The activities of the virtues are concerned with what conduces to the end; virtue, then, is in our power, and so is vice. Where it is in our power to act, it is also in our power not to act, and where saying 'No' is in our power, so is saying 'Yes'; so that if it is in our power to act when it would be noble, it will also be in our power not to act when it would be shameful, and if it is in our power not to act when it would be noble, it will also be in our power to act when it would be shameful. Now if it is in our power to do noble and shameful actions, and the same goes for not doing them, and if, as we saw, being good and bad consists in this, then it is in our power to be good or bad.

The saying, 'No one is voluntarily wicked, nor involuntarily blessed', seems partly false, and partly true. For no one is involuntarily blessed, but wickedness is voluntary; otherwise we shall have to disagree with what we have just said, and deny that a human being is a first principle or the begetter of his actions as he is of his children. But if it is clear that he is, and we cannot refer back to any other first principles beyond those within us, the actions whose first principles are within us will themselves also be in our power and voluntary.

45

This view seems to be backed up not only by each of us as private individuals, but also by legislators themselves. For they punish and penalize anyone who does wicked things, unless he acts by force or through ignorance for which he is not himself culpable, and they reward anyone who does noble things, as if encouraging the one while deterring the other. But no one is urged to do what is neither in our power nor voluntary; people assume it to be a waste of time to persuade us not to be hot or in pain or hungry or anything else like that, because we shall experience them anyway.

Indeed, legislators punish an offender for ignorance itself, if he is thought to be responsible for the ignorance. For example, there are double penalties for a drunken offender; the first principle lies in him, in that he had the power not to get drunk, and his getting drunk was the 1114a cause of his ignorance. And they punish those who are ignorant of any uncomplicated point of law that they ought to have known. The same sort of thing happens in other cases where people are thought to be ignorant through negligence, on the ground that it was in their power not to be ignorant, because it was up to them whether they took care.

Well, perhaps he is the sort of person not to take care. Nevertheless, people are themselves responsible for turning out like this, through the slackness of their lives – responsible for being unjust by doing wrong, or intemperate by spending their time in drinking and the like; in each sphere people's activities give them the corresponding character. This is clear from the case of people training for any competition or action, since they practise the relevant activity continually. A person would have to be utterly senseless not to know that states in each sphere arise from their corresponding activities.

Again, it is unreasonable to think that someone who does unjust actions does not wish to be unjust, or that someone who does intemperate actions does not wish to be intemperate. If a person does what he knows will make him unjust, he will be unjust voluntarily. It does not follow, however, that, if he wishes, he will stop being unjust and be just. For neither does the ill person become well like this; but he is ill voluntarily, by living incontinently and ignoring his doctors, if that was what happened. At that time, it was open to him not to be ill, but it is no longer so once he has thrown away his chance; similarly, one can no longer recover a stone once one has thrown it, though it was in one's power to throw it, because the first principle lay within one. So too from the start it was open to the unjust person and the intemperate person not to become such, so that they are what they are voluntarily; but now that they have become what they are, it is no longer possible for them to be otherwise.

But it is not only the vices of the soul that are voluntary; those of the body are too for some people, whom we go on to blame. For nobody blames someone unattractive by nature, but we do if he is so through not exercising and looking after himself. The same goes for weakness and disability; nobody would criticize a person blind by nature, or as the result of a disease or an injury, but rather pity him; everyone, however, would blame a person who was blind from drinking or some other intemperance. So bodily vices in our power are blamed, while those not in our power are not. And if so, then in other cases the vices that are blamed will be those in our power.

But suppose somebody argues: 'Everyone aims at what appears good to him, but over this appearance we have no control; rather, how the end 1114b appears to each person depends on what sort of person he is. So, if each person is in some way responsible for his own state, he will also be in some way responsible for how it appears. If he is not, however, then no one will be responsible for his own wrongdoing, but he will do these things through ignorance of the end, thinking that they will result in what is best for him. His aiming at the end is not up to him, but he must be born with a kind of vision, to enable him to judge nobly and to choose what is truly good. And a person is naturally good if he has this naturally noble capacity, since it is the greatest and noblest thing, and one cannot acquire or learn it from another; rather, his state will result from its natural character, and when it is naturally good and noble, this will be complete and true natural excellence.'

If this is true, how will virtue be any more voluntary than vice? For how the end appears and is determined – by nature or whatever – is the same for both the good and the bad person, and it is by referring everything else to this that they do whatever they do.

So whether it is not by nature that the end appears to each person in whatever way it does appear, but the person plays some role as well, or whether the end is fixed by nature, but virtue is voluntary because the good person does the remaining actions voluntarily, vice will be no less voluntary than virtue. For the part played by the person himself is found to the same extent in the actions of the bad person, even if not in the end.

If, then, as we suggested, virtues are voluntary (because we are in some way partly responsible for our states of character, and it is by our being the kind of people that we are that we assume such and such as our end), vices also will be voluntary; they are on the same footing.

With regard to virtues in general, then, we have given an outline account of their genus: they are means, they are states, they lead to actions that are in accordance with virtues and such as those from which they developed, they are in our power and voluntary, and they are as correct reason prescribes.

Actions and states, however, are not voluntary in the same way. For, being aware of the particulars we are in control of actions from the first 1115a principle to the end, but, though we control the first principle, the progress through the particular stages of states is not noticeable, as happens with illnesses; but, because it was in our power to behave in this way or that, states are voluntary.

Let us now resume consideration of the virtues, and one by one say what each is, what sort of things it is concerned with, and in what way; at the same time, it will be clear how many there are.

Chapter 6

First let us discuss courage. That it is a mean concerning feelings of fear and confidence we have already made clear. Obviously, what we fear are fearful things, and these are, without qualification, evils; this is why people define fear as an expectation of evil.

We fear all evils, such as disgrace, poverty, disease, friendlessness, and death, but not all of them seem to be the concern of the courageous person. For some things, like disgrace, it is right and noble to fear, and shameful not to fear: the person who fears this is good and properly disposed to feel shame, and the one who does not is shameless. Some people extend the term 'courage' to cover his case, since he has a degree of similarity to the courageous person, in that the latter is also a sort of fearless person.

Presumably, however, we ought not to fear poverty or disease, nor in general anything that does not arise from vice or through us. But the person who is fearless of these is still not courageous, though he too is described as such by transference of meaning, because some people who are cowards in the perils of battle are generous and face the loss of their money in good heart. Nor is a person a coward if he fears wanton violence against his wife and children or envy or anything like that. Nor is he courageous if he displays confidence when he is about to be flogged.

What sort of fearful things, then, do concern the courageous man? Surely the worst kind, since no one is more likely to stand his ground in the face of horrors? Death is the most fearful thing of all, since it is a limit, and when someone is dead nothing any longer seems good or bad for him. But not even death in all its forms, such as death at sea, or from illness, seems to be the concern of the courageous person. Which forms do concern him, then? Surely the most noble? These are deaths in battle, because they take place in the greatest and noblest danger; and this fits with the way honours are bestowed in cities and the courts of monarchs. So it is the person who does not fear a noble death, or the risks of immediate death, that should really be described as courageous; and risks in battle are most of all like this.

Nevertheless, the courageous person will also be fearless at sea and 1115b when he is ill, but not in the same way as seamen; for while courageous people have given up hope of safety and shudder at the idea of such a death, seamen are sanguine because of their experience. Again, while people act courageously in situations where there is a possibility of sturdy resistance or a noble death, in these sorts of disaster there is no room for either.

Chapter 7

Not everyone finds the same things fearful. But we do say that there are things beyond human endurance, which would be fearful to anyone – anyone sane that is. Things not beyond human endurance differ in scale and degree, and so do those that inspire confidence.

The courageous person will be undaunted so far as is humanly possible; so, though he will fear even the things not beyond human endurance, he will stand his ground for the sake of what is noble (since this is the end of virtue) in the right way and as reason requires. But one can fear these things to a greater or lesser degree, and even fear things that are not fearful as if they were. One kind of missing the mark is to fear the wrong thing, another to fear in the wrong way, another to fear at the wrong time, and so on; and the same goes for what inspires confidence. So the courageous person is the one who endures and fears – and likewise is confident about – the right things, for the right reason, in the right way, and at the right time; for the courageous person feels and acts in accordance with the merits of the case, and as reason requires.

The end of every activity is being in accordance with its state. To the courageous person, courage is noble; and so its end is also noble, since the character of everything is determined by its end. So it is for the sake of what is noble that the courageous person stands his ground and acts in accordance with courage.

Among the excessive, the person who exceeds in fearlessness has no name (we said before that many do not have a name), but if he feared nothing – not even an earthquake or rough seas, as people say of the Celts – he would be a sort of madman or insensible. The person who exceeds in confidence about fearful things is rash. But the rash person also seems to be a boaster and a pretender to courage; at any rate, in relation to what is fearful, he wishes to appear like the courageous person is in reality, and so imitates him when he can. This is why most of them are rash cowards; for on these occasions they put on a show of confidence, but they do not stand their ground against what is fearful.

1116a Rash people are impetuous, eager for danger before it arrives, but shrinking from it when it does; the courageous, however, are keen when the time for acting comes, but cool beforehand.

1115b The person who exceeds in fear is the coward, since he fears the
1116a wrong things, in the wrong way, and so on. He is also deficient in confidence, but he reveals himself more in his excessive pain. So, because he fears everything, he is a despondent sort. The contrary is true of the courageous person, because confidence is characteristic of a person of hope.

The coward, the rash person, and the courageous, then, are all concerned with the same things, but are in different states in relation to them; the first two exceed and fall short, while the state of the courageous person is intermediate and right.

As we have said, then, courage is a mean in relation to what inspires confidence and fear in the circumstances described; and it makes choices and stands its ground because it is noble to do so, or shameful not to. To commit suicide as a way of escaping poverty or love or anything painful is not characteristic of a courageous person, but rather of a coward; for it is softness to run away from problems, and such a person endures death not because it is noble, but to escape an evil.

Chapter 8

Courage, then, is something like this. But the name is applied to five other states of character as well.

First comes citizen courage, since this is most like courage proper: citizens are thought to endure danger because of the legal penalties and opprobrium if they do not, and because of the honours they receive. This is why the most courageous people are thought to be those among whom cowards are held in dishonour and courageous people honoured. Homer depicts people like this, such as Diomede and Hector:

> Polydamas will be the first to cast reproach on me[18]

and

> For one day Hector will proclaim among the Trojans
> 'By me the son of Tydeus . . .'[19]

This is most like what we described earlier, because it arises from virtue: it arises from shame and a desire for what is noble (honour, in other words), and aversion to opprobrium, for the disgrace it brings.

One might put in the same class those who are compelled by their commanders. But they are not as good, in so far as they act not through shame, but fear – avoiding not disgrace, but pain. Their superiors apply compulsion, as did Hector:

> If I see anyone skulking far away from the battle,
> He can be sure that he will not escape the dogs.[20]

The same thing is done by those who line their men up in front of 1116b them and beat them if they retreat, and those who position them in front of trenches or suchlike; they are all applying compulsion. But one ought to be courageous not under compulsion, but because it is noble.

Experience of particulars is also thought to be courage; this is why Socrates thought that courage is knowledge.[21] Some people have it in one situation, others in another, but in war professional soldiers have it;

---

[18] Homer, *Iliad* xxii.100.   [19] Homer, *Iliad* viii.148f.
[20] Cf. Homer, *Iliad* ii.391–3, xv.348–51.
[21] See Plato, *Laches* 199a–d; *Protagoras* 360d; *Meno* 88c–d.

for they have seen with their own eyes the many false alarms that seem to arise in war, and so they seem courageous, because others do not know what such alarms are like. Again, their experience makes them especially able in attack and defence, because they are proficient in the use of their weapons and have the sort that is best for attacking and defending. So they are like armed men contending against unarmed, or trained athletes against amateurs; for in contests like this too it is not the most courageous who are best at fighting, but those who are strongest and whose bodies are in the best condition.

Professional soldiers turn out to be cowards, however, when the danger is too much for them and they are inferior in numbers and equipment. They are first to run away, while the citizen troops stand fast and die, as happened at the temple of Hermes. This is because, to the citizens, running away is a disgrace, and death worth choosing in preference to saving one's life in such a way; but the professionals were facing the danger on the initial assumption that they were stronger, and when they find out the truth, fearing death more than disgrace, they run away; and the courageous person is not like this.

Spirit is also referred to as courage; those influenced by spirit, like wild animals charging at those who wound them, also seem to be courageous, since courageous people feel spirit as well. For spirit is readiest to rush headlong into danger, which explains Homer's 'into his spirit he put strength', 'might and spirit he aroused', 'bitter might in his nostrils', and 'his blood boiled'.[22] All such phrases seem to indicate the stir and impulse of spirit.

Now courageous people act for the sake of what is noble, but spirit does help them. Brutes, however, are influenced by pain; for it is being injured or frightened that influences them, as one can see from the fact that when they are in a forest, they do not come near us. So they are not courageous, because they rush into danger driven on by pain and spirit, and do not think of the horrors that await them. For otherwise even 1117a hungry donkeys would be courageous, because they will not stop eating even when they are beaten![23] Adulterers, as well, do many reckless things because of their appetite.

This form of courage caused by spirit, then, seems the most natural,

---

[22] Homer, *Iliad* ix.11, xiv.151, xvi.529; v.470, xv.232, 594; *Odyssey* xxiv.318f.; cf. Theocritus xx.15.
[23] See Homer, *Iliad* xi.557–62.

and to be courage if it is accompanied by rational choice and directed towards some end.

People too feel pain when they get angry, and pleasure when they retaliate. But those who fight for these reasons, though they may be good at fighting, are not courageous; they are doing so not for the sake of what is noble nor as reason requires, but because of feeling. Nevertheless, they do resemble courageous people quite closely.

Nor are hopeful people courageous, since they are confident in danger only because they have often been victorious over many enemies. They resemble the courageous, however, because both are confident; but courageous people are confident for the reasons given above, while the hopeful are so because they think that they are strongest and that no harm will come to them (drunks behave like this as well, because they become hopeful). And when things do not turn out as they expected, they run away; as we noticed, however, it is characteristic of the courageous person to endure what is – and appears – fearful for a human being, because it is noble to do so, and shameful not to.

It therefore seems to be characteristic of the more courageous person to be unafraid and unruffled in sudden alarms rather than to be so in those that are foreseen: it comes more from his state of character, because less from preparation. Foreseen actions can be rationally chosen on the basis of calculation and reason, but unforeseen ones only in virtue of one's state of character.

Those who act in ignorance also seem courageous; they are quite similar to the hopeful, but inferior to them in so far as the hopeful have a self-confidence that they lack. So, while the hopeful will stand firm for a time, those who are under a delusion, once they find out or suspect that the situation is other than they imagined, run away. This happened to the Argives, when they fell in with the Spartans and took them to be Sicyonians.[24]

We have now covered what courageous people, and those who seem to be courageous, are like.

Chapter 9

Courage is concerned with both confidence and fear, but not to the same degree with both – more with fearful things; for the person unruffled in

---

[24] In 392 BCE, in the battle at the Long Walls of Corinth.

the midst of them and with the right attitude to them is courageous more than the person like this in the face of things that inspire confidence. As we have said, then, people are called courageous for enduring what is painful; so courage involves pain, and is justly praised, since it is more difficult to endure what is painful than to abstain from what is pleasant.

1117b   Nevertheless, the end that courage aims at would seem to be pleasant, but to be obscured by what else is happening. This happens, for instance, in gymnastic competitions. For the end for boxers – their reason for doing what they do, namely, the crown and the honours – is pleasant, but, since they are flesh and blood, being hit is distressing and painful, as is all the hard exercise they do; and because of the number of these painful things, what they are aiming at, being small, seems to have nothing pleasant in it. And so, if this is true of courage as well, death and wounds will be painful for the courageous person, and he will face them involuntarily, but he will stand his ground against them because it is noble, or shameful not to.

And the more he is possessed of virtue as a whole and the happier he is, the more pain he will feel at the thought of death. For life is especially worth living for a person like this, and he knows that he is losing the greatest goods – and this is painful. But he is no less courageous for that, and is perhaps even more so, because he chooses what is noble in war at the cost of these goods. So it is not true, then, except in so far as one achieves the end, that the exercise of every virtue is pleasant.

It is quite possible, I suppose, that the best professional soldiers are not like this, but rather those who are less courageous and have nothing to lose; they are ready to face danger, and sell their lives cheaply.

So much, then, for courage. It should not be difficult to grasp what it is – in outline, at least – from what we have said.

Chapter 10

After courage, let us say something about temperance, since these two are thought to be the virtues of the parts without reason. Temperance is a mean concerned with pleasures, as we have already said; it is less concerned with pains, and in a different way. Intemperance also manifests itself in the same sphere. Let us now determine, then, what sort of pleasures they are concerned with.

A distinction should be drawn between pleasures of the body and those of the soul. As examples of the latter, consider love of honour and love of learning, since, in each case, when the person enjoys what he loves, it is not his body so much as his mind which is at all affected. People concerned with pleasures like this are described neither as temperate nor as intemperate. The same goes for those concerned with the other non-bodily pleasures: those who like telling stories and chatting, and spend their days on whatever comes along, we call idle 1118a gossips, but not intemperate, nor do we so describe people who feel pain at losing money or friends.

Temperance, then, will be concerned with bodily pleasures, but not even all of these. For people who enjoy what they see, such as colours, shapes, a painting, are called neither temperate nor intemperate; yet it would seem possible to enjoy even these in the right way, as well as excessively or deficiently. The same goes for what we hear; nobody describes people who enjoy music or acting to an inordinate degree as intemperate, nor as temperate those who do so in the right way. Nor do we do this in the case of smells, except incidentally. We describe as intemperate not those who enjoy the smells of apples, roses or incense, but rather those who enjoy the smells of perfumes and cooked dishes. These are what intemperate people enjoy, because they remind them of the objects of their appetites. One can see other people also, when they are hungry, enjoying the smell of food; but enjoying such things is characteristic of the intemperate person, since these are the objects of his appetites. Nor do other animals take pleasure in these senses, except incidentally. It is not the smell of hares that dogs enjoy, but eating them, and smell makes them aware of the presence of hares. Nor is it the lowing of an ox that a lion enjoys, but devouring it; he seems to enjoy the lowing because it was through it that he perceived that the ox was near. In the same way, it is not the sight of 'a deer or wild goat'[25] that he enjoys, but the fact that he is going to have a meal.

It is with pleasures like these, then, that temperance and intemperance are concerned – those in which other animals share; this is why they seem slavish and brutish. These pleasures are touch and taste; but even taste appears to have little or no role to play. For the job of taste is to discriminate flavours, as do wine-tasters, or cooks preparing dishes;

---

[25] Homer, *Iliad* iii.24.

but people do not really enjoy these sorts of thing – at least, intemperate people do not – but rather the gratification itself, which arises entirely through touch in the cases of food, drink and what people call the sexual pleasures. This is why a certain gourmet prayed that his throat might 1118b become longer than a crane's, demonstrating that it was the touching which gave him pleasure.

So the sense to which intemperance is related is the most widely shared, and seems justly subject to criticism, because it is something we have not in so far as we are human, but in so far as we are animals. To enjoy such things, then, and to love them most of all is brutish. The most genteel of the pleasures of touch – such as those produced in the gymnasium through massage and heat – are indeed exceptions here, since the sense of touch characteristic of the intemperate person is to do not with the body as a whole, but certain parts of it.

Chapter 11

Some appetites are thought to be common, others peculiar to particular individuals. That for sustenance, for example, is natural, since everyone who needs it has an appetite for food or drink, or sometimes both; and that for sex, when one is, as Homer puts it, young and blooming.[26] But not everyone has an appetite for this or that kind of sustenance or sex, nor the same kinds; so it seems to be a matter of personal taste. Nevertheless, there is also something natural in it, because one thing will please one kind of person, another another, and some things are more pleasant to everyone than certain others.

In the case of the natural appetites, the number of people who miss the mark is low, and they do so in only one direction, that of excess. To eat whatever is at hand or to drink until one is full to bursting is to exceed the amount that accords with nature, since natural appetite is the replenishment of what one lacks. This is why these people are called 'belly-crazy', since they fill their bellies beyond what is right; it is utterly slavish people who become like this.

In the case of the pleasures peculiar to particular individuals, however, many people miss the mark, and in many ways: people are called lovers of such and such because they enjoy the wrong things,

---

[26] Homer, *Iliad* xxiv.130f.

enjoy things more than most people do, or enjoy things in the wrong way. And intemperate people go to excess in all these ways; for they enjoy certain things they should not (because those things are detestable), and if they enjoy the sort of things that it is right to enjoy, they enjoy them more than is right or more than most people enjoy them.

Clearly, then, excess with regard to pleasures is intemperance and to be blamed. With regard to pains, however, one is not called temperate, as one is called courageous, for enduring them, nor intemperate for not doing so. Rather, the intemperate person is so called for being more pained than he ought to be when he fails to get pleasant things (even his pain being caused by pleasure), while the temperate is described as such because he is not pained at the absence of what is pleasant, or at abstaining from it.

The intemperate person, then, has an appetite for all pleasant things, 1119a or the most pleasant, and is led by his appetite to choose them at the cost of everything else. So he is pained both when he fails to get them and when he has an appetite for them, because appetite involves pain; but experiencing pain on account of pleasure seems absurd.

People who are deficient in relation to pleasures and enjoy them less than they ought are not generally found, since such insensibility is not a human characteristic. Even the other animals make discriminations between different kinds of food, and enjoy some but not others; and if there is anyone who finds nothing pleasant and is indifferent about everything, he must be far from being human. And because he is found so rarely, this sort of person has not been given a name.

The temperate person occupies a mean position with regard to pleasures. For he does not enjoy the things that the intemperate enjoys most – rather he actually dislikes them – nor, in general, pleasures it would be wrong to enjoy; nor does he enjoy any pleasure to excess; nor does he feel pain or appetite at the absence of pleasures, except perhaps in moderation, and not more than is right, at the wrong time, and so on. But things that are pleasant and conducive to health or vigour he desires in a moderate way, as is right, and other pleasant things as well, as long as they are not incompatible with health or vigour, contrary to what is noble, or beyond his means. For the person who fails to abide by these limitations enjoys such pleasures more than they deserve; the temperate person is not like this, but enjoys them as correct reason prescribes.

Chapter 12

Intemperance seems more of a voluntary matter than does cowardice, since it is caused by pleasure, which is to be chosen, while cowardice is caused by pain, which is to be avoided. And pain upsets and ruins the natural state of the person who is experiencing it, while pleasure does nothing of the sort. Intemperance, then, is more voluntary. So it is also more reprehensible, since it is easier to accustom oneself to resist pleasures; for there are many of them in life, and the modes of accustoming oneself are quite safe, while with fearful things the contrary is true.

It would seem, however, that cowardice is voluntary in a way that its particular instances are not. For it is itself painless, but particular instances upset people because of the pain, to the extent that they even throw away their arms and disgrace themselves in other ways. This is why they even seem to be forced. In the case of the intemperate, the contrary is true. The particular instances are voluntary (since he acts through appetite and desire), but taken as a whole the condition is less so, because nobody has an appetite for intemperance.

1119b We also apply the name intemperance to children's errors, because they have a certain resemblance. Which is called after which is not relevant to our present purpose, but it is clear that the posterior is called after the prior. The transfer of the name does not seem inapposite, since that which desires what is disgraceful and grows quickly ought to be disciplined. Appetites and children fall especially into this category, since children live in accordance with appetite, and the desire for what is pleasant is found especially in them.

If, then, it is not going to be obedient and subject to its ruler, it will get out of hand. For the desire of an irrational being for what is pleasant is insatiable and indiscriminate, and the activity of desire will strengthen the tendency he is born with. And if appetites are strong and excessive, they actually expel calculation. They should therefore be moderate and few in number, and in no kind of opposition to reason – this is what we mean by 'obedient' and 'disciplined' – and as the child ought to live in accordance with what his tutor prescribes, so ought the appetitive element in accordance with reason.

So the appetitive element in a temperate person ought to be in harmony with reason; for the aim of both is what is noble, and the temperate person's appetite is for the right thing, in the right way, and at the right time, and this is what reason requires as well.

So let us now conclude our discussion of temperance.

Book IV

Chapter 1

Next let us discuss generosity. It seems to be the mean in relation to wealth: the generous person is praised not in matters of war, nor in those that concern the temperate person, nor again in respect of his legal judgements, but rather with regard to the taking and giving of wealth, and more especially the giving. By wealth, I mean everything the value of which is measured in money.

Both wastefulness and stinginess are also excesses and deficiencies with regard to money. We always ascribe stinginess to people who take wealth more seriously than they should, but we sometimes use the term 'wasteful' with a wider connotation, calling wasteful those who are incontinent and spend their money on intemperate pursuits. These incontinent people are therefore thought to be the worst of characters, because they possess several vices at the same time. But this means they are not properly called wasteful, since 'wasteful' means a person with one vice, namely, that of wasting his property. This is because a wasteful person – one who is *asōtos*, 'not saved' – is a person who ruins himself, and the wasting of one's property seems to be a kind of ruining of oneself, since living depends on it. This, then, is how we understand wastefulness.

Things that have a use can be used both well and badly. Riches are among the things that can be used; and each thing is used best by the person with the relevant virtue. Riches, therefore, will be used best by the person who has the virtue concerned with them, and this is the generous person. The use of wealth seems to consist in spending and

1120a

60

giving, while taking and keeping are more a matter of possession. So it is more characteristic of the generous person to give to the right people than to take from the right people and not from the wrong people. For it is more characteristic of virtue to do good than to receive it, and to do noble actions than not to do shameful ones; and it is pretty clear that giving implies doing good and doing noble actions, while taking implies receiving good or not doing what is shameful.

Again, gratitude is directed towards the person who gives, not the one who refuses to take, and praise even more so. Also, it is easier not to take than to give, since people are less inclined to give away what belongs to them than not to take what belongs to someone else. Again, those who give are called generous, while those who do not take are not praised for generosity, though they are praised for their justice; and those who do take are not really praised at all. Of all those who are liked on the basis of their virtue, the generous are pretty much the best liked, because they are helpful, and their help consists in giving.

Actions done in accordance with virtue are noble and done for the sake of what is noble. So the generous person will give for the sake of what is noble and in the correct way – to the right people, in the right amounts, at the right time, and so on, with the other qualifications that attach to correct giving. And this he will do with pleasure, or at least without pain, because what is done in accordance with virtue is pleasant or painless, and certainly not painful. Someone who gives to the wrong people, however, or not for the sake of what is noble but for some other reason, will be called not generous but something else. Nor will the person who finds it painful to give be called generous, because he would choose wealth over noble action, and this is not characteristic of a generous person. But neither will the generous person take wealth from the wrong sources, since taking like this is not characteristic of a person who does not hold wealth in honour. Nor will he be the kind of person to ask for it, because it is not characteristic of the benefactor of others readily to accept benefits himself. But he will take money from the right sources, such as his own property, not because doing so is noble but 1120b because it is necessary if he is to have something to give. Nor will he neglect his own possessions, since he wants to use them to help others. And he will not give to just anybody, so that he might have something to give to the right people, at the right time, and where it is noble to do so. It is very typical of the generous person to be excessive in giving, so that too little is left for himself, since it is characteristic of him not to look to his own interests.

Generosity is spoken of as relative to a person's property. For what is generous depends not on the amount given, but on the state of the giver, and this is relative to his property. So nothing prevents the person who gives less being the more generous, if he has less to give.

People who have inherited their wealth instead of acquiring it themselves seem to be more generous: first, they have not had the experience of being in want; and, secondly, everyone – like parents and poets – is more attached to what he produces himself.

It is not easy for the generous person to be rich, since he is not the sort either to take wealth or to keep it, but rather to give it away, and he honours it not for itself, but because it enables him to give. (Hence the charge against fortune that the most deserving of wealth are the least wealthy. But this is only to be expected, since, as with everything, one cannot have money without taking trouble over it.) But he will not give to the wrong people, nor at the wrong time, and so on, because he would not then be acting in accordance with generosity, and if he were to spend his money on these things, he would have none left to spend on the right things. For, as we have said, the generous person is the one whose expenditure is in proportion to his property and on the right objects, while the one who goes to excess is wasteful. This is why we do not call tyrants wasteful, since it does not seem that their giving and spending could easily exceed what they possess.

So, since generosity is a mean concerned with the giving and spending of money, the generous person will give and spend the right amounts, on the right objects, in both small and large matters alike, and he will do it with pleasure. He will also take the right amounts from the right sources: because the virtue is a mean concerning both, he will do both as he ought. For taking in the right way implies giving in the right way, while the wrong sort of taking conflicts with it; and so the giving and taking that imply one another are found at the same time in the same
1121a person, while those that conflict clearly are not.

But if it should so happen that the generous person spends more or less than is right and noble, he will be pained, but only in a moderate way, as one ought. For it is a characteristic of virtue to be pleased and to be pained, at the right objects and in the right way.

Again, the generous person is easy to do financial business with. For he can be cheated, since he holds wealth in no great honour, and is more upset if he has not spent what he ought than pained if he has spent what he ought not; he does not agree with Simonides. The wasteful person misses the mark in these respects as well, since he is neither pleased nor pained at the right things, or in the right way. This will become clearer as we go on.

We have said that wastefulness and stinginess are excesses and deficiencies in two respects: giving and taking (spending we count as giving). Wastefulness exceeds in giving and not taking, and is deficient in taking, while stinginess is deficient in giving, and exceeds in taking, but only in small matters. The characteristics of wastefulness are rarely found together, since it is not easy to give to all when you take from none; for the resources of private citizens – which wasteful people are thought to be – soon dwindle as they are given away. Nevertheless, someone like this seems to be quite a lot better than a stingy person, because the wasteful person is easily cured both by age and by poverty, and can thus approach the mean; for he has the characteristics of the generous person, because he gives and does not take, though neither rightly nor well. So if he is changed by habituation or in some other way, he will be generous, since he will give to the right people, and not take from the wrong sources. He is therefore held not to be bad in character; for going to excess in giving and not taking is characteristic not of a wicked or despicable person, but of a foolish one. Someone wasteful in this way seems to be far better than the stingy person for the reasons given above, and because he benefits many people, while the stingy person benefits nobody, not even himself.

But most wasteful people, as we have said, also take from the wrong sources, and are in this respect stingy. They become acquisitive because they wish to spend; and they are not in a position to do this easily, since their resources soon run short, and so they are compelled to obtain 1121b provision from other sources. At the same time, because they think nothing of what is noble, they take money irresponsibly from any source; for they desire to give, and how they do so or from what source makes no difference to them. Their giving, then, is not generous, because it is not noble, nor aimed at what is noble, nor is it performed in the right way. Sometimes they make rich those who should be poor, and will give nothing to people with the right sort of characters, but a great deal to flatterers or providers of some other pleasure. This is why most of them are intemperate. For, because they find it easy to spend money, they lavish it on intemperate pursuits; and since they do not live with a view to what is noble, they incline towards pleasures.

Someone wasteful, left without guidance, turns into such a person; but if he is dealt with carefully, he could attain to the mean, that is, to what is right. Stinginess, however, is both incurable (it seems to be caused by old age and every sort of disability), and more a part of human nature than wastefulness; for the masses are fonder of getting money than giving it away. It also covers a large area and comes in many forms, since there seem to be many kinds of stinginess; for it consists of two things – deficiency in giving and excess in taking – and it does not occur as a single entity in every case, but is sometimes divided, some people being excessive in taking, others deficient in giving.

Those referred to as, say, miserly, penny-pinching, or close-fisted are all deficient in giving, but do not covet the possessions of others nor wish to take them. Some do this from a sense of decency of some kind and a concern to avoid what is disgraceful, because there are those who seem – at least, this is what they claim – to look after their money so that they may never be compelled to do anything disgraceful; into this class fall the cumin-splitter (so called from his extreme aversion to giving anything away) and everyone like that. Others, however, keep their hands off the property of other people from fear, thinking that it is not easy for one person to take another's property without their taking his; so they are content neither to take nor to give.

Others again are excessive in taking, by taking anything from any-where – for example, those with base occupations, such as brothel-keepers and everyone like this, and people who lend small sums of 1122a money at high rates of interest; all of these take the wrong amounts from the wrong sources. What they have in common, of course, is their disgraceful love of gain, since they all put up with opprobrium for the sake of gain, and no great gain at that. For those who take a great deal of what they should not, from the wrong sources, such as tyrants who sack cities and pillage temples, we call not stingy, but rather wicked, impious and unjust. The dice-player and the petty thief or robber, however, do fall into the category of the stingy, since they have a disgraceful love of profit. For both types exert themselves and put up with the opprobrium for profit, the one facing the greatest dangers for the loot, the other profiting at the expense of his friends, to whom he ought to be giving.

Both, then, because they wish to profit from the wrong sources are disgraceful lovers of gain; and all such forms of taking are stingy.

It is natural that stinginess should be described as the contrary of generosity; for not only is it a greater evil than wastefulness, but people miss the mark more in this direction than in that of wastefulness as we have described it.

So much, then, for generosity and the vices in opposition to it.

Chapter 2

Next in order of discussion would seem to be magnificence, since it also seems to be a virtue concerned with wealth. Unlike generosity, however, it covers not all those actions concerned with wealth, but only those concerned with heavy expenditure; and in this it surpasses generosity in its large scale.

For, as its name (*megaloprepeia*) implies, it is expenditure that is fitting in its large scale (*megathei prepousa*); but the scale is relative, since the expense of equipping a trireme is not the same as that of being chief ambassador in a state delegation. What is fitting, then, is relative to the agent, to the circumstances, and to the object.

If someone spends on small or ordinary matters what they merit, as in the line, 'Many times I gave to a wanderer',[27] he is not called magnificent, but only if he does this in important matters: while the magnificent person is generous, this does not mean that the generous person is magnificent.

The deficiency of this state is called niggardliness, and its excess vulgarity, lack of taste and the like, which are excessive not because of the largeness of the amount spent on the right objects, but because of ostentatious expenditure on the wrong things and in the wrong way. These vices we shall discuss later.

The magnificent person is like an expert, since he can see what is fitting and spend large amounts with good taste. As we said at the 1122b beginning, a state is determined by its activities and its objects; the expenditures of the magnificent person will be large and fitting; so too, then, are the results, since this will make the expense large and fitting to the result. So the result should be worthy of the expenditure, and the expenditure worthy of the result, or even in excess of it.

---

[27] Homer, *Odyssey* xvii.420.

The magnificent person will spend such amounts for the sake of what is noble, since this is a feature common to the virtues. Again, he will do it with pleasure and lavishly, because precise counting of the cost is niggardly; and he will think more about how he might achieve the most noble and fitting result than about the cost or the cheapest way to produce it.

The magnificent person, then, must also be generous, since the generous person too will spend the right amount in the right way. But it is in meeting these criteria that we see the greatness, the largeness of scale, of the magnificent person, these being the things with which generosity is concerned, and he will produce a more magnificent result even at the same expense. For the virtue of a possession is not the same as that of an achieved result; the most honourable possession is that which is worth most, such as gold, while the most honourable result is that which is great and noble, because the contemplation of such a thing excites admiration, and what is magnificent excites admiration. Virtue in an achieved result on a large scale – that is magnificence.

Magnificence is found among the sorts of expenditure we call honourable, such as those connected with the gods – votive offerings, temples, and sacrifices – and similarly those concerning religion as a whole; and all those that are appropriate objects of public-spirited ambition, such as when people somewhere decide that a splendid chorus or warship or feast for the city must be provided.

But in all cases, as we have said, the expenditure is to be seen as relative to the identity and resources of the agent; the amounts should be worthy of these, and fitting not only for the result but also for the person bringing it about. So a poor person could not be magnificent, because he does not have resources from which he can spend large sums in a fitting way; and anyone who tries is a fool, since he spends beyond what is worthy of him and what is right, whereas correct expenditure is that which is in accordance with virtue.

Great expenditure is appropriate to those who have the resources, either through their own efforts, or those of their ancestors or connections, and to those of high birth, high reputation, and so on; for all these involve greatness and distinction. In particular, then, the magnificent person is like this, and magnificence is shown in expenditures of this kind, as we have said, for these are the greatest and most honoured.

1123a But it is seen also on those private occasions that happen only once, at weddings and suchlike; and on those that might excite the whole city or those in high places – arrangements for receiving and sending off foreign guests, for gifts and reciprocal gifts. For the magnificent person spends not on himself but on the community, and his gifts are rather like votive offerings.

It is also typical of the magnificent person to furnish his house in a way appropriate to his wealth (even this is a sort of ornament), and to spend more on those results that will last for a long time (because they are the noblest), and in each case to spend what is fitting: what befits the gods is not the same as what befits human beings, what befits a temple not the same as what befits a tomb.

And since each expenditure will be great relative to its kind; and the expenditure most magnificent without qualification is when it is great and for a great object, and in a given case that which is great for that kind of case; and greatness in the result is different from that in the expense (for a very noble ball or oil-flask is magnificent as a gift for a child, though its cost is small and petty); since these things are so, it is characteristic of the magnificent person, whatever kind of thing he is producing, to do it in a magnificent way (because a result like this will not easily be surpassed) and so that it is worthy of the expenditure.

Such, then, is the magnificent person.

The person who goes to excess and is vulgar, as we have said, exceeds by spending more than he should. For in small matters, he spends a great deal and puts on an unharmonious display, feasting the members of his dining-club, for example, as if they were at a wedding; or, when funding the chorus for a comedy, bringing them onto the stage in purple, as they do at Megara. And all such things he will do, not for the sake of what is noble, but to show off his wealth and because he thinks it will win him admiration. Where he ought to spend much, he spends little, and where little, much.

The niggardly person, however, will be deficient in everything, and having spent the greatest sums will ruin something noble to save a tiny amount. In whatever he does, he is hesitant and considers how he may keep the cost as low as possible; he complains even about this, and thinks he is doing everything on a grander scale than is required.

These states are vices, but they do not bring opprobrium, because they are neither harmful to one's neighbours nor particularly offensive.

Chapter 3

Greatness of soul also seems from its name to be concerned with great
1123b things; let us first try to grasp what sort. It makes no difference whether
we consider the state or the person characterized by it.

A person is thought to be great-souled if he thinks himself worthy of
great things – and is indeed worthy of them (anyone who thinks like this
when he is not worthy is a fool, and no one who lives in accordance with
virtue is foolish or senseless); the great-souled person, then, is as we
have described. The person who is worthy of little and thinks himself to
be such is temperate, but not great-souled; for greatness of soul implies
grandness of scale, as beauty implies grandeur of body, and small people
can be pretty and well-proportioned, but not beautiful.

Someone who thinks himself worthy of great things when he is not is
vain; but not everyone who thinks himself worthy of greater things than
he is worthy of is vain. Someone who thinks himself worthy of lesser
things than he is worthy of, however, is small-souled, whether he is in
fact worthy of either great or ordinary things, or even whether he is
worthy of small things but thinks himself worthy of yet smaller ones.
The most small-souled would seem to be the one who is worthy of great
things: what would he have done if he had not in fact been worthy of so
much? The great-souled person, then, is an extreme with regard to the
grandness of his claims, but a mean with regard to their correctness; for
he reckons his own worth in accordance with his real merit, while the
others are excessive and deficient.

If, then, he thinks himself worthy of great things – and above all the
greatest – and if he is indeed so, he will be concerned with one thing in
particular. Worth is spoken of with reference to external goods; and
the greatest external good we should assume to be what we render to
the gods, the good most aimed at by people of worth, the prize for the
noblest achievements. Such is honour, since it is indeed the greatest
external good. The great-souled person, then, is concerned with
honours and dishonours in the right way.

In fact, it is obvious even without argument that great-souled people
are concerned with honour; for it is honour most of all that they think
themselves worthy of, and this accords with their real worth. The small-
souled person falls short both in relation to his own worth and the
great-souled person's estimate of his own worth, while the vain person

goes to excess in relation to his own worth, but his claims are not excessive in relation to the great-souled person. The great-souled person, since he is worthy of the greatest things, must be the best person of all. For the better a person is, the greater the things he is worthy of, and the best will be worthy of the greatest things; so the truly great-souled person must be good.

Again, greatness in every virtue would seem to be a characteristic of a great-souled person. It would be quite unfitting for him to run away with his arms swinging, or to commit an injustice. For what could prompt someone like this, to whom nothing is great, to act disgracefully? If one considers particular cases, it becomes obvious that the notion of a great-souled person who is not good is quite ridiculous. Nor would he be worthy of honour if he were bad, since honour is the prize of virtue, and it is conferred on those who are good. Greatness of soul, 1124a then, seems to be a sort of crown of the virtues, because it makes them greater and does not occur in isolation from them. This is why it is hard to be truly great-souled, since it is not possible without a noble and good character.

It is primarily with honours and dishonours, then, that the great-souled person is concerned. He will be pleased in a moderate way at great honours conferred by good people, thinking that he is getting what he deserves, or even less than he deserves, because there could be no honour worthy of total virtue. Nevertheless, he will accept such honours, on the ground that they have nothing greater to confer on him. But honour conferred by ordinary people or for unimportant reasons he will utterly despise, since it is beneath him. The same goes for dishonour, because it could not with justice be attributed to him.

Primarily, then, as we have said, the great-souled person will be concerned with honours, but he will also take a moderate view of wealth, power, and all kinds of good and bad fortune, whatever happens, in the sense that he will neither be excessively happy at good fortune nor excessively distressed at bad fortune. For he does not even view honour as a terribly important thing. Power and wealth are to be chosen for the honour they bring – at any rate, those who have them wish to be honoured on their account; thus, if honour matters little to a person, so will the rest. This is why great-souled people are thought to be supercilious.

The advantages of fortune, however, do seem to contribute to greatness of soul. For the well-born are thought worthy of honour, as are those of power and wealth, because they are in a position of superiority, and superiority in something good is in every case more honoured. So these things too make people more great-souled, in that they are honoured by some people for them. In truth, however, the good person alone is to be honoured; but the person who has both is more widely thought worthy of honour.

People who have the advantages of fortune, but lack virtue, cannot justly claim to be worthy of great things, nor are they rightly called great-souled; these are impossible without total virtue. But when they possess the advantages of fortune they become supercilious and wantonly violent, since in the absence of virtue it is not easy to carry such 1124b goods gracefully. Being unable to do this and thinking themselves superior to other people, they look down on them, and do as they please. Though they are not like the great-souled person, they imitate him whenever they can; so they do not act in accordance with virtue, but they do look down on others. The great-souled person looks down on others with justification, because he has the right opinion of himself, but the masses do so capriciously.

He does not face trivial dangers, nor, because he holds few things in honour, does he enjoy danger; but he will face great dangers, and when in danger will not spare his own life, thinking that the price of life can be too high. He is the sort of person to do good, but is ashamed to be a beneficiary himself, since doing good is characteristic of a superior, receiving it of an inferior. And he will repay benefits with interest, so that his original benefactor, in addition to being paid, will have become a debtor and a beneficiary. Great-souled people seem also to remember any benefits they have conferred, but not those they have received (since a beneficiary is inferior to a benefactor, and he wishes to be superior), and to hear of the former with pleasure, the latter with displeasure; this, it appears, is why Thetis did not speak to Zeus of the services she had done him,[28] and the Spartans did not mention their services to the Athenians, but rather those that had been done for them.

It is also characteristic of a great-souled person to ask for nothing, or almost nothing, but to help others readily; and to be dignified in his behaviour towards people of distinction or the well-off, but unassuming

---

[28] Aristotle is apparently misremembering Homer, *Iliad* i.503f.

towards people at the middle level. Superiority over the first group is difficult and impressive, but over the second it is easy, and attempting to impress the first group is not ill-bred, while in the case of humble people it is vulgar, like a show of strength against the weak.

Again, it is characteristic of him not to go for things that are generally held in honour, or things in which others excel. He is hesitant and slow to act except where there is great honour or a significant result at stake; and the actions he is inclined to perform are few, but great and renowned. He must also be open in his likes and dislikes, since hiding one's feelings is characteristic of a fearful person, and he cares more for the truth than for what people think. And he must speak and act openly; for the fact that he is inclined to look down on people and to speak the truth, except when he speaks self-deprecatingly to the masses, makes him free in his speech. He must be unable to live in dependence on another, unless he is a friend, because such behaviour is servile. This is 1125a why all flatterers are servile and lowly people are flatterers. Nor does he incline towards admiration, because in his eyes nothing is great, nor towards remembering evils, because it is not characteristic of a great-souled person to harbour memories, especially of evils, but rather to overlook them. Nor is he a gossip, and he will not speak about himself or about anyone else, because he does not care to have himself praised or others blamed. Nor is he the sort to praise people; and so he does not speak ill of others either, not even his enemies, unless wanton violence on their part gives him cause to do so.

When faced with necessary tasks or with minor problems, he is the last person to complain and to ask for assistance, because such behaviour is characteristic of a person who takes these things seriously. And he is the kind of person whose possessions are noble but unprofitable, rather than profitable and useful, since this is more indicative of self-sufficiency. His movements are thought slow, his voice deep, and his speech measured: since only a few things matter to him, he is not likely to be rushed. And since he puts no great weight on anything, he is not vehement when he speaks; it is rushing and vehemence that make for hastiness and a high-pitched voice.

Such a person, then, is the great-souled. The deficient person is small-souled, and the excessive vain; because what they do is not evil, these people are thought not to be bad either, but to be missing the mark. For the small-souled person is worthy of good things, but deprives himself of what he is worthy of. There does seem something bad about him in his not thinking himself worthy of good things; and he seems not to know himself, since otherwise he would have striven for the things of which he was worthy, because they are good. Nevertheless these people are thought to be not so much foolish as timid. But their view of themselves seems to make them even worse, because each sort of person aims at what is in accordance with his worth, and these people abstain from noble actions and projects, and similarly from external goods, because they feel unworthy of them.

Vain people, however, are foolish, and ignorant of themselves – quite obviously so. For they try for honours when they are unworthy of them, and are then found out; and they dress themselves up and put on airs and so on, and, since they wish for good fortune and that their good fortune be well known, talk about it in the hope of being honoured for it. Smallness of soul is more opposed than vanity to greatness of soul, because it is more common, as well as worse.

Greatness of soul, then, as we have said, is concerned with honour on a grand scale.

Chapter 4

1125b As we said at the beginning, there seems also to be a kind of virtue concerned with honour and apparently related to greatness of soul as generosity is to magnificence. Neither of them has to do with anything great, but they dispose us in the right way towards matters of moderate or little importance; and as in the giving and taking of money there is a mean, an excess, and a deficiency, so also we can desire honour more or less than is right, and from the right source, and in the right way. For we blame both the honour-lover, for seeking honour more than is right and from the wrong sources, and the person uninterested in it, for not rationally choosing to be honoured even for noble things. But sometimes we praise the honour-lover for being manly and a lover of what is noble, and the person uninterested in honour for being moderate and temperate, as we said at the beginning.

Clearly, since a person can be described as a lover of such and such in a number of senses, we do not always apply the term 'honour-loving' to the same thing; rather, we use it to praise loving honour more than the masses, and to blame loving it more than is right. Since the mean is nameless, it seems as if the extremes are competing for it as if it were unoccupied territory.

But wherever there is an excess and a deficiency, there is also a mean; and since people desire honour both to a greater and to a lesser degree than they should, there is a right way to do so. It is this state, then, that is praised, in that, though nameless, it is a mean concerned with honour. Compared with love of honour, it seems like lack of interest in it, and compared with lack of interest, like love of it, while compared with both, it seems in a sense to be like both. This seems to happen in the case of the other virtues as well; but here it is the fact that the person at the mean has no name that makes the extremes appear in opposition only to one another.

Chapter 5

Even temper is a mean concerned with anger. The mean is nameless, and the extremes pretty much so, but we apply the name 'even temper' to the mean, though it inclines towards the deficiency, which is also nameless. The excess might be called a kind of irascibility, since the feeling here is anger, though the things that produce it are many and various.

There is praise for someone who gets angry at the right things and with the right people, as well as in the right way, at the right time, and for the right length of time. This, then, will be the even-tempered person, since it is his even temper that is praised. The even-tempered person professes to be calm and not carried away by his feelings, but to 1126a be cross only in the way, at the things, and for the length of time that reason directs. And he is thought to miss the mark more in the direction of the deficiency, because the even-tempered person is inclined not to revenge so much as to forgiveness.

The deficiency, whether it is a kind of non-irascibility or whatever, is blamed, because people who do not get angry at things that they ought to get angry at are thought to be foolish, as are those who do so in the wrong way, at the wrong time, and with the wrong people. Such a person seems to be insensible and to feel no pain, and, because he does not get angry, not the sort to stick up for himself; and it is slavish to put up with being insulted oneself or to overlook insults to those close to one.

The excess occurs in all these respects – in getting angry with the wrong people, for the wrong reasons, as well as to a greater degree, more quickly, and for a longer time than is right. But not all of them will be found in the same person; indeed, they could not, since evil destroys even itself, and if it is perfect, it becomes intolerable.

Irascible people get angry quickly, with the wrong people, at the wrong things, and to a greater degree than they should, but they are also quick to calm down – which is the best thing about them. This happens because they do not repress their anger but, since they are quick-tempered, retaliate openly and then stop.

Irritable people are excessively quick-tempered; they get angry at anything in any situation, which is the origin of their name.

Sulky people are hard to make up with, and remain angry for a long time, because they repress their spirit. It stops, however, when they retaliate, since revenge relieves their anger, by substituting pleasure for pain. Otherwise, they retain their grudge; because it does not manifest itself, no one persuades them out of it, and it takes time to digest one's anger in oneself. People like this cause terrible trouble to themselves and their close friends.

We call cross those who get cross at the wrong things, and to a greater degree and for a longer time than is right, and will not make up before vengeance or punishment has been inflicted. We place the excess in greater opposition to even temper, because it is more common (revenge being more human), and because cross people are harder to live with.

What we have just said makes clear what we said before: it is not easy to determine how, with whom, at what, and how long one should be angry, and the limits of acting rightly and missing the mark. For the person who strays a little from the right path, whether towards excess or

1126b deficiency, is not blamed: sometimes we praise as even-tempered those who fall short, and those who get cross as manly in that they can influence others.

So it is not easy to articulate how far a person has to go in getting angry, and in what way, before he is liable to blame; such things depend on the particular circumstances, and judgement lies in perception. But so much at least is clear, that the mean state – in virtue of which we get angry with the right people, at the right things, in the right way, and so on – is praiseworthy, while the excesses and deficiencies are to be blamed – only slightly if they are minor, more so if they are more serious, and very much so if they are major. Obviously, then, we should keep close to the mean state.

So much, then, for the states concerned with anger.

Chapter 6

In private relations with others – both in living together and in participating in discussions and actions – some people seem obsequious; in an attempt to please us, they praise everything and are never obstructive, thinking that they must not cause any pain to those they meet. At the opposite extreme, people who obstruct everything and think nothing of causing pain are called bad-tempered and belligerent.

It is quite clear that the states we have mentioned are blameworthy, and that the mean – on the basis of which a person will accept the right things, and in the right way, and likewise reject them – is praiseworthy. It has not been given a name, but it seems most like friendship; for the person corresponding to the mean state is the sort we mean when we talk of a good friend, though this does imply affection. It differs from friendship, in that it does not involve feeling and affection for those with whom one associates: this person accepts the right things not because he is a friend or an enemy, but because his character is as it is. For he will act in the same fashion towards strangers and those he knows, towards people with whom he is familiar and those with whom he is not, except that in each case he will do what suits the occasion; it is not appropriate to take the same trouble over – or to cause the same amount of pain to – close acquaintances and strangers.

Generally, then, we have said that he will associate with people in the right way, but it is by reference to what is noble and what is useful that he will aim at not causing pain to others or at pleasing them. For he seems to be concerned with the pleasures and pains that arise in private relations with others; and whenever it is not noble for him to add to the enjoyment of others, or is harmful to do so, he will object to doing it, and rationally choose to cause them pain. Again, if the other's doing something would bring great disgrace on him, or cause him some harm, while opposition would cause only slight pain, the person with virtue will not accept the action, but object to it.

He will associate with people of distinction differently from ordinary people, and with people he knows better differently from those he 1127a

75

knows less well, and similarly as regards the other differences between people, rendering to each what is appropriate.

What he will rationally choose for itself is pleasing others while taking care not to cause them pain. But he will not ignore the consequences, if these are more important, namely, what is noble and what is useful. And he will also inflict small pains for the sake of a great pleasure in the future.

The person with the mean state, then, is as we have described, but he is without a name. In the case of the type who makes others happy, the person who is pleasant with no ulterior motive is obsequious, while he who is so with a view to benefiting himself with money or what it buys is a flatterer. We have already said that the person who objects to everything is bad-tempered and belligerent. The extremes seem to be directly opposed to one another because the mean has no name.

Chapter 7

The mean between boastfulness and its contrary is concerned with almost the same things; and it too does not have a name. It is worth running through nameless states like this, since, if we do go through particular aspects of character individually, we shall know more about them, and we shall be sure that each virtue is a mean if we see it to be so in all cases.

As regards social life, then, we have talked about those who associate with others with a view to causing pleasure and pain; let us now speak of those who pursue truth and falsity in what they say and do – in other words, in what they are claiming.

The boastful person, then, seems to be the sort to lay claim to esteemed qualities that he either does not have or has to a lesser degree than he claims. The self-deprecating person, on the other hand, seems to disclaim those he has or to play them down. The person at the mean, however, is straightforward, and truthful in life and in what he says, since he acknowledges no more and no less than the qualities he has.

Each of these things can be done with or without an ulterior motive; and each person – if he is not acting for an ulterior motive – speaks, acts, and lives in accordance with his character. Falsehood is in itself bad and blameworthy, while the truth is noble and praiseworthy; so the truthful person, because of his intermediate position, is praiseworthy, while the dissemblers are both blameworthy, especially the boastful person.

Before we discuss each extreme, let us first consider the truthful person. We are not talking about someone truthful in his agreements or in matters of injustice or justice, since these are the concern of another 1127b virtue, but someone who, when nothing like this is at stake, is truthful in what he says and the way he lives because that is what his state of character is like. A person such as this would seem to be good. For someone who loves truth, and is truthful when nothing is at stake, will be all the more truthful when something is at stake, since he will avoid falsehood as something disgraceful, having already avoided it in itself. And a person like this is praiseworthy. He inclines more towards understatement than overstatement, because this seems to be in better taste, exaggeration being a tiresome thing.

Someone who pointlessly pretends to greater qualities than he in fact has does seem bad (otherwise he would not enjoy telling lies), but he is really more foolish than bad. If he does it for a reason like reputation or honour, he is not to be blamed too much, but if he does it for money or for what money can buy, he is an uglier character (it is not a capacity that makes one boastful, but rather the rational choice; a person is boastful in accordance with his state of character, by being a person of a certain type). In the same way, a liar can be either one who enjoys the very lie itself, or one who desires honour or gain.

Those who boast for the sake of reputation lay claim to qualities that win praise or a name for happiness, while those who do it for gain claim qualities that are advantageous to others and the non-existence of which cannot be proven, such as the powers of a doctor or wise prophet. This is why it is things like this, since they have the characteristics mentioned, that most people claim and boast about.

Self-deprecating people, because they play down their qualities, appear to have more attractive characters. For they seem to speak, not for gain, but in order to avoid pomposity. And it is especially qualities held in esteem that they disclaim, as Socrates used to do.

People who disclaim minor everyday qualities are called humbugs and are more contemptible. Sometimes this appears to be boastfulness, as in the case of Spartan dress, since an extreme deficiency is boastful as well as an excess. But people seem attractive who are moderate in their self-depreciation and play down qualities that are not too everyday and obvious. And it is the boastful person, because he is the worse, who appears to be the contrary of the truthful.

Chapter 8

Since relaxation is a part of life, and one element of this is amusing 1128a diversion, here too it seems that there is a form of tasteful social conduct, namely, saying, and similarly listening to, the right thing in the right way. The kind of people to whom one talks or listens also makes a difference. Clearly we find here also an excess and a deficiency in relation to the mean.

Those who go too far in their humour are thought to be common buffoons who will do anything to raise a laugh, and care more about this than about speaking decently and not offending those who are the butt of their jokes; while those who do not make jokes themselves and object to others' doing so are thought to be boorish and austere.

Those who joke in a tasteful way are described as quick-witted (*eutrapelos*), as if they are quick-to-turn (*eutropos*). For such jokes are thought to be movements of the character, and characters, like bodies, are judged by their movements. Material for humour, however, is always near at hand, and most people enjoy fun and jokes more than they should; so buffoons, since they are thought amusing, are described as quick-witted. But that there is a difference, and no small one at that, is clear from what we have said.

In addition, seemliness is proper to the mean state. It is characteristic of a seemly person to say and to listen to the sort of things that are suitable for a gentleman of good character. For there are some things that it is appropriate for such a person to say and to listen to by way of amusement, and the amusement of a gentleman differs from that of a slavish person, and that of an educated person from that of an uneducated. One can also see this from old and new comedies: to the earlier writers, bad language was what was funny, while, to the later, it was innuendo, which is far more decent. Should we distinguish the person who jokes well, then, by his saying what is not unbecoming to a gentleman, or by his not causing pain to, or even pleasing, his listener? Or is this, at any rate, indefinite, since different things are hateful and pleasant to different people? The kind of thing he will listen to will be the same, since he puts up with hearing the kind of remarks he seems to make himself. He will not, then, indulge in every kind of humour. For joking is a kind of abuse, and law-givers forbid us to abuse certain things; perhaps they should have included joking as well. The sophisticated gentleman, then, will be like this, as a sort of law unto himself.

Such, then, is the intermediate person, whether he is called seemly or quick-witted.

The buffoon cannot resist a joke, sparing neither himself nor anyone else if he can raise a laugh, and saying things that a person of taste would never say, and some that he would not even listen to. 1128b

The boor is useless in such social intercourse. For he contributes nothing and takes objection to everything, even though relaxation and amusement are thought to be a necessary part of life.

Three means in life have been described, then, and they are all concerned with social interaction in various kinds of of conversation and actions. They differ in so far as one is concerned with truth, the other two with what is pleasant. Of those concerned with pleasure, one is found in amusements, the other in the remaining kinds of social intercourse of life.

Chapter 9

Shame is not properly spoken of as a virtue, since it is more like a feeling than a state of character. Anyway, it is defined as a kind of fear of disrepute, and it has an effect very like that produced by the fear of something horrible: people blush when they feel disgrace, and turn pale when they are afraid of death. So both seem to be in some way bodily conditions, and this seems to be more characteristic of a feeling than a state.

This feeling is appropriate not to every age, but only to youth. For we think that young people should be properly disposed to feel shame, because they live by feeling and so make many errors, but are restrained by shame. And we praise the young for being properly disposed to feel shame, but no one would praise an older person for having a sense of shame, since we think that he should do nothing to feel shame for. A feeling of disgrace is not characteristic of a good person, since it arises from bad actions; for these should not be done, and it makes no difference whether some actions are genuinely disgraceful, while others are only believed to be so – neither should be done, so no disgrace should be felt. A feeling of disgrace is characteristic of a bad person, because he is the sort to do disgraceful things. To be disposed to feel disgrace on doing any disgraceful actions like this, and on this basis to think oneself good, is absurd, since it is for voluntary actions that shame is felt, and a good person will never do bad actions voluntarily. Shame might be a good thing conditionally: if a good person were to do this, then he would feel disgrace; but this does not apply to the virtues. And if not feeling shame and disgrace at doing disgraceful actions is bad, that does not make it good for someone to do them and then feel shame.

Continence is not a virtue either, but is, as it were, mixed; it will be explained later. For now, let us discuss justice.

Book V

Chapter 1

We must consider justice and injustice – what sort of actions they are concerned with, what kind of mean justice is, and what are the extremes between which the just is a mean. Let our inquiry be conducted in the same way as our preceding discussions.

We see that everyone means by justice the same kind of state, namely, that which disposes people to do just actions, act justly, and wish for what is just. In the same way, by injustice they mean the state that makes people act unjustly and wish for what is unjust. So let us too begin with these assumptions as a rough basis for our discussion.

What is true of sciences and capacities is not true of states, since it seems that contraries can both be the concern of the same capacity or science, while a state does not produce results contrary to itself. For example, as a result of health, we do not do actions contrary to health, but only those that are healthy; we say that we are walking healthily when we walk as a healthy person would.

One can often identify a contrary state from its contrary, and states from their subjects. If it is clear what the good state is, then the bad state also becomes clear, and the good state is identified from the things that are in that state, and they from it: if the good state is firmness of flesh, then the bad state must be flabbiness, and what conduces to the good state must be what produces firmness of flesh. It generally follows that if one contrary is spoken of in more than one way, so is the other; if the just, for example, is spoken of in more than one way, so is the unjust. It seems, in fact, that justice and injustice are spoken of in more than one way, but

81

because the different senses of each are close to one another, their homonymy passes unnoticed and is not so obvious as it is in cases when the two are far apart. For example (and here the difference in outward appearance is a large one), the word 'key' is used homonymously for the collar-bone of an animal and for that which people use to lock doors.

Let us acquire some grasp, then, of how many ways there are in which a person is said to be unjust. Both the lawless person and the greedy and unfair person seem to be unjust. Obviously, then, both the lawful person and the fair person will be just; and thus the just is the lawful and the fair, and the unjust is the lawless and the unfair.

1129b Since the unjust person is greedy, he will be concerned with goods – not all goods, but those with which good and bad fortune are concerned; these are always good without qualification, but not always for a particular individual. (People pray for and pursue these things, but they should not; rather, they should pray that those goods that are good without qualification may also be good for them, and they should choose things that are good for them.)

The unjust person does not always choose more, but, in the case of things that are bad without qualification, he chooses less. But because the lesser evil itself seems to be a kind of good, and greed is for what is good, he therefore seems to be greedy. He is indeed unfair, this being an inclusive term that covers both.

Since, as we saw, the lawless person is unjust and the lawful just, it is clear that whatever is lawful is in some way just; for the things laid down by legislative science are lawful, and each of these we describe as just. The laws have something to say about everything, their aim being the common interest either of all the citizens, or of the best, or of those in power, or of some other such group. So, in one sense, we call anything just that tends to produce or to preserve happiness and its constituents for the community of a city.

Law requires us to do the acts of a courageous person – not, for example, to desert our post, run away or throw down our weapons – as well as those of a temperate person – such as not to commit adultery or wanton violence – and those of an even-tempered person – not to hit or slander anyone, for instance. And similarly it demands actions in accordance with the other virtues, and forbids those in accordance with the vices, correctly if it is correctly established, less well if it is carelessly produced.

Justice in this sense, then, is complete virtue, not without qualification, but in relation to another person. For this reason, it is often held that justice is the greatest of the virtues, and that 'neither evening star nor morning star is such a wonder'.[29] We express this in the proverb, 'In justice is all virtue combined'.[30]

And it is complete virtue in the fullest sense, because it is the exercise of complete virtue. It is complete because he who possesses it can exercise his virtue in relation to another person, not only himself. There are many people who can exercise virtue in their own affairs, but are 1130a unable to do so in their relations with others. This is why the aphorism of Bias,[31] 'Office will reveal the man', seems a good one, since an official is, by reason of his position, engaged in relations with other people and the community at large. For the same reason, justice is the only virtue considered to be the good of another,[32] because it is exercised in relation to others: it does what is beneficial for another, whether he is in office over one or is a fellow-citizen.

So the worst person is the one who exercises his wickedness in relation to himself and in relation to his friends, and the best is not he who exercises his virtue in relation to himself but the one who exercises it in relation to others, since this is a difficult thing to do. Justice in this sense, then, is not a part of virtue, but the whole of virtue, and the injustice contrary to it is not a part of vice, but vice as a whole. The difference between virtue and justice in this sense is clear from what we have said. For they are the same, but what it is to be each of them is different. In so far as it is seen in relation to others, it is justice, while as an unqualified state, it is virtue.

Chapter 2

But, since we say there is such a thing, we are looking for the justice that is a part of virtue and similarly for the injustice that is a part of vice.

There is evidence that such a particular form exists. In all other cases of wickedness, the person who exercises it acts unjustly, but is not at all greedy (the person who throws away his shield through cowardice, for example, or speaks abusively through bad temper, or refuses financial

---

[29] Euripides, *The Wise Melanippe*, fr. 486 Nauck.
[30] Theognis, 147. Late seventh-century (or mid-sixth century) elegaic poet, from Megara.
[31] One of the Seven Sages.   [32] Cf. Plato, *Republic* 343c.

assistance through stinginess). But when someone is greedy, his action is often not in accordance with any of these forms of wickedness, still less all of them; but, since we blame him, it is in accordance with some form of wickedness, namely, injustice. There is, then, another kind of injustice, which is part of injustice as a whole, and what is unjust can here be seen as part of the whole of what is unjust in the sense of being contrary to law.

Again, someone who commits adultery for gain and makes money out of it would seem unjust, but not intemperate, while another who does so through appetite, though it costs him and he loses money for it, would seem to be intemperate rather than greedy. Obviously, this is because the first acts for gain.

Again, all other unjust acts are always attributed to some form of wickedness, such as adultery to intemperance, desertion of a comrade in battle to cowardice, physical assault to anger. But if the person gains by what he does, it is attributed to no other form of wickedness than injustice.

Clearly, then, besides universal justice, there is another form of injustice – particular injustice; it has the same name, because its 1130b definition falls under the same genus, both being effective in relation to somebody else. But, whereas the one is concerned with honour or money or security – or that which includes all of these, if we had a name for it – and is motivated by the pleasure that results from gain, the other is concerned with all the things with which the good person is concerned.

Clearly, then, there are several kinds of justice, and there is one that is distinct from virtue as a whole; we must ascertain what it is and what sort of thing it is.

What is unjust has been divided into what is unlawful and what is unfair, and what is just into what is lawful and what is fair. Injustice in the sense above corresponds to what is unlawful. But what is unfair is not the same as what is unlawful, but differs as part from whole (since everything that is unlawful is unfair, while not everything that is unfair is unlawful); and so what is unjust, and injustice in the sense of unfairness, are not the same as what is unjust and injustice in the other sense, but differ as parts from wholes. For this injustice is a part of injustice as a whole, and similarly particular justice a part of justice as a whole. So we must discuss justice and injustice in the particular sense, and similarly what is just and unjust. Let us therefore put aside the justice and injustice that correspond to virtue as a whole, the one being the exercise of virtue as a whole in relation to another, the other of vice.

It is obvious, too, how we should distinguish what is just and what is unjust in accordance with these types of justice and injustice, since most acts required by law, we might say, are enjoined from the point of view of virtue as a whole. For law requires us to live in accordance with each single virtue and forbids us to live in accordance with each form of wickedness. And the things that tend to produce virtue as a whole are the actions required by law that are laid down for education in good citizenship. But any decision must be delayed as to whether the education of the individual as such, on the basis of which he is a good person without qualification, is a branch of political science or of some other science; for, presumably, being a good person is not in every case the same as being a good citizen.

One type of particular justice, and of what is just in that same sense, is that found in distributions of honour or money or the other things that have to be shared among members of the political community (since here one person can have a share equal or unequal to another's).

Another type is that which plays a rectificatory role in transactions. 1131a This type divides into two, since some transactions are voluntary, others involuntary. The voluntary transactions are things like selling, buying, lending at interest, pledging, lending without interest, depositing, and letting (they are called voluntary because the first principle in these transactions is voluntary). The involuntary ones are either secret – such as theft, adultery, poisoning, procuring, enticing away slaves, treacherous murder, and false witness – or involve force, such as assault, imprisonment, murder, robbery, maiming, slander, and insult.

Chapter 3

Since the unjust person is unfair, or unequal, and what is unjust is unfair, or unequal, it is clear that there is a mean in respect of what is unfair, namely, what is fair, or equal. In any kind of action in which there is a more and a less, there is also an equal. So if what is unjust is unequal, what is just must be equal – something that everyone thinks, even without argument.

Since what is equal is a mean, the just will be some sort of mean.

Because equality requires at least two terms, what is just must be a mean, and equal, and relative, namely, just for certain people. And, in so far as it is a mean, it must be between certain extremes (excess and deficiency); in so far as it is equal, it must involve two terms; and in so far as it is just, it must be so for certain people. So what is just requires at least four terms: the persons for whom it is just are two, and the shares in which its justice consists are two. There will be the same level of equality between persons as between shares, because the shares will be in the same ratio to one another as the persons. For if the persons are not equal, they will not receive equal shares; in fact quarrels and complaints arise either when equals receive unequal shares in an allocation, or unequals receive equal shares.

This is clear also from the principle of distribution according to merit. For everyone agrees that justice in distribution must be in accordance with some kind of merit, but not everyone means the same by merit; democrats think that it is being a free citizen, oligarchs that it is wealth or noble birth, and aristocrats that it is virtue.

So the just is a sort of proportion. Being proportionate is not a property peculiar to abstract number, but belongs to number in general, since proportion is an equality of ratios, and involves at least four terms. Now it is obvious that discrete proportion involves four terms. But the same is true of continuous proportion, since it treats one term as two, mentioning it twice; for example, as the line A is to the line B, so is B to C. B, then, has been mentioned twice; so if B is set down twice, the proportional terms will be four.

1131b

What is just will also involve at least four terms, and the ratio is the same, since the persons and the shares are divided in the same ratio. As the term A, then, is to the term B, so will C be to D, and consequently, in permutation, as A is to C, so B is to D. And so whole will bear the same ratio to whole. It is this combination which the distribution brings about, and, if the terms be united in this way, brings about justly.

What is just in distribution, therefore, is the conjunction of the term A with the term C, and of the term B with the term D. And the just in this sense is a mean, and the unjust violates the proportion, since what is proportionate is a mean, and the just is proportionate. Mathematicians call this kind of proportion geometrical, because in geometrical proportion what happens is that whole is to whole as each part is to each part. But this proportion is not continuous, since there is not a single numerical term for person and share.

What is just in this sense, then, is what is proportionate. And what is unjust is what violates the proportion: one side becomes too large, the other too small, which is actually what happens in practice, since the one who acts unjustly gets more of what is good, while the one treated unjustly gets less. In the case of evil, the reverse is the case, since the lesser evil is counted as a good in comparison with the greater evil; the lesser evil is more worthy of choice than the greater, what is worthy of choice is a good, and what is more worthy of choice is a greater good.

This, then, is the first species of what is just.

Chapter 4

The other kind of justice is rectificatory, which is found in both voluntary and involuntary transactions. It belongs to a different species from that above. For the just in distribution of common property is always in accordance with the proportion stated above, since if the distribution is from common funds, it will be in the same ratio as are the corresponding investments to one another. And the injustice that is opposed to this kind of justice is what violates the proportion.

What is just in transactions is nevertheless a kind of equality, and what is unjust a kind of inequality, in accordance, however, not with that kind of proportion, but with arithmetical proportion. For it makes no difference whether it is a good person who has defrauded a bad or a bad person a good, nor whether it is a good or bad person that has committed adultery. The law looks only to the difference made by the injury, and treats the parties as equals, if one is committing injustice, and the other suffering it – that is, if one has harmed, and the other been harmed. So the judge, since this kind of injustice is an inequality, tries to equalize it. For even when one party is struck, and the other strikes, or one kills, and the other is killed, the suffering and the action are divided unequally. The judge tries to equalize them with the penalty, decreasing the gain that has been made. For the word 'gain' is generally employed in such cases, even if it is not appropriate for some of them, such as assault, and the same goes for the use of the word 'loss' of the victim. At any rate, when the damage has been assessed, the one is called loss, the other gain.

What is equal is therefore a mean between the greater and the less, but the gain and the loss constitute the greater and the less in contrary ways: more good and less evil constitute gain, while the contraries constitute loss. And the mean between them, as we saw, is what is equal, which we say is just. So what is just in rectification will be the mean between loss and gain.

1132b   These names, 'loss' and 'gain', are in fact derived from voluntary exchange. For having more than one's share is called gaining, while having less than one had at the beginning is called losing – in buying and selling, for example, and other transactions in which the law has left people free to decide their own terms. But when neither party gets too much or too little, and both get what they gave, they say that they have what belongs to them, and that they neither lose nor gain. It follows that in voluntary transactions the just is a mean between some kind of gain and loss; it consists in having an equal amount both before and after the

1132a   transaction. This is why, when people are in dispute, they turn to a judge. To appeal to a judge is to appeal to what is just, because a judge is meant to be, as it were, justice personified. They seek the judge also as an intermediary, and some people even call them mediators, on the basis that if they are awarded what is intermediate, they will be awarded what is just. What is just, then, is intermediate, since the judge is so. The judge restores equality. It is as if there were a line divided into unequal parts, and he takes away that by which the greater segment exceeds the half, and adds it to the smaller segment. And when the whole has been equally divided in two – when the parties have equal shares – then they say that they have what belongs to them. It is for this reason that it is called just (*dikaios*), because it is a division into two parts (*dicha*), just as if one were to call it divided in two (*dichaios*), and the judge (*dikastēs*) is a divider in two (*dichastēs*).

What is equal is a mean between the greater and the less according to arithmetical proportion, because when a certain amount is subtracted from one of two equals and added to the other, the other exceeds the first by double that amount; for if the amount had been subtracted, but

1132b   not added to the other, it would have exceeded it by only once that amount. It therefore exceeds the mean by once the amount, and the mean exceeds by once the amount that from which the amount was subtracted.

In this way, then, we shall work out what we must subtract from the party with more, and add to the party with less; for we must add to the party with less the amount by which the mean exceeds what he has, and subtract from the greatest quantity the amount by which it exceeds the mean. Let the lines AA', BB' and CC' be equal to one another. From the line AA', let the segment AE be subtracted, and the segment CD added to the line CC', so that the whole line DCC' exceeds the line EA' by the segment CD and the segment CF; thus it exceeds the line BB' by the segment CD.

Chapter 5

Some hold that reciprocity is just without qualification. This was the claim of the Pythagoreans, since they defined, without qualification, what is just as reciprocity with another.

Reciprocity, however, fits neither distributive nor rectificatory justice (though people do take even the justice of Rhadamanthus[33] to be a conception of rectificatory justice: 'If a person should suffer what he did, right justice would be done'[34]), since often they conflict. For example, if a person in authority strikes someone, he should not be struck in return, but if someone has wounded an official, he should not only be struck in return, but receive an additional punishment. Again, voluntariness and involuntariness make a great difference.

When people associate with one another for the purpose of exchange, however, this kind of justice – reciprocity in accordance with proportion, not equality – is what binds them together, since a city is kept together by proportionate reciprocation. For people seek to return either evil for evil – otherwise they feel like slaves – or good for good – 1133a otherwise no exchange takes place, and it is exchange that holds them together. This is why they erect a temple of the Graces in a conspicuous place, so that benefits might be repaid. This is the special characteristic of grace, because one ought both to perform a return service to someone who has been gracious, and another time to make the first move by being gracious oneself.

It is a diagonal conjunction that produces proportionate reciprocation. Let A represent a builder, B a shoemaker, C a house, and D a shoe. The builder must get from the shoemaker the product of his labour, and

---

[33] Mythical son of Zeus and Europe, one of the judges of the dead in Elysium.
[34] Hesiod, fr. 174 MW.

must hand over his own in return. If, first, proportionate equality is established, and then reciprocation takes place, the result we mentioned will follow. If not, there is no equality, and the bargain falls through, since there is no reason why what one produces should not be more valuable than what the other produces, and the products must therefore be equated.

This is the case with the other crafts as well. For they would have been ruined if what the passive party received were not the same in quantity and quality as what the active party produced; it is not two doctors who associate for exchange, but rather a doctor and a farmer, and, in general, people who are different and unequal, and must be made equal. This is why everything that is exchanged must be in some way commensurable. This is where money comes in; it functions as a kind of mean, since it is a measure of everything, including, therefore, excess and deficiency. It can tell us, for example, how many shoes are equal to a house or some food. Then, as builder is to shoemaker, so must the number of shoes be to a house. For without this, there can be no exchange and no association; and it will not come about unless the products are in some sense equal. Everything, then, must be measured by some one standard, as we said before. This standard is in fact demand, which holds everything together; for if people needed nothing, or needed things to different degrees, either there would be no exchange or it would not be the same as it now is. But by social convention money has come to serve as a representative of demand. And this is why money is called *nomisma*, because it exists not by nature but by convention (*nomos*), and it is in our power to change its value and to render it worthless.

There will be reciprocity, then, when the equation has been made, so that the shoemaker's product is to the farmer's as farmer is to shoe-
1133b maker. But we must bring them into the form of a proportion not after they have exchanged goods, but when they still have their own; otherwise one extreme will have both excesses. In this situation, they are equals and capable of association, because it is possible to establish this kind of equality between them. Let A be a farmer, C some food, B a shoemaker, and D his product equated to C; if this kind of reciprocity had been impossible, the two would not have entered into an association with one another.

That demand holds things together as a single entity is obvious from the fact that whenever people – either both, or one of a pair – have no need of one another, they do not enter into exchange. This is what happens whenever someone wants something that one has not got oneself – when, for example, people offer an export licence for corn in return for wine. It is imperative, therefore, that this equation be made.

Money is, as it were, our guarantor for future exchange: if we do not need a thing now, we can have it if ever we do need it, since we must be able to get it if we pay. The same thing happens to money as to other commodities, in that its value is not always the same, but it does tend to be more stable. Everything, then, must have a value put on it, because then there will always be exchange, and if exchange, association between people.

So money makes things commensurable as a measure does, and equates them; for without exchange there would be no association between people, without equality no exchange, and without commensurability no equality. It is impossible that things differing to such a degree should become truly commensurable, but in relation to demand they can become commensurable enough. So there must be some one standard, and it must be on an agreed basis – which is why money is called *nomisma*. Money makes all things commensurable, since everything is measured by money. Let A be a house, B ten minae, C a bed. A is half of B, if the house is worth, or equal to, five minae; and C, the bed, is worth one tenth of B. It is obvious, then, how many beds are equivalent to a house, namely, five. This is clearly how exchange took place before the existence of money, since it makes no difference whether you pay five beds for a house, or the value of five beds.

We have now described the nature of what is just and unjust. The distinctions we have drawn make it clear that acting justly is a mean between committing injustice and suffering it, since the one is having more than one's share, while the other is having less.

Justice is a kind of mean – not in the same way as the other virtues, but because it is concerned with a mean, while injustice is concerned 1134a with extremes. And justice is the state in accordance with which the just person is said to be the kind of person who is disposed to do just actions in accordance with rational choice, and to distribute goods – either between himself and another or between two others – so as to assign not more of what is worth choosing to himself and less to his neighbour (and conversely with what is harmful), but what is proportionately equal; and similarly in distributing between two other people.

Injustice, on the contrary, is concerned with what is unjust, that is, a disproportionate excess or deficiency of what is beneficial or harmful; so injustice is an excess and a deficiency, because it is concerned with excess and deficiency. In one's own case, this is an excess of what is unqualifiedly beneficial, and a deficiency of what is harmful; in the case of others, though the general result is the same, the proportion may be violated in either direction. In an unjust action, to have too little is to suffer injustice, while to have too much is to commit it.

This, then, can be taken as an adequate account of the nature of justice and injustice, and similarly of what is just and unjust in general.

Chapter 6

We have stated above how reciprocity is related to justice. But we must not forget that what we are investigating is not only justice in the unequal sense, but political justice. This is found among people who associate in life to achieve self-sufficiency, people who are free and either proportionately or arithmetically equal. So between people who are not like this there is nothing politically just, but only something just by approximation. For what is just exists only among people whose relations are governed by law, and law only among those liable to injustice, since legal justice consists in judgement between what is just and what is unjust. Among those liable to injustice will also be found the committing of injustice, though injustice is not found among all those who commit injustice. Committing injustice consists in assigning to oneself too large a share of what is good without qualification, and too little of what is bad without qualification.

1134b This is why it is not a person that we allow to rule, but rather law, because a person does so in his own interests and becomes a tyrant. The magistrate, however, is a guardian of what is just, and so of what is equal as well. If he is just, he seems not to have more than his share, since he does not assign to himself a greater share of what is unqualifiedly good, unless it is in proportion to his deserts. He thus seems to labour for others, which is why people say that justice is the good of another, as we mentioned above. He ought therefore to receive some sort of reward, namely, honour and privilege; and people who find these insufficient are the ones who become tyrants.

What is just for a master and for a father are not the same as this, though they are similar. For there is no unqualified injustice in relation to what is one's own, and a man's property, as well as his child until it reaches a certain age and becomes independent, are, as it were, a part of him; and no one rationally chooses to harm himself, which is why there is no injustice in relation to oneself. So nothing politically just or unjust is possible here, because, as we saw, they depend on law, and exist only among people where law is natural, namely, those who share equally in ruling and being ruled. There is therefore more of what is just in relation to one's wife than one's children or possessions, since this is what is just in households; but this too is distinct from what is politically just.

Chapter 7

As regards what is politically just, one part is natural, the other legal. What is natural is what has the same force everywhere and does not depend on people's thinking. What is legal is what originally makes no difference whether it takes one form or another, but does matter when people have adopted it; for example, that the ransom for a prisoner be one mina, or that a goat be sacrificed and not two sheep, and all the laws that people lay down for particular occasions, such as that sacrifices be carried out for Brasidas,[35] and decisions made by special decree.

Some people think that everything just is like this, since what is natural is unchangeable and has the same force everywhere, as fire burns both here and in Persia, while they see what is just as changing. As it stands, this is false, though it is true in a sense. Among the gods, indeed, it is probably not true at all, but among us, though there is such a thing as what is natural, everything is nevertheless changeable; but still some things are so by nature, and others are not.

It is obvious, in the case of contingent things, which sort are by nature, and which are not, but are legal and conventional, assuming that both are similarly changeable. And the same distinction will hold in other cases: by nature, the right hand is superior, but it is still possible for everyone to become ambidextrous.

---

[35] d. 422 BCE. Distinguished Spartan general.

1135a   The sorts of things that are just in accordance with convention and expedience are like standard measures. For measures for wine and corn are not the same everywhere, but are larger in wholesale markets, smaller in retail. Similarly, things that are not just by nature, but are just for a particular group of people, are not the same everywhere, since political systems are not the same either, though only one is naturally the best everywhere.

Each type of what is just and legal stands as a universal in relation to particulars; for the actions done in virtue of them are many, but each of them is a single entity, since it is a universal.

There is a difference between an unjust act and what is unjust, and between a just act and what is just. For what is unjust is so by nature or by ordinance; this, once done, is an unjust act, but before that it is not yet an unjust act, though it is unjust. The same goes for a just act, though here the general type is more usually called an act of justice, and what is called a just act is what rectifies an unjust act.

Later we must examine each of these actions, to see what sort and how many are their species, and what they are concerned with.

Chapter 8

Given that just and unjust actions are as we described, a person acts unjustly or justly whenever he does these things voluntarily; when he acts involuntarily, he does not do so unjustly or justly, except incidentally, since the actions he performs are incidentally just or unjust.

Whether something is an unjust or a just act is determined by what is voluntary and what is involuntary. For when it is voluntary, it is blamed, and is thereby also an unjust act. So there will be things that are unjust, but not yet unjust acts, unless voluntariness is present as well. By voluntariness I mean, as I have said, that which lies in an agent's power and which he does knowingly, that is, not in ignorance of the person affected, the instrument used, or the end of the action – for example, whom he is striking, with what, and to what end; and each such action must be neither incidentally just nor done through compulsion (for example, if someone were to take the hand of another and use it to strike a third party, the second person would not be acting voluntarily, since the action did not lie within his control). The person struck may be the agent's father, though the agent knows only that he is a human being or one of the people present, and is unaware that he is his father. A similar distinction may be made in the case of the end, and with regard to the action as a whole. An involuntary action, then, is one performed in ignorance, or, if not in ignorance, beyond the agent's control or under compulsion; there are plenty of things in the course of nature that we do 1135b and suffer knowingly, and which have nothing voluntary or involuntary about them, such as growing old or dying.

Both unjust and just actions alike may be incidentally just. For if someone returned a deposit involuntarily and through fear, we should say that he is neither doing just actions nor acting justly, except incidentally. In the same way, we should say that someone who is forced involuntarily into not returning a deposit is only incidentally acting unjustly and doing unjust actions. Some of our voluntary actions we do with rational choice, namely, those that are the consequence of previous deliberation; others, those that are not the consequence of such deliberation, we do without rational choice.

So there are three ways in which people can injure one another when they associate. What is done in ignorance is an error, when the person affected, the nature of the act, the instrument used or the end is different from what the agent supposed. He thought, for example, that he was not hitting anyone, or not with this object, or not this person, or not for this end; but the result turned out to be different from what he had thought (he meant, for instance, only to prick the other person, not wound him), or the person hit or the object used was different.

When the injury occurs contrary to reasonable expectation, it is a misadventure. When, however, it is not contrary to reasonable expectation, but is without malice, it is an error (someone makes an error when the first principle of the cause is in him, but when it is external he is unfortunate). When the agent acts knowingly, but without previous deliberation, it is an injustice; for example, actions done from spirit and the other feelings that are necessary and natural for human beings. For people who inflict these sorts of harm and make these errors are committing injustice, and their actions are injustices, but it does not follow that the agents are unjust or wicked, because the harm is not due to wickedness.

Since one can commit injustice without yet being an unjust person, 1134a what sort of unjust acts make the person who commits them, such as a thief, an adulterer, or a pirate, unjust in each type of injustice? Or is the quality of the act irrelevant? For a person might have sex with a woman knowing who she was, but through feeling rather than the first principle of rational choice. So he commits injustice, but he is not unjust; a person is not a thief, for example, though he stole, or an adulterer, though he committed adultery, and so on. But a person who acts like this from rational choice is unjust and wicked. This is why actions done from spirit are rightly thought to be unpremeditated, because the first principle is not in the person who acts from spirit, but in the one who made him angry.

Again, the dispute is not about whether the action took place or not, but about its justice, since it is an apparent injustice that has given rise to the anger. For they are not disputing the fact, as people do in contracts, where one of the parties must be wicked unless the dispute arises from forgetfulness. Rather they agree about the fact, and dispute about which action was just (whereas a person who has deliberately harmed another is not ignorant of this), so that the one thinks he is being treated unjustly, while the other disagrees.

But if a person harms another by rational choice, he does act unjustly; and it is committing these acts of injustice, when they violate proportionality or equality, which make a person unjust. Similarly, a person is just when he acts justly by rational choice, but acts justly if he merely acts voluntarily.

Some involuntary acts are pardonable, others not. Errors that people make not only in ignorance but through ignorance are pardonable; those made in ignorance through a feeling that is neither natural nor human, and not through ignorance, are not pardonable.

Chapter 9

Assuming our definitions of suffering and committing injustice are adequate, someone might wonder, first of all, whether things are as Euripides suggests in the odd lines:

'I killed my mother; that's my story in brief.'
'Both voluntarily, or involuntarily both?'.[36]

For is it really possible to suffer injustice voluntarily, or is it always

---

[36] Euripides, *Alcmaeon* fr. 68 Nauck.

involuntary, as acting unjustly is always voluntary? And is it always one or the other, or sometimes voluntary, sometimes involuntary? The same goes for being treated justly. Acting justly is always voluntary, so it would be reasonable to expect a like opposition in either case – that suffering injustice and being treated justly are either both voluntary or both involuntary. But it would seem absurd even in the case of being treated justly for it always to be voluntary, since some people are involuntarily treated justly.

Someone might go on to ask the further question whether everyone who has been dealt an injustice is being treated unjustly, or whether the case is the same in suffering injustice as it is in doing it. For it is possible in both doing and suffering to participate in what is just incidentally; and clearly the same goes for what is unjust, since doing something unjust is not the same as acting unjustly, and suffering something unjust is not the same as being treated unjustly. The same goes for acting justly and being treated justly; it is impossible to be treated unjustly unless someone is acting unjustly, or to be treated justly unless someone is acting justly.

But if acting unjustly, without qualification, is inflicting harm voluntarily – in the sense of having knowledge of the person acted upon, the thing used in the action, and the way it was performed – and if the incontinent person voluntarily harms himself, then he would voluntarily be treated unjustly, as well as being able to treat himself unjustly (this is also one of the questions raised, whether a person can treat himself 1136b unjustly). Moreover, someone could, through incontinence, voluntarily be harmed by another who was acting voluntarily, so that it would be possible to be treated unjustly voluntarily. Or is it rather that our definition is not correct, and that to 'harming someone with knowledge of the person acted upon, the thing used in the action, and the way it was performed' we should add that the action be 'against the wish of the person acted upon'?

Someone can, then, be harmed and suffer injustice voluntarily, but no one is voluntarily treated unjustly. For no one wishes this, not even the incontinent man. Rather, he acts contrary to his wish, because no one wishes for what he does not think is good, and what the incontinent does is not what he thinks he ought to do.

The person who gives away his own property, as Homer says Glaucus gave to Diomede 'gold arms for bronze, the worth of a hundred oxen for that of nine',[37] does not suffer injustice. To give is in his power, but to suffer injustice is not; there must be someone to treat him unjustly. Clearly, then, suffering injustice is not voluntary.

Two of the topics we rationally chose to discuss still remain, namely, whether it is the person who distributes more to someone than he deserves who is committing injustice or the person who receives it, and whether a person can treat himself unjustly.

If the first suggestion is possible, and it is the distributor who acts unjustly and not the person who has more than he should, and if someone can knowingly and voluntarily assign more to someone else than to himself, this is a case of a person's treating himself unjustly. And indeed this is what moderate people seem to do, since a good person will tend to take less than his share. Or is this too simple? For perhaps he is greedy for some other good, such as honour or what is unqualifiedly noble. Again, a solution to the problem can be found in our definition of acting unjustly. He does not suffer anything contrary to his own wish, so that he is not unjustly treated in this respect at any rate; and if he does suffer anything, it is only harm.

Clearly it is the distributor who acts unjustly, and not always the person who receives more than his share. For it is not the person who possesses what is unjust who acts unjustly, but he who voluntarily does what is unjust, namely, the person in whom we find the first principle of the action – and this is in the distributor, not the recipient.

Also, since doing is spoken of in many different ways, and there is a sense in which soulless things, or a hand, or a slave at the order of his master can kill, the recipient does not act unjustly, though he does do something unjust.

Again, if the distributor gave judgement in ignorance, he does not act unjustly as far as legal justice goes, nor is his judgement unjust, except in a sense (legal justice and primary justice being different). But if he 1137a knew what he was doing when he judged unjustly, then he himself is also greedy, either for favour or for revenge. The person who has judged unjustly for these reasons, then, has more than his share, quite as though he has a share of the unjust award: when he judges on that condition about land, he took not land but money.

People think that acting unjustly is within their power, and therefore

---

[37] Homer, *Iliad* vi.236.

that justice is an easy matter, when in fact it is not. While having sex with a neighbour's wife, punching the person next to us, putting money in somebody's hands, are easy and in our power, doing these things through having a certain character is neither easy nor in our power.

In the same way, people think that knowing what is just and what is unjust does not require any wisdom, because it is not difficult to grasp what the laws say, though the acts they prescribe are not just other than in an incidental way. But knowing how acts are to be done and distributions to be effected if they are to be just is more of a job than knowing what health requires. Though, even in the case of health, knowing about honey, wine, hellebore, cautery and surgery may be easy, knowing how one should prescribe them to make people healthy, and to whom and at what time, is as demanding a task as it is to be a doctor.

Again, for this same reason, people suppose that acting unjustly is no less a characterstic of a just person than of an unjust, because the just person would be no less but even more able to do each act. For he could have sex with a woman or hit somebody; and a courageous person could throw away his shield and turn to run in either direction. But to act in a cowardly or unjust way is not to do things of this kind, except incidentally, but to do them on the basis of having a certain character. In the same way, being a doctor or curing a patient is a matter not merely of operating or not operating, of prescribing or not prescribing, but of doing them in a particular way.

What is just is found among people who have a share of things that are good without qualification, and whose share can be excessive or deficient. No share can be excessive for some – for example, I suppose, the gods – and for others – those who are incurably vicious – none of them is beneficial, but they are all harmful; there are yet others for whom they are beneficial up to a point. So what is just is a human affair.

Chapter 10

We have next to say something about equity and what is equitable – about how equity is related to justice, and what is equitable to what is just. On examination they seem to be neither without qualification the same nor generically different. Sometimes we praise what is equitable and the person with that quality, so that when we are praising someone 1137b
for other things we even transfer the term 'equitable', as an equivalent

to 'good', showing that what is more equitable is better. At other times, however, when we follow through the logical implications, it seems odd that what is equitable, if it is something beyond what is just, should be praiseworthy. For if they are different, one or other of what is just and what is equitable is not good; or if they are both good, they are the same.

These, then, are roughly the claims causing the puzzle about what is equitable; but, in a sense, they are all correct and do not conflict with one another. For what is equitable, though superior to one kind of what is just, is nevertheless just, and it is not by being a different genus that it is superior to justice. The same thing, then, is just and equitable, and while both are good, what is equitable is superior. What makes for the puzzle is that what is equitable is just, but not what is legally just – rather a correction of it. The reason is that all law is universal, and there are some things about which one cannot speak correctly in universal terms. In those areas, then, in which it is necessary to make universal statements but not possible to do so correctly, the law takes account of what happens more often, though it is not unaware that it can be in error. And it is no less correct for doing this; for the error is attributable not to the law, nor to the law-giver, but to the nature of the case, since the subject–matter of action is like this in its essence.

So when law speaks universally, and a particular case arises as an exception to the universal rule, then it is right – where the law-giver fails us and has made an error by speaking without qualification – to correct the omission. This will be by saying what the lawgiver would himself have said had he been present, and would have included within the law had he known. What is equitable, therefore, is just, and better than one kind of justice. But it is not better than unqualified justice, only better than the error that results from its lacking qualification. And this is the very nature of what is equitable – a correction of law, where it is deficient on account of its universality.

This is also the reason why not everything is regulated by law: about some things it is impossible to legislate, so that a special decree is required. For when the object is indeterminate, so also is the rule, like the leaden rule of Lesbian architecture. Just as this rule adapts to fit the shape of the stone and does not remain rigid, so the special decree adapts to fit the circumstances.

The nature of what is equitable, then, is clear, as is the fact that it is just and superior to one kind of justice. It is also evident from this who the equitable person is. He is the kind of person who chooses rationally and who does equitable things; he does not stand on his rights in a bad 1138a way, but tends to accept less than his share, though he has law on his side. This is the equitable person, and his state of character is equity, which is a sort of justice, not some distinct state.

Chapter 11

Whether a person can treat himself unjustly or not is evident from what we have said.

First, some just acts are legal requirements in accordance with virtue as a whole; for example, law does not allow a person to kill himself, and what it does not allow, it forbids. Again, when a person voluntarily harms another illegally, and he is not acting in retaliation, he acts unjustly, a voluntary agent being one who knows the person affected and the instrument used. A person who cuts his throat in a fit of anger is doing this voluntarily, contrary to correct reason, and the law does not allow this; so he is acting unjustly. But towards whom? Surely towards the city, not himself, since he suffers voluntarily, and no one voluntarily suffers injustice? This is why the city imposes a penalty, and a kind of dishonour attaches to the person who has done away with himself, on the ground that he has perpetrated an injustice against the city.

Again, in so far as the person acting unjustly is merely unjust and not altogether bad, it is impossible for him to treat himself unjustly (this is different from the other type of injustice, in that there is a sense in which the unjust person is wicked in the same way as the cowardly person, not by possessing wickedness in its entirety, so that his acting unjustly is not in accordance with wickedness in its entirety either). For this would be for the same thing to have been subtracted from and added to the same person at the same time, and that is impossible. Rather, justice and injustice must always involve more than one person.

In addition, an unjust act is voluntary and done from rational choice, and prior in the sense that a sufferer of injustice who retaliates in kind is not thought to be acting unjustly; but when a person harms himself, he suffers and does the same things at the same time.

Again, it would mean that a person could voluntarily be treated unjustly.

Besides, no one acts unjustly without committing particular acts of injustice. And no one commits adultery with his own wife, burgles his own house, or steals his own property.

In general, the question of whether a person can treat himself unjustly is to be resolved in line with the distinction we made concerning the voluntary suffering of injustice.

It is obvious too that both acting unjustly and suffering injustice are bad (because the former is to have less than the mean, the latter more, the mean here playing a role similar to that of what is healthy in medicine and that of what conduces to bodily fitness in physical training). Nevertheless, acting unjustly is the worse, because it is blameworthy and implies vice that is either complete and without qualification or nearly so (since not every voluntary act of injustice involves injustice), while suffering injustice involves neither vice nor injustice. In 1138b itself, then, suffering injustice is less bad, but nothing prevents its being the greater evil in an incidental way. What is incidental, however, is not the concern of a skill; rather, the skill says that pleurisy is more serious than a stumble, even though the latter may turn out incidentally to be the more serious, if the fall it causes incidentally leads to one's being taken prisoner or put to death by the enemy.

By transference of meaning and by resemblance there is a kind of justice not between a person and himself, but between certain parts of him. This is not full-blooded justice, however, but the sort one finds between master and slave, or in the management of a household. For in theories of this kind, the part of the soul with reason is distinguished from the part without. It does seem to people who take this point of view that there can actually be such a thing as injustice to oneself, because it is possible for each of the parts to suffer things that are contrary to their desires; so there is something just in their relations with one another, as there is in those between ruler and ruled.

This may be taken, then, as our account of justice and the other virtues of character.

Book VI

Chapter 1

Since we have already stated that one should rationally choose the mean, not the excess or the deficiency, and that the mean is as correct reason prescribes, let us now analyse this prescription.

In all the states of character we have mentioned, and in the others as well, there is a sort of target, and it is with his eye on this that the person with reason tightens or loosens his string. There is also a sort of standard for the mean states, which, as we say, lie between excess and deficiency and are in accordance with correct reason.

But to say this, though true, is not at all clear. For in all other practices of which there is a science it is true to say that one should exert oneself and relax neither too much nor too little, but to the extent of the mean that is prescribed by correct reason. But having grasped only this, someone would be none the wiser; for example, you would not know what sort of treatments to use on your body if someone were to say that you should employ those that medicine requires, and in the way that a medical practitioner employs them. With states of the soul as well, then, we must not only offer this truism, but also determine what correct reason is and what its standard is.

When we had classified the virtues of the soul, we said that some are 1139a virtues of character, others of thought. We have discussed the virtues of character; so let us now speak as follows of those that remain, having first made some remarks about the soul.

We said earlier, then, that there are two parts of the soul, one with reason and the other without. We must now make a similar division of the part with reason. Let us assume that there are two sub-parts with reason, one with which we contemplate those things whose first principles cannot be otherwise, and another those things whose first principles can be otherwise. For when the objects are different in kind, the part of the soul naturally related to each is different in kind, since they gain their understanding through a certain similarity and relationship between them and their objects. Let us call the one the scientific part, the other the calculative part, since deliberating and calculating are the same, and no one deliberates about what cannot be otherwise. So the calculative is one part, as it were, of the part of the soul with reason.

We must therefore work out what is the best state of each of these sub-parts, because this will be the virtue of each. And the virtue of a thing is related to its own proper characteristic activity.

Chapter 2

There are three things in the soul controlling action and truth: perception, intellect, and desire. Of these, perception is clearly not the first principle of any action, since animals have perception, but no share in action.

Pursuit and avoidance in the sphere of desire correspond to affirmation and denial in that of thought. So, since virtue of character is a state involving rational choice, and rational choice is deliberative desire, the reason must be true and the desire correct, if the rational choice is to be good, and desire must pursue what reason asserts.

Such thought and truth are practical. In the case of thought concerned with contemplation, however, which is neither practical nor productive, what constitute its being good or bad are truth and falsity, because truth is the characteristic activity of everything concerned with thought. But in the case of what is practical and concerned with thought, its being good consists in truth in agreement with correct desire.

The first principle of action – its moving cause, not its goal – is rational choice; and that of rational choice is desire, and goal-directed reason. This is why rational choice involves not only intellect and thought, but a state of character; for acting well and its contrary require thought and character.

Mere thought, however, moves nothing; it must be goal-directed and practical. Such thought governs productive thought as well, in that 1139b everyone who produces aims at some goal, and the product is not the goal without qualification, but only relative to something, and instrumental to something; for the goal without qualification is what is done, because acting well is the goal, and the object of desire. So rational choice is either desire-related intellect or thought-related desire, and such a first principle is a human being.

Nothing that is past is an object of rational choice; no one, for example, rationally chooses to have sacked Troy, because nobody deliberates about the past, but rather about the future and what can turn out in one way or another; and it is not possible for the past not to have happened. So Agathon was right to say:

> Of this one thing is even god deprived,
> To make what has been done not to have happened.[38]

The characteristic activity of each of the parts related to intellect, then, is truth; and so the virtues of each will be those states on the basis of which it will most of all arrive at the truth.

Chapter 3

Let us begin again, then, and discuss these states of soul. Let us assume that there are five ways in which the soul arrives at truth by affirmation or denial, namely, skill, scientific knowledge, practical wisdom, wisdom, and intellect; for supposition and belief can be mistaken.

The nature of scientific knowledge – if we must give a precise account and not be led astray by similar uses of the word – will be clear from the following. We all assume that what is scientifically known cannot be otherwise; and when what can be otherwise lies beyond our observation, we cannot tell whether it exists or not. So the object of scientific knowledge is necessary. Therefore it is eternal, because everything that is necessary, without qualification, is eternal, and what is eternal does not come into being or cease to be.

Again, every science seems to be teachable, and its object learnable. And all teaching begins from what is already known, as we say in the *Analytics* as well, because some teaching is through induction, some through deductive inference.

---

[38] Agathon, fr. 5 Snell. *c.* 450–400 BCE. Highly celebrated Athenian tragic poet.

Induction leads to the first principle, that is, the universal, while deductive inference proceeds from universals. Therefore there are first principles from which deductive inference proceeds and which are not reached by deductive inference; so they are reached by induction.

Scientific knowledge, then, is a state by which we demonstrate, and has all the other distinguishing characteristics we add in the *Analytics*. For it is when a person believes in a certain way and understands the first principles that he has scientific knowledge: if he fails to understand the first principles better than the conclusion, he will have scientific knowledge only in an incidental way.

Let this, then, be our definition of scientific knowledge.

Chapter 4

1140a Included within the class of what can be otherwise are what is produced and what is done. Production and action are different (we can rely here also on our popular accounts). So the practical state involving reason is different from the productive state involving reason. Neither, therefore, is included in the other, since action is not production, nor production action.

Since building is one of the skills, and is essentially a productive state involving reason, and since there is neither any skill that is not a productive state involving reason, nor any such state that is not a skill, skill is the same as a productive state involving true reason.

Every skill is to do with coming into being, and the exercise of the skill lies in considering how something that is capable of either being or not being, and the first principle of which is in the producer and not the product, may come into being; for skill is not concerned with things that are or come into being by necessity, or with things that are by nature (since they have their first principle within themselves).

Since production and action are different, skill must be a matter of production, not action.

There is a sense in which fortune and skill are concerned with the same things, as Agathon says: 'Skill loved fortune, and fortune skill.'[39]

Skill, then, as we have said, is a productive state involving true reason;

---

[39] Agathon, fr. 6 Snell.

and its contrary, lack of skill, is a productive state involving false reason. Both are concerned with what can be otherwise.

Chapter 5

We may grasp what practical wisdom is by considering the sort of people we describe as practically wise. It seems to be characteristic of the practically wise person to be able to deliberate nobly about what is good and beneficial for himself, not in particular respects, such as what conduces to health or strength, but about what conduces to living well as a whole.

An indication of this is the fact that we call people practically wise in some particular respect whenever they calculate well to promote some good end that lies outside the ambit of a skill; so, where living well as a whole is concerned, the person capable of deliberation will also be practically wise.

No one deliberates about what cannot be otherwise, or about things he cannot do. So, if scientific knowledge involves demonstration, but there is no demonstration of anything whose first principles can be otherwise (since every such thing might be otherwise), and if one cannot 1140b deliberate about what is necessary, then practical wisdom cannot be scientific knowledge. Nor can it be skill. It is not scientific knowledge because what is done can be otherwise; and it is not skill because action and production are generically different.

It remains therefore that it is a true and practical state involving reason, concerned with what is good and bad for a human being. For while production has an end distinct from itself, this could not be so with action, since the end here is acting well itself. This is why we think Pericles and people like him are practically wise, because they can see what is good for themselves and what is good for people in general; and we consider household managers and politicians to be like this.

This is also how temperance (*sōphrosunē*) got its name, because it preserves (*sōzein*) practical wisdom (*phronēsis*). It preserves the kind of supposition we have described; it is not every supposition that is ruined and distorted by what is pleasant or painful – not, for example, the supposition that a triangle does or does not have not two right angles – but rather those about what is done. For the first principle of what is done consists in the goal it seeks. But if a person has been ruined by pleasure or pain, it follows that this first principle will not be evident to him, nor the fact that this ought to be the goal and cause of everything he chooses and does; for vice tends to destroy the first principle.

Practical wisdom, then, must be a true state involving reason, concerned with action in relation to human goods. Moreover, while there is a virtue in skill, there is none in practical wisdom. In skill the person who misses the mark voluntarily is preferable, but with practical wisdom, as with the virtues, the reverse is true. Clearly, then, practical wisdom is a virtue and not a skill. And since there are two parts of the soul that possess reason, it will be the virtue of one of them, namely, that which forms beliefs, both belief and practical wisdom being concerned with what can be otherwise. Moreover it is not merely a state involving reason; an indication of this is the fact that such a state can be forgotten, but practical wisdom cannot.

Chapter 6

Scientific knowledge is supposition about things that are universal and necessary. And there are first principles of what is demonstrable, and of every science, since scientific knowledge involves a rational account. So the first principle of what is known cannot be an object of scientific knowledge, or skill, or practical wisdom, because what can be known by
1141a scientific knowledge is demonstrable, and skill and practical wisdom are concerned with what can be otherwise. Nor are these first principles the concern of wisdom, because it is characteristic of the wise person to employ demonstration in certain cases.

So if the states through which we arrive at the truth and by which we are never deceived about what can or what cannot be otherwise are scientific knowledge, practical wisdom, wisdom, and intellect, and if it cannot be any of the first three (that is, practical wisdom, scientific knowledge, or wisdom), it is intellect that remains as the state concerned with first principles.

Chapter 7

Wisdom in skills we attribute to their most exacting practitioners; for example, we call Pheidias a wise sculptor and Polycleitus a wise maker of statues, meaning nothing by wisdom other than virtue in a skill. But

some people we think are wise in general, not in some particular sphere
or wise in any other respect, as Homer says in the *Margites*:

> Neither a digger nor a ploughman did the gods make him,
> Nor wise in anything else.[40]

Clearly, then, wisdom will be the most precise of the sciences. So the
wise person must not only know what follows from the first principles
of a science, but also have a true understanding of those first principles.
Wisdom, therefore, will be intellect in combination with scientific
knowledge; it is scientific knowledge of the most honourable matters
which, as it were, 'retains its head'.

It would be absurd for someone to think that political science or
practical wisdom is the best science, unless human beings are the best
thing in the cosmos. Now if what is healthy or good is different for
people and for fish, but what is white or straight is always the same,
everyone would say that what is wise is the same, while what is
practically wise is different. For when something considers well its own
peculiar interests they call that a practically wise person, and entrust
such matters to him. This is why people say that certain animals are also
practically wise, namely, those that appear capable of forethought about
their own lives.

It is obvious as well that wisdom and political science could not be the
same. For if we are to say that the science that concerns our own
particular advantage is wisdom, there will be many wisdoms; for there is
not a single science concerned with the good of all creatures, but each
kind of good has a different science – just as there is not a single science
of medicine for all beings.

It makes no difference if it is claimed that a human being is superior
to all the other animals. For there are other things far more divine in   1141b
nature than human beings, such as – to take the most obvious example –
the things constituting the cosmos.

From what we have said, then, it is clear that wisdom is scientific
knowledge, combined with intellect, of what is by nature most honourable. This is why people say that Anaxagoras,[41] Thales,[42] and people
like them are wise, but not practically wise, when they are seen to be

---

[40] Homer (?), *Margites*, fr. 2 Allen.
[41] 500–428 BCE. The first philosopher known to have moved to Athens.
[42] Early sixth-century Milesian. Aristotle believed him to be the first natural philosopher.

ignorant of what is in their own interest; and that their knowledge is extraordinary, wonderful, abstruse, godlike, but useless, because it is not human goods they are looking for.

Practical wisdom, on the other hand, is concerned with human affairs, namely, with what we can deliberate about. For deliberating well, we say, is the characteristic activity of the practically wise person above all; but no one deliberates about what cannot be otherwise, or about what has no goal that consists in a good achievable in action. The person unqualifiedly good at deliberation is the one who tends to aim, in accordance with his calculation, at the best of the goods for a human being that are achievable in action.

Nor is practical wisdom concerned only with universals. An under-standing of particulars is also required, since it is practical, and action is concerned with particulars. This is why some without knowledge – especially those with experience – are more effective in action than those with it. For if someone knew that light meats are digestible and wholesome, but did not know which kinds are light, he would not produce health; rather, the person who knows that chicken is wholesome will be better at producing health. And since practical wisdom is practical, one needs both kinds of knowledge, but especially the particular kind. Here too, however, there must be some master science.

Chapter 8

Political science and practical wisdom are the same state, but their being is different.

There are two sides to practical wisdom as concerned with the city; that which co-ordinates is legislative science, while that concerned with particulars has the name 'political science', which properly belongs to both. That concerned with particulars is practical and deliberative, since a decree is to be acted on, as the last thing reached in deliberation. This is why it is only people exhibiting this kind of practical wisdom who are said to participate in politics: they are the only ones who practise politics in the way that craftsmen practise.

Practical wisdom is also thought of especially in terms of that form of it that is concerned with oneself, the individual; it has the name 'practical wisdom', which properly is common to the various kinds, namely, household management, legislative science, and political science, the latter being subdivided into deliberative and judicial science.

One species of practical wisdom will indeed be knowledge of what is in one's own interests, but there is much disagreement about it.

The person who knows his own interests and makes these his concern 1142a seems to be a practically wise person, while politicians are seen as busybodies. So Euripides says:

> How can I be a practically wise person, when I might have lived free
>   from business,
> Counted among the masses in the army,
> And have had an equal share?
> For people who are out of the ordinary and busy themselves too
>   much . . .[43]

For people do seek their own good, and think that this course of action is what is required. So from this belief has arisen the notion that people like this are practically wise. Nevertheless, one's own good will presumably not exist without the management of a household and without a political system.

Besides, how one should manage one's own affairs is not clear, and ought to be considered. What I have said is supported by the fact that, though the young become proficient in geometry and mathematics, and wise in matters like these, they do not seem to become practically wise. The reason is that practical wisdom is concerned also with particular facts, and particulars come to be known from experience; and a young person is not experienced, since experience takes a long time to produce.

Indeed, one might ask this question as well: why a boy can become accomplished in mathematics, but not in wisdom or natural science. Surely it is because mathematics is a matter of abstraction, while the first principles of the latter two come from experience? The young speak of them, but without conviction, while the essence of mathematical things is clear enough to them.

Again, error in deliberation can concern either the universal or the particular; for example, thinking that all kinds of water that are heavier than usual are bad, or that this particular water is heavier than usual.

It is obvious that practical wisdom is not scientific knowledge; for, as

---

[43] Euripides, *Philoctetes* frr. 787, 788 Nauck.

we have said, it is concerned with the last thing, since this is what is done. It is therefore opposed to intellect, since intellect is concerned with the first terms, of which there is no rational account to be given, while practical wisdom is concerned with the last thing; and this is the object of perception, not of scientific knowledge. This is not the perception concerned with objects peculiar to any particular sense, but like that with which we perceive that the last mathematical object is a triangle; for it will stop here as well. But this is more perception than practical wisdom, though it is another species of perception.

Chapter 9

Inquiry is not the same as deliberation, since deliberation is a kind of inquiry. We must also grasp the nature of good deliberation, and see whether it is some kind of science, or belief, or good guesswork, or some other sort of thing.

1142b First, it is not scientific knowledge, since people do not inquire about what they know; but good deliberation is a kind of deliberation, and a person who deliberates is engaged in inquiry and calculation.

Nor, moreover, is it good guesswork. Good guesswork does not involve reason and is done quickly, whereas people deliberate for a long time, and say that one should act quickly on the result of one's deliberation, but deliberate slowly. Again, readiness of mind is different from good deliberation, and readiness of mind is a kind of good guesswork.

Nor is good deliberation any kind of belief. But since the person who deliberates badly is in error, while he who deliberates well does things correctly, good deliberation is clearly some kind of correctness; but it is not correctness in knowledge or belief. For there is no such thing as correctness in knowledge, since there is no such thing as error in it either; and correctness of belief is truth. Besides, everything that is an object of belief is already determined.

But excellence in deliberation does involve reason. What remains, then, is that it is correctness in thought, since this is not yet assertion. For belief is not inquiry, but already a kind of assertion, while the person who deliberates, whether he does so well or badly, is inquiring into something and calculating.

But since good deliberation is a kind of correctness in deliberation, we must first inquire into the nature and sphere of deliberation. Since there are various kinds of correctness, it is clear that good deliberation does not consist in every kind. For the incontinent or the bad person will achieve by calculation what he proposes as required, so that, though he will have deliberated correctly, he will have gained a great evil. Having deliberated well, however, seems to be something good, since the sort of correctness in deliberation that comprises good deliberation is the sort that achieves something good. But it is also possible to achieve something good through false inference, that is, to achieve the right result, but not by the right steps, the middle term being false. So this kind of correctness, on the basis of which we achieve the right result, but not by the right steps, is not yet good deliberation either.

Again, one person may achieve the right result after a long period of deliberation, another after a short period. So long deliberation is not enough for good deliberation, which is rather correctness regarding what is beneficial, about the right thing, in the right way, and at the right time.

Again, it is possible to have deliberated well either in an unqualified sense or towards some particular end. Good deliberation in the unqualified sense, then, is what succeeds in relation to the end in the unqualified sense, good deliberation in the particular sense in relation to some particular end.

If, then, it is characteristic of practically wise people to have deliberated well, good deliberation will be correctness with regard to what is useful towards the end, about which practical wisdom is true supposition.

Chapter 10

Judgement, that is good judgement, in virtue of which people are said to 1143a have judgement or good judgement, is not the same as knowledge in general, or the same as belief (since then everyone would have been a person of judgement); nor is it any one of the particular sciences, such as medicine, which has health as its concern, or geometry, which has spatial dimensions. Judgement is concerned not with what is eternal and unchanging, nor with what comes into being, but with what someone might puzzle and deliberate about. For this reason it is concerned with the same things as practical wisdom.

But judgement and practical wisdom are not the same. Practical wisdom gives commands, since its end is what should or should not be done, while judgement only judges. Judgement and good judgement are the same, as are those with judgement and those with good judgement.

Judgement, then, is neither the possession nor the acquisition of practical wisdom. But just as understanding is called judging, when one employs scientific knowledge, so we also call judging what is involved in employing belief to judge what someone else says about what concerns practical wisdom (and it must judge it nobly, since judging it well is the same as judging it nobly). From this use of the word judgement in the case of understanding is derived the sense in virtue of which people are described as having good judgement, since we often say that understanding is judging.

Chapter 11

What is called discernment, in virtue of which we say that people are discerning and have discernment, is correct judgement of what is equitable. This is indicated by the fact that we say that the equitable person is especially discerning, and that it is equitable to be discerning in certain circumstances. Discernment is correctly discerning judgement of what is equitable; and correct discernment is that which judges what is true.

All these states naturally tend in the same direction. For we attribute discernment, judgement, practical wisdom, and intellect to the same people, saying that they have discernment and thereby intellect, and that they are practically wise and have judgement. For all these capacities are to do with the last things – particular things – and being a person of judgement, a person of sound discernment, or a discerning person, consists in the capacity to judge in those matters that are of concern to the practically wise person. For what is equitable is the common concern of all good people in their relations with others.

Everything that is done is one of the particular and last things; for the practically wise person must understand these, and judgement and discernment are concerned with what is done, and this is one of the last things.

Intellect is also concerned with the last things, and in both directions; 1143b there is intellection, not a rational account, of both the first terms and the last. The intellect related to demonstrations is concerned with the first and unchanging terms, while in practical questions intellect is concerned with the last term, which can be otherwise, that is, with the minor premise. For these last terms are the first principles for achieving the end, since universals are arrived at from particulars. We ought, then, to have perception of these, and this is intellection.

This is why these states seem to be natural endowments, and why no one is held to be wise by nature, though he may by nature have discernment, judgement and intellect. An indication of this is our thinking that these qualities are related to one's time of life, and the fact that intellect and discernment belong to a particular time of life, which implies that nature is the cause. So we should attend to the undemonstrated words and beliefs of experienced and older people or of practically wise people, no less than to demonstrations, because their experienced eye enables them to see correctly.

We have now stated what practical wisdom and wisdom are, what each is concerned with, and that each is a virtue of a different part of the soul.

Chapter 12

Someone might wonder what use these states are. Wisdom, since it is not concerned with any process of coming into being, will not consider any of the things that make a human being happy, and though practical wisdom does do this, what do we need it for? Practical wisdom is concerned with acts that are just, noble, and good for a human being, but these are characteristic of the good person, and we are no more able to do them through knowing about them, since the virtues are states of character. In the same way, we are no more able to do what is healthy and invigorating – in the sense not of what produces a healthy state but of what results from it – with knowledge alone; for we are no more able to act merely through having scientific knowledge of medicine or of gymnastics.

If we are to say, however, that practical wisdom is useful not for this purpose, but for becoming good, then it will be of no use to those who are good already. Again, it will not actually be useful to people who are not good, since it will make no difference whether they possess it themselves or take the advice of others who possess it; it would be enough for us to do what we do in the case of health – we wish to be healthy, yet we do not learn medicine.

In addition, given that a productive science does govern each product and issue commands about it, it will seem odd if practical wisdom, which is inferior to wisdom, is to be put in control of it.

These, then, are the things we must discuss, since up to now we have only raised the puzzles about them.

1144a First, then, let us say that these states must be worthy of choice in themselves, even if neither produces anything whatsoever, since each is a virtue of one of the two parts of the soul.

Secondly, they do in fact produce something. Wisdom produces happiness, not as medicine produces health, but as health does. For by being a part of virtue as a whole, it makes a person happy through its being possessed and being exercised.

Again, our characteristic activity is achieved in accordance with practical wisdom and virtue of character; for virtue makes the aim right, and practical wisdom the things towards it. There is no such virtue of the fourth, nutritive part of the soul, because there is nothing it has the power to do or not to do.

As regards the claim that practical wisdom does not increase our capacity for just and noble acts, we should begin a little further back, taking the following as our first principle. We say that some people who do just actions are not yet just; for example, those who do what is laid down by the laws either involuntarily or through ignorance or for some other reason, and not for the sake of the actions themselves (though they do indeed do what they should and what a good person is required to do). Similarly, it seems that there is a way in which a person can do each action so as to be good, namely, as the result of rational choice and for the sake of the actions themselves.

Virtue makes the rational choice right, but the actions of the natural stages in the achievement of that choice are the concern not of virtue but of another capacity – and we must understand these more clearly before proceeding with our discussion.

There is a capacity that people call cleverness. This is such as to be able to do the actions that tend towards the aim we have set before ourselves, and to achieve it. If the aim is noble, then the cleverness is praiseworthy; if it is bad, then it is villainy. This is why both practically wise and villainous people are called clever.

Practical wisdom is not the same as this capacity, though it does involve it. And, as we have said and as is clear, virtue is involved in this eye of the soul's reaching its developed state. For practical syllogisms have a first principle: 'Since such-and-such is the end or chief good', whatever it is (let it be anything you like for the sake of argument). And this is evident to the good person alone, since wickedness distorts our vision and thoroughly deceives us about the first principles of actions.

Manifestly, then, one cannot be practically wise without being good.   1144b

Chapter 13

We must therefore also consider virtue again, because it is related in almost the same way: as practical wisdom is to cleverness – they are not the same, but similar – so natural virtue is to real virtue.

Each of us seems to possess the character he has in some sense by nature, since right from birth we are just, prone to temperance, courageous, and the rest. Nevertheless we expect to find that what is really good is something different, and that we shall possess these qualities in another way. For both children and animals have the natural states, but without intellect they are obviously harmful. This, at least, does seem an observed fact, that just as a strongly built person, if he is deprived of sight, is apt to stumble heavily when he moves around, because he cannot see, so too with virtue. But if the agent acquires intellect, then his action is quite different; his state, while similar to what it was, will then be real virtue.

So, as there are two states, cleverness and practical wisdom, in the part of the soul related to belief, so there are two in the part related to character – natural virtue and real virtue; and of these real virtue does not develop without practical wisdom.

This is why some people say that all the virtues are forms of practical wisdom, and why Socrates was partly right and partly wrong in his inquiry. He was wrong to think that all the virtues are forms of practical wisdom, but correct in saying that they involve practical wisdom. There is evidence for this in the fact that whenever people now define virtue, they all say what state it is and what its objects are, and then add that it is a state in accordance with right reason. Right reason is that which is in accordance with practical wisdom; everyone, then, seems in some way to divine that the state like this, in accordance with practical wisdom, is virtue.

But we need to go a little further. Virtue is not merely the state in accordance with right reason, but that which involves it. And practical wisdom is right reason about such matters. Socrates, then, thought that the virtues were forms of reason (since he believed them all to be forms of knowledge), while we think that they involve reason.

It is clear from what we have said, then, that we cannot be really good without practical wisdom, or practically wise without virtue of character.

(Moreover, on these lines one might also meet the dialectical argument that could be used to suggest that the virtues exist in isolation from one another. The same person, it might be argued, is not best suited by nature for all the virtues, so that he will already have acquired one before he has acquired another. This is possible in respect of the 1145a natural virtues, but not in respect of those on the basis of which a person is said to be really good; for he will possess all of them as soon as he acquires the one, practical wisdom.)

Clearly, even if practical wisdom were not of value in action, it would be needed, since it is the virtue of this part of the soul; and clearly too rational choice will not be correct in the absence of either practical wisdom or virtue. For the one sets the end, while the other makes us do what is towards the end.

Moreover, practical wisdom is not in control of wisdom or the superior part of the soul, just as medicine is not in control of health. For it does not make use of health, but provides for its coming into being; it therefore issues prescriptions for the sake of health, but not to it. Besides, saying this would be like saying that political science governs the gods, since it issues prescriptions about everything in the city.

Book VII

Chapter 1

Next we must make a fresh start, stating that there are three types of character to be avoided, namely, vice, incontinence, and brutishness. The contraries of two of these are clear; we call one virtue and the other self-control. What is contrary to brutishness might most appropriately be described as superhuman virtue, a virtue heroic and godlike; thus Homer depicts Priam saying of Hector that he was good in the extreme: 'For he seemed not to be a child of a mortal man but of a god.'[44]

So if, as they say, people become gods through superlative virtue, this must clearly be the sort of state opposed to brutishness. Just as no brute possesses vice or virtue, neither does a god; but the god's state is more honourable than virtue, while that of the brute is in a different class from vice.

And, since it is unusual for a man to be godlike (as the Spartans are wont in their dialect to call someone they particularly admire, saying 'He is a godlike fellow'), so the brutish person is also uncommon among human beings. He is found chiefly among non-Greeks, though some cases arise through disease and disability. We also use the term derogatorily to refer to those who surpass other human beings in their vice.

But we shall have to make some mention of this kind of disposition later; we have spoken of vice above. Now we must discuss incontinence, softness and effeminacy, as well as self-control and endurance; for we 1145b

---

[44] Homer, *Iliad* xxiv.258f.

must not suppose either of the two to be concerned with the same states as virtue and vice, nor to belong to a different genus.

As in our other discussions, we must first set out the way things appear to people, and then, having gone through the puzzles, proceed to prove the received opinions about these ways of being affected – at best, all of them, or, failing that, most, and the most authoritative. For if the problems are resolved, and received opinions remain, we shall have offered sufficient proof.

Both self-control and endurance seem to be good and praiseworthy things, while incontinence and softness seem to be bad and blame-worthy. And the self-controlled person seems to be the same as someone who tends to stand by his calculation, the incontinent the same as someone who tends to depart from it.

The incontinent person knows what he does is bad, but does it because of what affects him, while the self-controlled person, knowing that his appetites are bad, because of reason does not follow them.

The temperate person is thought to be self-controlled and prone to endurance. Some believe that anyone with these qualities is temperate, while others do not. Some call the intemperate person incontinent and the incontinent person intemperate indiscriminately, while others claim they are different.

Sometimes it is said that the practically wise person cannot be incontinent, sometimes that certain people who are practically wise and clever are incontinent.

Again, people are described as incontinent with respect to spirit, honour, and gain.

These, then, are the claims people make.

Chapter 2

Someone might raise the puzzle of what kind of correct supposition a person has when he acts incontinently.

Some people deny that he can have knowledge, because it would be strange, as Socrates thought, for knowledge to be in a person, but mastered by something else and dragged around like a slave. Socrates was wholeheartedly opposed to this view, since he thought there was no such thing as incontinence: no one who acts against what is best does so on the supposition that he is doing so; rather it occurs through ignorance.

This view is plainly at variance with the way things appear to people. We have to look into what affects him: if he acts through ignorance, what manner of ignorance? For it is obvious that before he is affected, at any rate, the person who acts incontinently does not think he should.

But there are people who accept some of Socrates' arguments, but reject others. They agree that nothing is superior to knowledge, but deny that no one acts contrary to his belief about what is the better course; and for this reason they claim that the incontinent has, not knowledge, but belief when he succumbs to pleasure.

But if it is belief and not knowledge – if it is not a strong supposition 1146a that offers resistance, but a weak one like that found in those who are doubtful – we shall pardon a person's failure to stand by his beliefs in the face of strong appetites; but we do not forgive wickedness, or any of the other blameworthy states.

Is it, then, practical wisdom that is in opposition, since it is the strongest? But this is absurd, because the same person will be at the same time practically wise and incontinent, and no one would say that it was a characteristic of the practically wise person to do the worst actions voluntarily. Besides, it has been shown above that the practically wise person is the sort to act, since he is concerned with the last things to be done, and to be in possession of the other virtues as well.

Again, if the self-controlled person must have strong and bad appetites, the temperate person will not be self-controlled, nor the self-controlled person temperate. For a temperate person is not the sort to have excessive or bad appetites, while a self-controlled person must have both. For if his appetites are sound, the state that prevents his following them must be bad, so that not all self-control would be good. And if the appetites are weak and not bad, there is nothing especially wonderful in resisting them, while if they are bad and weak, it is no great achievement either.

Again, if self-control makes a person disposed to stand by all of his beliefs, it is a bad thing if, for example, it makes him stand by even a false belief. And if incontinence makes a person likely to depart from anything that he believes, then there will be a good form of incontinence. For example, Neoptolemus in Sophocles' *Philoctetes* is to be praised for not abiding by what Odysseus persuaded him to do, because it pains him to lie.[45]

Again, there is the puzzle in the argument used by the sophists. Because they wish to refute an opponent by producing paradoxical conclusions from his views, so as to appear clever when they succeed, the deduction that follows becomes a puzzle. One's thought is quite tied up, since it is unhappy with the conclusion and so does not want to remain where it is, but is unable to progress because it cannot resolve the argument. It follows from one of their arguments that foolishness combined with incontinence is a virtue. For, because of incontinence, the person acts in the way contrary to that in which he supposes he should act; and because he supposes that good things are bad and that he should not do them, he will do good actions and not bad ones.

Again, a person who does or pursues what is pleasant through conviction and from rational choice might be thought superior to one who does the same as the result not of calculation, but of incontinence. For he is easier to cure, because he could be persuaded otherwise; but the incontinent person exemplifies the proverb, 'When water chokes 1146b you, what do you need to wash it down?' For if he had been persuaded to do what he is doing, he would have stopped when he was persuaded to act otherwise; but in fact he now acts in one way though already persuaded that he should act in another.

Again, if incontinence and self-control are concerned with everything, who is the unqualifiedly incontinent person? No one has every form of incontinence, and yet we do say that some people are unqualifiedly so.

Such, then, are the sorts of puzzle that occur. Some of these claims must be rejected, and others retained, since the resolution of the puzzle is discovery of the truth.

Chapter 3

First, then, we should consider whether they do act with knowledge or not, and with knowledge in what sense. Secondly, what sort of things should we set down as the concern of the incontinent and of the self-controlled person – every pleasure and pain, or some limited range? And are the self-controlled person and the person prone to endurance

---

[45] Sophocles, *Philoctetes* 906.

the same or different? Similarly we must consider the other issues related to this inquiry.

We begin our investigation with the question whether the self-controlled person and the incontinent person differ from other people in what they are concerned with, or in the manner of their concern – that is, whether the incontinent person is incontinent merely because he is concerned with these particular things, or rather because he is concerned with them in a certain way, or both.

The unqualifiedly incontinent person is concerned not with everything, but with the same things as the intemperate person. Nor is he incontinent by being inclined towards them without qualification (this would be the same as intemperance), but by being inclined towards them in the following way. The intemperate is led on by rational choice, believing he ought always to pursue the present pleasure, while the incontinent thinks the opposite, but pursues it nevertheless.

The view that people are incontinent in the face of true belief but not knowledge is irrelevant to our argument. Some people hold beliefs without doubting them at all, thinking that they have precise knowledge. So if it is because of the weakness of their conviction that those who believe are more likely to act against their supposition than those who know, knowledge will be no different from belief. For some people are no less convinced of what they believe than are others of what they know. Heraclitus makes that clear.

But since we speak of knowing in two senses (the person who has knowledge but is not using it, and the person who is using it, are both said to know), it will make a difference whether someone doing what he should not has knowledge but is not attending to it, or is attending to it. The latter seems extraordinary, but not if he is not attending to it.

Again, since there are two kinds of premise, it is quite possible for 1147a someone to have both of them and to act contrary to what he knows, by using his knowledge of the universal but not that of the particular – because things to be done are particulars.

There are also different types of universal. One refers to the agent himself, the other to the object; for example, that dry foods are good for all humans, and that the agent himself is a human, or that this sort of food is dry; but he either does not have the knowledge whether this particular food is of this sort, or is not exercising it. Between these two ways of knowing, then, there will be a huge difference, so that to know in one way seems not at all strange, while in the other way it would be quite remarkable.

Again, human beings can have knowledge in another way besides those that have been mentioned. In the case of having knowledge without using it we see a different kind of having, so that one can in a sense both have and not have it – for example, if one is asleep, mad or drunk. Now this is the condition of people under the influence of the ways they are affected; for spirited feelings, sexual appetites, and some other such things clearly alter our bodily condition as well, and in some people even produce attacks of madness.

It is obvious, then, that we should say that incontinent people have knowledge in a similar way to these people. The fact that they use words that have their origin in knowledge proves nothing. For people under the influence of these feelings even recite proofs and verses of Empedocles,[46] and those who have just begun to learn can string words together, but do not yet know; it must grow into them, and this takes time. So we must suppose that incontinent people speak just like actors.

Again, one could look at the cause as follows, in relation to facts of nature. One belief is universal, while the other is concerned with particulars, a sphere controlled by perception. When a single belief emerges from the combination of these two, the soul must in one kind of case affirm the conclusion, while in matters of production it must immediately act. If, for example, everything sweet must be tasted, and this is sweet, in that it is one example of particular sweet things, a person who is capable and not prevented must act on this immediately.

But when the one universal belief is present in the person deterring him from tasting, along with the other that everything sweet is pleasant, as well as the belief that this is sweet – and it is the latter that is activated – and when appetite happens to be present within him, one belief bids him avoid this, but appetite leads him on, since it can move each of our bodily parts.

1147b So it happens that reason and belief in a way make him act incontinently; and the belief is not in itself contrary to correct reason, but only incidentally so, since it is appetite, not belief, that is contrary. So this is also why animals are not incontinent, because they have no universal supposition, but only mental imagery and memory of particulars.

---

[46] *c.* 492–432 BCE. Sicilian philosopher.

The explanation of how the ignorance is dispelled and the incontinent recovers his knowledge is the same as in the case of the person who is drunk or asleep, and is not peculiar to this way of being affected. We must refer here to the natural scientists.

Since the last premise is both a belief about what is perceived, and controls actions, it must be this that he does not have when he is being affected, or this that he has in such a way that the having of it amounts not to knowing it, as we saw, but saying the words as the drunk speaks the words of Empedocles.

And because the last term does not seem to be universal, or related to knowledge in the same way as the universal term, the result Socrates was seeking seems to follow. The knowledge present when someone comes to be affected by incontinence, and that is 'dragged about' because he is affected, is not what is thought to be real knowledge, but only perceptual knowledge.

So much, then, for knowing and not knowing, and for how we can know and yet act incontinently.

Chapter 4

Next we must discuss whether anyone is incontinent without qualification, or whether all incontinent people are such in a particular respect; and if anyone is unqualifiedly incontinent, we must say what sorts of things he is concerned with.

First, it is obvious that it is pleasures and pains that concern both self-controlled people and those prone to endurance, as well as the incontinent and the soft. Some sources of pleasure are necessary, while others are worth choosing in themselves, but can be taken to excess. The necessary ones are bodily – I mean those concerned with things like nourishment and our sexual needs, that is, the bodily sources of pleasure we took as the sphere of intemperance and temperance; the others are not necessary but worth choosing in themselves, such as victory, honour, wealth, and other such good and pleasant things.

Now if people indulge excessively in these, beyond the correct reason within them, we do not describe them as incontinent without qualification, but specify that they are incontinent in respect of money, gain, honour or spirit. We refrain from calling them incontinent without qualification, on the ground that they are different and are called incontinent by resemblance (like the victor at the Olympic Games called 1148a *Anthrōpos* ('Human Being') – in his case, the general definition of human being differed little from that peculiar to him, but it was different none the less). This is indicated by the fact that incontinence is blamed not only as an error but as a sort of vice, whether it is incontinence without qualification or in some particular respect, while none of the states we mentioned is so blamed.

Of the pleasures concerned with those bodily indulgences we say are the concern of the temperate person and the intemperate, he who pursues them to excess and avoids excessive pains (hunger, thirst, heat, cold, and all those to do with touch and taste), not from rational choice but in opposition to it and his thinking, is called incontinent; no qualification 'in respect of something', such as anger, is added, but he is called simply incontinent without qualification. There is evidence for this in the fact that people are called soft in respect of these pleasures and pains, but not in respect of any of those that are not necessary.

For this reason, also, we class together the incontinent and the intemperate person, as well as the self-controlled and the temperate, but not those who are incontinent in some particular respect, because incontinence and intemperance are concerned with what amount to the same pleasures and pains. But though they are concerned with the same things, they are not concerned with them in the same way; one type acts from rational choice, while the other does not.

This is why, if a person has no appetite or only mild appetite for excesses, but still pursues them and avoids moderate pains, we should describe him as more intemperate than the person who does so on account of his strong appetite. For what would the one with the mild appetite do, if he were also to develop a mighty appetite, and serious pain at the lack of necessities?

Some pleasant things are naturally worth choosing, others the contrary, and yet others in between, as we distinguished them above; thus certain things noble and good in kind, such as money, gain, victory, and honour, are objects of appetite and sources of pleasure. In relation to all these or the kind in between, people are blamed not for being affected by them, feeling an appetite for them, and liking them, but only for doing so in a particular way, namely, to excess. (Some people succumb to or pursue one of these naturally noble and good things in opposition to reason. Take, for example, those who care too much for honour or children or parents; for though these are good, and people are praised for caring for them, nevertheless even in these cases one can go to excess. It would be excessive if one were to be like Niobe and fight even with the gods,[47] or care for one's father as did Satyr, nicknamed Fatherlover,[48] who seemed an utter fool about it.)   1148b

There is no wickedness, then, involved in these pleasures, for the reason stated above, that each of them is naturally worthy of choice in itself; but excessive indulgence in them is bad and to be avoided. Similarly there is no incontinence here either, since incontinence is not only to be avoided but also blameworthy. But because of a resemblance in the way one is affected, people use the name incontinence, qualifying it in each case; in the same way, they might describe someone as a bad doctor or a bad actor, though, because each of these states is not a vice but merely resembles one, they would not describe him as bad without qualification.

In the same way, it is clear that we should take as incontinence or self-control only the states concerned with the same things as temperance and intemperance. We use the words in relation to spirit only from a resemblance, which is why we add the qualification and say 'incontinent in respect of spirit', just as we say 'in respect of honour', or 'in respect of gain'.

Chapter 5

Some things are naturally pleasant, and of these some are unqualifiedly pleasant, others in relation to classes of animals and human beings. Other things are not naturally pleasant, but some of them become so because of a disability, one's habits, or a wicked nature; and we can see similar states concerned with each of these things. By brutish states I mean, for example, the female human who people say rips open pregnant women and devours their babies; or the pleasures of some of the savages that live around the Black Sea, who are alleged to eat raw flesh, or human flesh, or to lend their children to one another to feast upon; or the story of Phalaris.[49]

---

[47] Niobe had a large family, and boasted that she was superior to Leto, who had only two. Leto charged her children to avenge the insult by killing those of Niobe.

[48] Satyrus was said to have committed suicide on hearing of the death of his father.

[49] The first major Sicilian tyrant (*c.* 570–549 BCE).

These states are brutish, but others develop through disease, and in some cases madness, as in the case of the person who sacrificed and ate his mother, or the one who ate the liver of his fellow slave. There are others that arise from diseased states or habit, such as pulling out one's hair, nibbling one's nails, or even charcoal or earth, and sodomy too. These occur naturally in some people, and in others from habit, as in the case of those who have been sexually abused since childhood.

If nature is the cause, no one would call these people incontinent, any more than one would call women incontinent on the ground that they play a passive rather than an active role in sexual intercourse. The same goes for those who are in a diseased state through habit. Possessing each 1149a of these states, then, is beyond the bounds of vice, just as brutishness is; and if the person who has them is overcoming them or succumbing to them, this is not unqualified incontinence, but incontinence by resemblance, just as someone in this state in respect of spirited feelings should be described as incontinent in relation to his feelings, not just as incontinent.

Every excessive state, whether it is foolishness, cowardice, intemperance, or ill-temper, is either brutish or diseased. The person who is naturally the sort to be afraid of everything, even the squeak of a mouse, is a coward with a brutish kind of cowardice, while disease made the person afraid of the weasel.

Of foolish people, those who are naturally lacking in reason and live by perception alone are, like some of the far distant non-Greek races, brutish; those foolish through bouts of disease, such as epilepsy, or fits of madness, are diseased.

It is sometimes possible to have some of these states and not to be overcome by them; I mean, for example, if Phalaris had an appetite to eat a baby or for a deviant sexual pleasure, and restrained himself. But it is also possible not merely to have them, but to be overcome by them as well.

One sort of wickedness is human, and this is called wickedness without qualification, while other types are described not without qualification but with the addition of 'brutish' or 'diseased'. In the same way, it is clear that one sort of incontinence is brutish, another diseased, but only that related to human intemperance is incontinence without qualification.

It is clear, then, that incontinence and self-control are concerned only with the same things as intemperance and temperance, and that what is concerned with other things is another kind of incontinence, so called by a transference of meaning and not without qualification.

Chapter 6

Let us now consider the fact that incontinence in respect of spirit is less shameful than that in respect of appetites. For spirit seems to listen to reason to some extent, but to hear it incorrectly; it is like hasty servants who rush off before they have heard everything that is being asked of them and then fail to do it, and dogs that bark at a mere noise, before looking to see whether it is a friend. In the same way, spirit, because of its heated and hasty nature, does hear, but does not hear the command, and so rushes into taking revenge. For reason or mental imagery has shown that we have been wantonly insulted or slighted, and spirit, as though it had deduced that one should treat such a person as an enemy, loses its temper. Appetite, however, needs only reason or perception to say that something is pleasant before it rushes off to enjoy it. So spirit 1149b obeys reason in a sense, but appetite does not, and is therefore more shameful. For if someone is incontinent in respect of spirit, he is in a sense overcome by reason, while the other kind of person is overcome by appetite, and not reason.

Again, we are more inclined to pardon someone who follows natural desires, since we are more inclined to pardon someone who pursues appetites common to all, in so far as they are common. Spirit and bad temper are more natural than excessive and unnecessary appetites. It is like the case of the son defending himself for striking his father: 'He did it to his father', he said, 'and his father did it to his'; and, pointing to his own son, he said, 'And he will do it to me when he grows up; it runs in the family.' Or it is like the father who, when he was being dragged out of the house by his son, used to order him to stop when they reached the front door, since that was as far as he had dragged his own father.

Again, people who are more treacherous are more unjust. But a person of spirit is not treacherous, nor is spirit; rather it is open. But appetite is like what they say of Aphrodite: 'a weaver of guile, sprung from Cyprus';[50] and what Homer says of her embroidered girdle:

---

[50] Unknown.

Allurement, which steals the mind of the wise, shrewd though it is.[51]

So if this kind of incontinence is more unjust and shameful than that in respect of spirit, it is incontinence without qualification, and in a sense a vice.

Again, no one feels pain at acting with wanton violence, indeed people do it with pleasure, while everyone feels pain at acting from anger. So if the more unjust acts are the ones it is more just to be angry at, incontinence due to appetite is more unjust, since there is no wanton violence in spirit.

It is clear, then, how incontinence in respect of appetite is more shameful than that concerned with spirit, and that self-control and incontinence are concerned with bodily appetites and pleasures. But we must grasp the differences between the latter; as we said at the beginning, some are human and natural in their kind and extent, some brutish, and some due to disabilities and diseases. Temperance and intemperance are concerned only with the first of these. This is why we do not call animals temperate or intemperate other than through a transference of meaning, and if some one kind of animal as a whole stands apart from another in its wanton violence, its destructiveness, or its voracious appetite. They have no capacity for rational choice or calculation, but are degenerations from nature, like the insane among human beings.

1150a

Brutishness is not as bad as vice, though it is more to be feared, because it consists not in the corruption of the superior element, as in human beings, but in its absence. So it is like comparing something without a soul to something with one, to see which is worse; for the badness of what does not have a first principle is always less destructive, and intellect is a first principle. It is, then, very like comparing injustice with an unjust human being: each is worse in a way, since a bad human being can do ten thousand times as much evil as a brute.

Chapter 7

Earlier we defined intemperance and temperance as concerned with the pleasures and pains arising from touch and taste, and the appetites for them and aversions to them. One can be so disposed as to succumb even

[51] Homer, *Iliad* xiv.214, 217.

to those that most people rise superior to, or to master even those that most people succumb to. Of these varieties, the people concerned with pleasures are the incontinent and the self-controlled, while those concerned with pains are the soft and the person prone to endurance. The state of most people lies in between, though they may incline more in the direction of the worse states.

Some pleasures are necessary, while others are not. The necessary ones are necessary only up to a point, while their excesses and deficiencies are not; and this is equally true of appetites and pains. So the person who pursues excessive pleasures from rational choice, for their own sake and not for any further consequence, is intemperate; such a person is bound to be without regrets, and thus incurable, since anyone without regrets is incurable. The deficient person is the contrary, while the intermediate person is temperate. The same goes for the person who avoids bodily pains not because he is overcome by them, but from rational choice.

Of those who do not do such acts from rational choice, one kind of person is led on for the sake of the pleasure, the other for the sake of avoiding the pain that comes from appetite; so these two differ from one another.

Now everyone would think worse of someone who does something disgraceful when appetite is absent or weak than someone who does such a thing when his appetite is intense; and worse of someone who strikes another when he is not angry than someone who strikes when he is. For what would he have done if he had been affected? This is why the intemperate person is worse than the incontinent.

Of the states mentioned, then, one is more a species of softness, while the other person is intemperate. The self-controlled person is opposed to the incontinent, and the person prone to endurance to the soft. For enduring consists in resisting, while self-control consists in overcoming; and resisting and overcoming are different, just as not being beaten is different from winning. This is why self-control is also more worthy of 1150b choice than endurance.

The person deficient in resisting what most people resist, and are able to resist, is soft and effeminate, since effeminacy is a kind of softness. Such a person trails his cloak to avoid the pain and burden of lifting it, and pretends to be suffering, though he has no thought that he really is wretched – he merely resembles someone wretched.

Much the same goes for self-control and incontinence. For there is nothing surprising in a person's succumbing to violent and excessive pleasures or pains; indeed, we shall pardon him if he resists, as do Theodectes' Philoctetes when bitten by the viper,[52] or Carcinus' Cercyon in the *Alope*,[53] and people who try to restrain their laughter and then let it out in a guffaw, as happened to Xenophantus.[54] But it is surprising if a person succumbs to pleasures that the majority can resist, and is unable to hold out against them, when this is not due to his hereditary nature or to disease, as is, for example, the hereditary softness one finds in Scythian kings, and that which distinguishes the female sex from the male.

The lover of amusement also seems to be intemperate, but really he is soft. For amusement is relaxation, since it consists in rest, and the lover of amusement is one of those who go to excess in this.

One kind of incontinence is impetuosity, the other is weakness. Weak people deliberate, but because of the way they are affected fail to stand by their decision, while impetuous people are led on by the way they are affected because they have not deliberated. For some people resemble those who are not tickled because they have tickled the other person beforehand; by noticing and seeing what is coming, and rousing themselves and their capacity for calculation, they do not succumb to what affects them, whether the thing is pleasant or painful.

Excitable and passionate people are especially prone to impetuous incontinence. The excitable are too hasty, and the passionate too intense, to wait for reason, since they are disposed to follow their own mental impressions.

Chapter 8

The intemperate person, as we said, is not the sort to have regrets, since he stands by his rational choice. But every incontinent person is the sort to have regrets. This is why things are not as we suggested in going through the puzzles, but the intemperate person is incurable, while the incontinent is curable. Wickedness is a chronically bad condition, and

[52] Theodectes, fr. 5b Snell. Lycian poet, orator, and rhetorician, who probably lived mainly in Athens, where he influenced Aristotle.
[53] Carcinus, fr. 1b Snell. Carcinus the younger was a fourth-century tragic poet, often cited by Aristotle. Cercyon was distressed by his daughter's seduction.
[54] Musician in Alexander's court.

thus like a disease such as dropsy or consumption, while incontinence is not chronic, and thus like epilepsy. And in general incontinence and vice are of different kinds, since an agent is not aware of his vice, whereas he is of his incontinence.

Among incontinent people, those who are carried away are superior to 1151a those who have reason but do not stand by it. For those who do not stand by reason succumb to a weaker way of being affected, and do not, like the other type, act without previous deliberation. The incontinent person is like those who quickly get drunk on a small amount of wine, that is, on less than most people.

Clearly, then, incontinence is not a vice (other than in a qualified sense, presumably), because incontinence is contrary to rational choice, while vice is in accordance with it. There is, however, a similarity in the actions that issue from them, as in the lines of Demodocus on the Milesians:

> Milesians are not stupid,
> But they do what stupid people do.[55]

So also incontinent people are not unjust, but they will do unjust things.

The incontinent person is the sort to pursue bodily pleasures that are excessive and contrary to correct reason, but not out of conviction; the intemperate person, however, does pursue them out of conviction, because he is just the sort to pursue them. So the incontinent can easily be persuaded to change his ways, while the intemperate cannot. For virtue preserves the first principle, while wickedness ruins it, and in actions the end for which we act is the first principle, as assumptions are in mathematics. In mathematics, it is not reason that teaches first principles, nor is it in actions; rather it is virtue, either natural or habituated, that enables us to think correctly about the first principle.

A person like this, then, is temperate, and his contrary intemperate. But there is a type who tends to be carried away contrary to correct reason because of the ways he is affected. They overcome him to the extent that he does not act in accordance with correct reason, but not so that he becomes the sort to be convinced that he ought to pursue such pleasures unrestrainedly. This is the incontinent person, superior to the intemperate person, and not unqualifiedly bad; for in him the best thing, the first principle, is preserved.

---

[55] Demodocus, fr. 1 Diehl. Early writer of satirical epigrams.

Contrary to this is another kind of person, the sort to stand by his convictions and not be carried away, at least not because of the ways he is affected. It is evident from these considerations that the state of the self-controlled person is good, and that of the incontinent is bad.

Chapter 9

We shall now consider a puzzle we raised before. Is a person self-controlled if he stands by just any reason and any rational choice, or must it be by the right rational choice? And is a person incontinent if he fails to stand by just any rational choice or any reason, or must it be reason that is not false, and correct rational choice? Or does the one stand, and the other fail to stand, incidentally by any rational choice, but in itself by true reason and the right rational choice? For if anyone 1151b chooses or pursues one thing for the sake of another, he pursues and chooses the second thing in itself, and the first incidentally. By 'in itself' I mean 'without qualification'; so in a sense it is just any belief that the one stands by and the other abandons, but without qualification it is the true one.

There are some who tend to stand by their belief and whom we call obstinate, in that they are hard to persuade of anything and not easily persuaded to change their minds. To some extent they are similar to the self-controlled person, as the wasteful is to the generous, and the rash to the confident; but in many ways they are different. It is by the ways he is affected and by appetite that the self-controlled person refuses to be swayed, since he is easy to persuade when the occasion arises. But obstinate people refuse to be swayed by reason, since they acquire appetites, and many of them are led on by pleasures. The obstinate include the self-opinionated, the ignorant, and the boorish. The self-opinionated owe their character to pleasure and pain: they enjoy the sense of victory if they are not persuaded to change their minds, and feel pain if their own views are annulled like decrees. So they are more like the incontinent person than like the self-controlled.

There are some people, however, who fail to stand by their beliefs for reasons other than incontinence; for example, Neoptolemus in Sophocles' *Philoctetes*. It was because of pleasure that he failed to remain resolute, but it was a noble pleasure, since telling the truth was noble to him, but he had been persuaded by Odysseus to tell a lie. Not everyone who does something for the sake of pleasure is intemperate, bad or incontinent, but only someone who does it for the sake of a shameful pleasure.

Since there is also a sort of person who finds less enjoyment in bodily pleasures than he should and fails to stand by reason, the self-controlled person is intermediate between him and the incontinent. For the incontinent fails to stand by reason through enjoying things too much, this person through enjoying things too little; but the self-controlled person does stand by it and does not change his course in either direction.

If self-control is a good thing, both the contrary states must be bad, as they do in fact appear to be. But because the other extreme is manifested rarely and only in a few people, self-control seems contrary only to incontinence, just as temperance seems contrary only to intemperance.

Many terms being based on a resemblance, it is from a resemblance that we have come to speak of the self-control of the temperate person. For both the self-controlled and the temperate person are the sort to do 1152a nothing contrary to reason for the sake of bodily pleasures. But the self-controlled person has bad appetites, while the temperate person does not; and the temperate person is the sort to feel no pleasure contrary to reason, while the self-controlled person is the sort to feel such pleasure but not to be led on by it.

The incontinent and the intemperate person are like one another as well. Though they are different, they both pursue bodily pleasures; but the intemperate person thinks that it is right to do so, while the incontinent does not.

Chapter 10

The same person cannot be practically wise and incontinent at the same time. We have shown that a practically wise person is at the same time good in character. Again, a person is practically wise not only by knowing, but also by being disposed to act; and the incontinent person is not disposed to act.

(Nothing prevents a clever person being incontinent. This is why certain people sometimes seem to be practically wise but incontinent, because cleverness and practical wisdom differ in the way we suggested at the beginning; they are close in respect of reason, but differ in respect of rational choice.)

And the incontinent person is not like someone who knows and is attending to his knowledge, but like someone asleep or drunk. He acts voluntarily (because he knows in a way what he is doing and for what end), but he is not wicked; his rational choice is good, so that he is only half-wicked. Nor is he unjust, since he does not plan his misdeeds. Of the two, one type is not disposed to stand by the results of his deliberation, while the other, the excitable person, does not do wrong deliberately at all.

So the incontinent person is like a city that passes all the right decrees and has good laws, but makes no use of them, as in Anaxandrides' joke: 'The city willed it, which cares nothing for laws.'[56] The wicked person, however, is like a city that implements its laws, but implements wicked ones.

Incontinence and self-control are concerned with what exceeds the state of most people; the self-controlled person stands firm more than most people can, the incontinent less.

The kind of incontinence exhibited by excitable people is easier to cure than that of people who deliberate but do not stand by the result. And those incontinent through habituation are easier to cure than those who are so naturally, because it is easier to change a habit than one's nature. Indeed, the reason why habit is also hard to alter is that it is like one's nature, as Euenus says:

I tell you, my friend, it is long-lasting training
And this ends up as nature for human beings.[57]

So we have said what continence, incontinence, endurance and softness are, and how these states are related to one another.

Chapter 11

1152b It is part of the job of the political philosopher to study pleasure and pain, since he is the architect of the end, with an eye on which we call one thing unqualifiedly bad, another good.

Again, examining them is also one of the things we must do, because one of our assumptions was that virtue of character, and vice, are concerned with pains and pleasures, and because most people claim that

---

[56] Anaxandrides, fr. 66 KA. Fourth-century comic poet, possibly from Rhodes.
[57] Euenus, fr. 9 Diehl. Fifth-century rhetorician and sophist, from Paros.

happiness involves pleasure; this is why people call the blessed (*ma-karios*) person by that name, from *chairein* (to enjoy).

Some people think that no pleasure is a good, either in itself or incidentally, on the ground that the good and pleasure are not the same. Others think that some pleasures are good, but that most are bad. Again, there is a third point of view, that even if all pleasures are good, nevertheless the chief good cannot be pleasure.

The reasons offered for the view that pleasure is not a good at all are that every pleasure is a perceived coming-to-be towards a natural state, and that no coming-to-be is in the same genus as its ends – no instance of building, for example, is in the same genus as what is built. Again, a temperate person avoids pleasures. Again, the practically wise person pursues what is painless, not what is pleasant. Again, pleasures are a hindrance to thought, the more so the more one enjoys them: sexual pleasure, for example – no one could think of anything in the midst of that. Again, there is no skill of pleasure, whereas every good thing is the product of a skill. Again, children and animals pursue pleasures.

The reasons offered for the view that not all pleasures are good are that there are shameful and reprehensible pleasures, and that there are harmful pleasures, since some pleasant things make people ill.

The reason offered for the view that pleasure is not the chief good is that it is not an end, but a coming-to-be.

These, then, are roughly the views people express.

Chapter 12

It is clear, however, from the following considerations that these arguments do not show that pleasure is not a good, or even that it is not the chief good.

First, since things are called good in two senses (good without qualification, and good for somebody), it follows that natures and states, and hence also processes and comings-to-be, will be called good in these ways. And so, of those that seem to be bad, some are bad without qualification, but not bad for a particular person, and indeed, for this person, worthy of choice. Some are not even worthy of choice for a particular person, but nevertheless are so sometimes and for a short period, though not without qualification. Others are not even pleasures, but appear to be, namely, all those that involve pain and are remedial, such as those in sick people.

Again, since one kind of good is an activity, while another is a state, the processes that restore a person to his natural state are only incidentally pleasant. The activity in the appetites is the activity of the

1153a state and nature that remain, since there are also pleasures that do not involve pain and appetite, such as those of contemplation, in which case one's nature is not lacking in anything. An indication of this is the fact that people do not enjoy the same pleasure when their natural state is being replenished as they do when it has been restored. Once it is restored, they enjoy things pleasant without qualification; but while it is being replenished they enjoy even quite the contrary. They even enjoy sharp and bitter things, none of which are pleasant either by nature or without qualification; nor, therefore, are the pleasures, since as pleasant things differ from each other, so also do the pleasures arising from them.

Again, it is not necessary that there be something else better than pleasure, as the end, according to some, is better than the coming-to-be. For pleasures are not comings-to-be, nor do they all even involve coming-to-be, but they are activities and constitute an end; nor do they result from our coming to be something, but from our exercising our capacities. And not all pleasures have an end distinct from themselves, but only those of people who are being led to the completion of their nature.

This is why it is wrong to say that pleasure is a perceived coming-to-be. What we should rather say is that it is an activity of one's natural state, and that it is unimpeded rather than perceived. It is because it is a good in the real sense that some people think it is a coming-to-be, believing that an activity is a coming-to-be; whereas in fact they are different.

Saying that pleasures are bad because some pleasant things are unhealthy is like saying that healthy things are bad because some are bad for business. Both are bad in the sense mentioned, but that is not to say that they are bad, since even contemplation is sometimes damaging to one's health.

Neither practical wisdom nor any other state is impeded by the pleasure arising from itself, but only by extraneous pleasures. For the pleasures arising from contemplation and learning will make us contemplate and learn all the more.

The fact that no pleasure is the product of a skill is as one would expect, since there is no skill of any other activity either, but only of the corresponding capacity. But in fact the perfumer's and chef's skills are thought to be skills of pleasure.

The arguments that the temperate person avoids pleasure, that the practically wise person seeks a life free from pain, and that children and brutes pursue pleasure, are all dealt with in the same way. We have said in what ways pleasures are good without qualification, as well as how not all pleasures are good – and it is these that brutes and children pursue, and it is freedom from the pain related to these that the practically wise person pursues. They are the pleasures involving appetite and pain, namely, the bodily pleasures (since they are like this) and their excesses, in respect of which the intemperate person is intemperate. This is why the temperate person avoids them, since the temperate person has his own pleasures as well.

Chapter 13

Again, it is also agreed that pain is an evil, and to be avoided; for one 1153b type of pain is unqualifiedly bad, while another is bad in a particular way, through its tendency to impede. But the contrary of what is to be avoided, in so far as it is something bad and to be avoided, is a good; pleasure, then, must be a good. The solution of Speusippus – that it is like the case of the greater, which is contrary both to the less and to the equal – does not work, because he would not say that pleasure is something essentially evil. And even if certain pleasures are bad, there is no reason why some pleasure or other should not be the chief good, just as one kind of knowledge might be, though some kinds are bad. And if there are unimpeded activities of each state, whether the activity of all of them or of one in particular constitutes happiness when unimpeded, that one must presumably be the most worthy of choice. But pleasure is an unimpeded activity, so the chief good might be some kind of pleasure, even if it so happens that most pleasures are bad without qualification.

And this is why everyone thinks that the happy life is pleasant, and weaves pleasure into happiness – reasonably enough, since no activity is complete when it is impeded, and happiness is something complete. The happy person therefore also needs bodily goods, external goods and good fortune, so that he will not be impeded in these respects. People who claim that the person being tortured, or the person who has fallen on very bad times, is happy if he is good are, whether voluntarily or involuntarily, talking nonsense.

Because we need fortune as well, some people think that good fortune is the same as happiness. But it is not, since even that in excess can be an impediment, and presumably should by rights no longer be called good fortune, its limits of application being defined in relation to happiness.

And the fact that all things, both brutes and human beings, pursue pleasure is some sort of evidence for its being in some sense the chief good: 'No utterance is wholly lost, that many peoples ...'.[58] But since no one nature or state either is or is held to be best for all, it is not the same pleasure that they all pursue, but they do all pursue pleasure. And perhaps they do in fact pursue the same pleasure, and not the one they think or would say that they pursue, since everything by nature has something divine in it.

But the bodily pleasures have taken possession of the name because it is those that people steer for most often, and all share in them; and so, 1154a because these are the only pleasures they know, people think that they are the only pleasures.

It is obvious, too, that, if pleasure – that activity – is not a good, it will not be true that the happy person has a pleasant life. For why would he need pleasure if it is not a good, and he can even live a life of pain? For pain is neither an evil nor a good if pleasure is not, so why would he avoid it? And in that case the life of the good person will not be more pleasant, if his activities are not also more pleasant.

Chapter 14

With regard to bodily pleasures, those who say that some pleasures, such as noble ones, are especially worthy of choice, but not the bodily pleasures, with which the intemperate person is concerned, should consider the following question: why are the pains contrary to them bad? For the contrary of an evil is a good.

Or are the necessary pleasures good in the sense in which what is not bad is good? Or are they good up to a point? For in the case of some

---

[58] Hesiod, *Works and Days* 763f.

states and processes, there can be no excess of what is better, and so no excess of pleasure either; while in cases where there can be an excess of what is better, there can be an excess of pleasure as well. In the case of bodily goods, there can be an excess, and it is pursuit of this excess, not the necessary pleasures, that makes a person bad; for everyone enjoys fine food and wine and sexual intercourse in some way, but not everyone in the way he ought.

With pain the contrary is true. It is not just the excess that the bad person avoids, but he avoids it altogether. For the pain opposed to excessive pleasure is not pain at all except to someone who is pursuing excessive pleasure.

We ought not only to state the true view, but also to explain the false one, since this helps to produce conviction. For when it is made to appear reasonable why a view appears to be true that is not, this makes people more firmly convinced of the true one. So we have to say why bodily pleasures appear more worthy of choice.

First, then, it is because such pleasure expels pain. Excessive pain makes people pursue excessive pleasure, and bodily pleasure in general, as a remedy. Remedial pleasures become intense – which is why they are pursued – because they stand out against their contraries.

Indeed, these are the two grounds for the view that pleasure is not a good thing, as we said. Some of them are the actions of a bad nature, either congenitally bad, like that of a brute, or bad by habituation, like the actions of bad people. Others, meanwhile, are remedies of what is lacking, and being in the state is better than coming to be in it. These 1154b pleasures arise from a process towards completion, and so are good only incidentally.

Again, bodily pleasures are pursued because of their intensity by those incapable of enjoying other kinds. At any rate, they contrive various thirsts for themselves, which is unobjectionable when the thirsts do no harm, but bad when they are harmful. For they have nothing else to enjoy, and the nature of many people is such that a condition of neutrality is painful to them. This is because every animal is always in a state of tension, as the natural scientists also affirm, since they claim that seeing and hearing are painful; but, they suggest, we have by now become accustomed to this. Similarly, because they are growing, young people are in a condition rather like drunkenness, and so youth is pleasant. People of an excitable nature, however, are always in need of remedial pleasure, because their make-up puts their body under constant affliction, and they are always in a state of intense desire. Pain is driven out by the pleasure contrary to it, indeed any chance pleasure, if it is strong enough; and for these reasons they become intemperate and bad.

Pleasures that do not involve pains, however, do not admit of excess. These are among the things pleasant by nature and not incidentally. By things pleasant incidentally, I mean those that are remedial; for the remedy is effected during action of that part of us that remains healthy, and because of this it seems pleasant. Things pleasant by nature, however, are those that produce action in a healthy nature.

The reason why the same one thing cannot always be pleasant is that our nature is not simple. There is another element in us, which makes us perishable, so that if one of these elements is acting, this is contrary to nature for the other nature within us; and when the two are balanced, what is done seems neither painful nor pleasant. If anything had a simple nature, the same action would always be the most pleasant.

This is why god enjoys a single simple pleasure always. There is an activity not only of movement, but of lack of movement; and indeed there is pleasure in rest more than in movement. 'Change in all things is sweet',[59] as the poet says, because of a fault of some kind; as among humans it is the faulty ones who are easy to change, so also the nature requiring change is faulty, because it is neither simple nor good.

Our discussion has covered self-control and incontinence, and pleasure and pain, both what each is and how some of them are good, others bad. It remains for us now to speak of friendship.

---

[59] Euripides, *Orestes* 234.

Book VIII

Chapter 1

After this, the next step would be a discussion of friendship, since it is a virtue or involves virtue, and is an absolute necessity in life. No one would choose to live without friends, even if he had all the other goods. Indeed, rich people and those who have attained high office and power seem to stand in special need of friends. For what use is such prosperity if there is no opportunity for beneficence, which is exercised mainly and in its most commendable form towards friends? Or how could their prosperity be watched over and kept safe without friends? The greater it is, the greater the danger it is in. In poverty, too, and in other misfortunes, people think friends are the only resort.

Friendship benefits the young by keeping them from making mistakes, and the old by caring for them and helping them to finish jobs they are unable to finish themselves because of their weakness. And it benefits those in their prime by helping them to do noble actions – 'two going together'[60] – since with friends they are more capable of thinking and acting.

And there seems to be a natural friendship of a parent for a child, and of a child for a parent, and this occurs not only among human beings, but among birds and most animals. It also seems to exist naturally among members of the same species in relation to one another, particularly among human beings, which is why we praise people who

---

[60] Homer, *Iliad* x.224.

143

are lovers of humanity. And one can see in one's travels how akin and friendly every human being is to every other.

Friendship seems also to hold cities together, and lawgivers to care more about it than about justice; for concord seems to be something like friendship, and this is what they aim at most of all, while taking special pains to eliminate civil conflict as something hostile. And when people are friends, they have no need of justice, while when they are just, they need friendship as well; and the highest form of justice seems to be a matter of friendship.

It is not only a necessary thing, but a noble one as well. We praise those who love their friends, and having many friends seems to be something noble. Again, we think that the same people are good and are friends.

There is a great deal of disagreement about friendship. Some people assume that it is a kind of likeness, that people who are alike are friends. Hence the sayings, 'Like to like',[61] and 'Birds of a feather', and so on. Others claim, on the contrary, that people who are alike are 'like potters to one another'.[62] Some people inquire into these questions more deeply and in a way that is more proper to natural science. Euripides claims that:

Parched earth loves the rain,
And the revered heaven, when filled with rain, loves to fall to earth.[63]

And Heraclitus says, 'Opposition is a helper', and, 'From discord comes the noblest harmony,' and, 'Everything comes to be through strife.'[64] Others, such as Empedocles, say that, on the contrary, like seeks like.[65]

The problems proper to natural science we can put to one side, since they are not germane to the present inquiry; let us consider those that are human and relate to character and feeling. For instance, can friendship arise between all kinds of people, or is it impossible for wicked people to be friends? Is there one species of friendship or several? Some think there is only one, because it admits of degrees, but their conviction is based on insufficient evidence; for things of different species also admit of variations of degree.

1155b

---

[61] Homer, *Iliad* xvii.218.   [62] Hesiod, *Works and Days* 25.
[63] Euripides, fr. 898 Nauck.   [64] Heraclitus, 22 B 8 DK.
[65] Cf. Empedocles, frr. 31 B 22, 62, 90 DK.

Chapter 2

Perhaps the matter will be clarified if we can understand what it is that is worthy of love. It seems that not everything is loved, but only what is worthy of love, and this is what is good, pleasant or useful. What is useful, however, would seem to be what is instrumental to some good or pleasure, so that what are worthy of love as ends are the good and the pleasant.

So do people love what is good, or what is good for them, since these are occasionally at variance (as happens also with what is pleasant)? Each person, it seems, loves what is good for him, and while what is good is unqualifiedly worthy of love, what is worthy of love for each individual is what is good for him. In fact, each person loves not what is good for him, but what seems good; this, however, will make no difference, since we shall say that this is what seems worthy of love. There are three reasons, then, for loving something.

Affection for soulless objects is not called friendship, since the affection is not mutual, nor is there any wishing good to the object (it would presumably be absurd to wish good to one's wine – if anything, one wishes that it keep, so that one may have it oneself). But people say that we ought to wish good things to a friend for his own sake. People describe those who do wish good things in this way, when the wish is not reciprocated, as having goodwill. For goodwill is said to count as friendship only when it is reciprocated.

Perhaps we should add 'and when it does not go unrecognized', since many have goodwill towards people they have not seen, but suppose to 1156a be good or useful; and the same feeling may exist in the other direction. They appear, then, to have goodwill to each other, but how could anyone call them friends when they are unaware of their attitude to one another? So they must have goodwill to each other, wish good things to each other for one of the reasons given, and not be unaware of it.

Chapter 3

Since these reasons differ from one another in species, so do the forms of affection and friendship. There are, then, three species of friendship, equal in number to the objects worthy of it. In the case of each object there is a corresponding mutual affection that does not go unrecognized, and those who love each other wish good things to each other in that respect in which they love one another.

Those who love one another for utility love the other not in himself, but only in so far as they will obtain some good for themselves from him. The same goes for those who love for pleasure; they do not like a witty person because of his character, but because they find him pleasing to themselves. So those who love for utility are fond of the other because of what is good for themselves, and those who love for pleasure because of what is pleasant for themselves, not in so far as the person they love is who he is, but in so far as he is useful or pleasant.

These friendships, then, are also incidental, since the person is loved not in so far as he is who he is, but in so far as he provides some good or pleasure. Such friendships are thus easily dissolved, when the parties to them do not remain unchanged; for if one party is no longer pleasant or useful, the other stops loving him.

What is useful does not remain the same, but differs according to different circumstances. So when the reason for their being friends has gone, the friendship is dissolved as well, since it existed only for that reason. This kind of friendship seems to come about among older people in particular, because at that age they are pursuing what is useful, not what is pleasant, and also among those in their prime or their youth who are pursuing their own advantage.

Nor do such people live in each other's company very much; for sometimes they do not even find each other pleasant. They have no further need of such association, unless they are useful to each other, because each finds the other pleasant only to the extent that he hopes for some good from him. In this class people also put the friendship between host and guest.

Friendship between the young seems to be for pleasure, since they live in accordance with their feelings, and pursue in particular what is pleasant for themselves and what is immediate. As they get older, however, what they find pleasant begins to change. This is why they are quick to become friends and quick to stop; their friendship fluctuates along with what they find pleasant, and this sort of pleasure is subject to rapid change. The young are also prone to erotic friendship, since it is generally a matter of following one's feelings, and aims at pleasure; they therefore quickly fall in love and quickly stop, often changing in one day. But they do wish to spend their days together and to live in one

1156b

another's company, since this is how they attain what accords with their friendship.

Complete friendship is that of good people, those who are alike in their virtue: they each alike wish good things to each other in so far as they are good, and they are good in themselves. Those who wish good things to a friend for his own sake are friends most of all, since they are disposed in this way towards each other because of what they are, not for any incidental reason. So their friendship lasts as long as they are good, and virtue is an enduring thing. Each of them is good without qualification and good for his friend, since good people are both good without qualification and beneficial to each other. They are similarly pleasant as well, since good people are pleasant both without qualification and to each other; for each person finds his own actions and others like them pleasant, and the actions of good people are the same or alike.

Such friendship is, as one might expect, lasting, since in it are combined all the qualities that friends should have: every friendship is for a good or for pleasure, either without qualification or for the person who loves, and is based on some similarity. To this kind of friendship belong all the qualities we have mentioned, in virtue of the participants themselves, for they are alike in this way, and their friendship has the other qualities – what is unqualifiedly good and what is unqualifiedly pleasant – and these are most of all worthy of love. Love and friendship, then, are found most of all among people like this, and in their best form.

Naturally, such friendships are rare, because people of this kind are few. Besides, they require time and familiarity. As the saying goes, they cannot know each other until they have eaten the proverbial salt together; nor can they accept each other or be friends until each has shown himself to be worthy of love and gained the other's confidence. Those who are quick to show the signs of friendship to one another wish to be friends, but are not, unless they are worthy of friendship and know it. For though the wish for friendship arises quickly, friendship does not.

Chapter 4

This kind of friendship, then, is complete both in respect of its duration and in the other respects. Each gets from each the same or similar

1157a benefits, in every way, as ought to happen among friends. Friendship for pleasure bears a resemblance to this kind, since good people are pleasing to each other. The same sort of thing applies in the case of friendship for utility, since good people are useful to each other.

These lesser friendships, too, are especially lasting when each receives the same benefit – such as pleasure – from the other, and not merely that, but from the same source, as happens with witty people, and not with lover and beloved. For lover and beloved do not take pleasure in the same things, but the one in seeing the beloved, the other in the attentions of the lover. And sometimes, as the bloom of youth fades, the friendship fades too, since the lover does not find the sight of his beloved pleasing, while the beloved does not receive his attentions. But many do remain friends, if they are alike in character and have come to be fond of each other's characters through familiarity with them. But those lovers who exchange not pleasure but utility are friends to a lesser degree and less constant. Friends for utility part when the advantage disappears, because they were friends not of each other, but of gain.

For pleasure or for utility, then, even bad people can be friends with each other, or good people with bad, or one who is neither good nor bad with a person of any sort. But clearly only good people can be friends for the sake of the other person himself, because bad people do not enjoy each other's company unless there is some benefit in it for them.

Also, it is only the friendship of good people that provides protection against slander. For it is not easy to trust criticism of a person whom one has proved oneself over a long period of time; between good people there is trust, the feeling that the other would never do an injustice to one, and all the other things that are expected in true friendship. In the other kinds of friendship, however, there is nothing to prevent bad things like this happening.

People do describe as friends also those whose motive is utility, as cities are said to be friendly (since it seems to be for their own advantage that cities form alliances), and those who are fond of each other for pleasure, as children are. So presumably we ought also to say that such people are friends, but that there are several kinds of friendship. Friendship in the primary and real sense will be the friendship of good people in so far as they are good, while the rest will be friendships by being like it; it is in virtue of something good and something like what is found in true friendship that they are friends, because what is pleasant is good to lovers of pleasure. These friendships, however, are not very likely to coincide, and the same people do not become friends for both utility and pleasure; for things that are incidental are not often combined.

Friendship being divided into these species, then, it is bad people who 1157b will tend to be friends for pleasure or utility, since this is the respect in which they are alike. But good people will be friends for each other's sake, because they are friends in so far as they are good. These people, therefore, are friends without qualification, while the others are friends incidentally and through being like them.

Chapter 5

Just as with virtues some are called good in respect of a state of character, others in respect of an activity, so it is with friendship. For some people find their enjoyment in living in each other's company, and bestow good things on each other. Others, however, are asleep or separated by distance, and so do not engage in these activities of friendship, but nevertheless have a disposition to do so; for distance does not dissolve friendship without qualification, but it does dissolve its activity. But if the absence is a long one, it seems to make people forget their friendship. Hence the proverb: 'Many friendships has lack of conversation dissolved.'

Neither old nor ill-tempered people seem inclined to friendship. For little pleasure is to be found in them, and nobody can spend his days with someone he finds painful, or even not pleasing, since nature seems above all to avoid what is painful and aim at what is pleasant.

People who approve of each other but do not live in each other's company seem to have goodwill rather than friendship. For there is nothing so characteristic of friends as living in each other's company (because while people in need desire benefit, even the blessed desire to spend their days together, since solitude suits them least of all). But people cannot spend time together if they are not pleasing to each other and do not enjoy the same things, as comrades seem to.

Friendship in the fullest sense, then, is that between good people, as we have said a number of times already. For what is worthy of love and of choice seems to be what is good or pleasant without qualification, and what is worthy of love and of choice for each person seems to be what is good or pleasant for him; and a good person is worthy of love and of choice for another good person on both these grounds.

Affection seems to be a feeling, but friendship a state. For affection occurs no less towards soulless things, while mutual friendship involves rational choice, and rational choice comes from a state; and it is a state, not a feeling, that makes people wish good things to those they love, for their sake. And in loving their friend they love what is good for themselves; for the good person, in coming to be a friend, comes to be a good for his friend. Each, then, both loves what is good for himself, and returns like for like in what he wishes and in giving pleasure: friendship, 1158a people say, is equality, and both of these are found most of all in the friendship of the good.

Chapter 6

Friendship arises to a lesser degree between sour or elderly people, in so far as they are less good-tempered and find less enjoyment in mixing with others; and it is these qualities that seem to be especially characteristic and productive of friendship. This is why young people become friends quickly, but old people do not, since they do not become friends with those whose company they do not enjoy; likewise, nor do sour people. But they can have goodwill to each other, since they wish good to one another and meet one another's needs; but they are not really friends, because they do not spend their days together or enjoy each other's company, and these seem especially characteristic of friendship.

One cannot be a friend – in the sense of complete friendship – to many people, just as one cannot be in love with many people at the same time (love is like an excess, and such a thing arises naturally towards one individual). And it is not easy for the same person at the same time to please many people a great deal, or, presumably, to be good in relations with them. He must have experience of them as well, and become familiar with them, which is very difficult. But when the friendship is for utility or pleasure, it is possible to please many people, since many people can be pleased like this, and the services do not take long.

Of these two kinds, that for pleasure is more like friendship, when both parties make the same contribution and enjoy each other's company or the same things. The friendships of the young are like this, since one finds more of a generosity of spirit in these friendships. Friendship for utility, on the other hand, is for common tradesmen.

The blessed, too, though they have no need of useful friends, do need pleasant ones. For they wish to spend their lives in the company of others, and while they can bear what is painful for a short time, nobody could endure it continuously – not even the Good Itself, if it were painful to him. This is why they seek friends who are pleasant. But presumably they ought to seek friends who are good as well, and also good for them, because they will then have what friends should have.

People in high office seem to have friends of different types; some people are useful to them, and others pleasant, but it is rare for the same people to be both. For they are not looking for people whose pleasantness is accompanied by virtue as well, or those who are useful for noble actions, but witty individuals if it is pleasure they seek, or people clever at doing what they are told; and rarely do these qualities occur in the same person.

Though we have indeed said that the good person is both pleasant and useful at the same time, he does not become a friend to a superior unless the latter is superior in virtue as well; otherwise he does not attain equality by being proportionately inferior. But superiors like this are rare.

The friendships we have discussed, then, are based on equality, since 1158b both sides get the same and wish the same to each other, or exchange one thing for another, such as pleasure for benefit. As we have said, however, these are lesser friendships and less lasting. But it is because of their similarity and dissimilarity to the same thing that they seem both to be and not to be friendships. It is because of their similarity to friendship based on virtue that they appear to be friendships (one of them involves pleasure and the other utility, and these are characteristics of friendship based on virtue as well); while it is because friendship based on virtue involves a refusal to listen to slander and is lasting, but these friendships change quickly and differ in many other ways as well, that they do not appear to be friendships – that is, because of their dissimilarity to friendship based on virtue.

Chapter 7

There is another species of friendship, that involving superiority – for example, that of father to son, and of older to younger in general, of man to woman, and of any ruler to his subject.

These friendships also differ from one another. That of parents to children is not the same as that of rulers to ruled; nor is that of father to son the same as that of son to father, or that of man to woman the same as that of woman to man. For the virtue of each of these is different, the characteristic activity is different, and so are the reasons for their becoming friends; and therefore the affection and the friendship differ as well. Each, then, does not get the same from the other, nor should they seek it; but when chidren give to parents what they ought to give to those who brought them into being, and parents give what they ought to their children, the friendship between them will be lasting and good.

In all friendships involving superiority, the affection must be proportional as well. The better, that is to say, must be loved more than he loves, and so must the more useful, and each of the others likewise; when the affection is in accordance with merit, then a kind of equality results, which is of course thought to be a mark of friendship.

But what is equal does not seem to be the same in friendship as it is in just actions. For in just actions what is equal in the primary sense is what is in accordance with merit, while quantitative equality is secondary, whereas in friendship quantitative equality is primary and that in accordance with merit secondary. This becomes clear if a large gap develops in respect of virtue, vice, wealth or something else: then they are no longer friends, nor do they even expect to be. This is most obvious in the case of the gods, since they are the most superior to us in 1159a all good things. But it is clear also in the case of kings, since people who are much inferior do not expect to be friends with them, nor do worthless people expect to be friends with the best or the wisest.

In cases like this there is no precise point at which people cannot remain friends. For friendship can survive many losses, but when one side is removed at a great distance – as god is – then it is no longer possible. This is the source of the puzzle whether friends really wish one another the greatest good – to be gods – because they will no longer have them as friends, nor as goods (friends being goods). If, then, we were right to say that one friend wishes goods to the other for the other's sake, the latter must remain as he is, whatever that may be. So it is to the other as a human being that a friend will wish the greatest goods, though presumably not all of them, since it is for himself most of all that each person wishes what is good.

Chapter 8

The masses, because of their love of honour, seem to wish to be loved more than to love, which is why they like flattery. For a flatterer is a friend who is inferior, or who pretends to be such and to love more than he is loved; being loved seems close to being honoured, and this is indeed what the masses aim at.

But it does not appear to be for its own sake that people choose honour, but incidentally. For the masses enjoy being honoured by those in high office because of their expectations (they think that they will get anything they want from them, and enjoy the honour as a sign of future indulgence). Those, however, who desire honour from good people familiar with them are seeking to have their own opinion of themselves confirmed; they enjoy honour, then, because they are confident of their own goodness on the strength of the judgement of those who say they are good. Being loved, however, they enjoy for its own sake. So it would seem to be better than being honoured, and friendship to be worth choosing for its own sake.

But friendship seems to consist more in loving than in being loved, as is indicated by the enjoyment a mother finds in love. Sometimes she will give her own child to others to bring up, and though she loves him because she knows him, she does not seek to be loved in return, if it is impossible to have both. It seems enough for her to see the child doing well, and she loves him even if, because he does not know her, he gives her none of the things appropriate to a mother.

Since friendship consists more in loving, and we praise those who love their friends, it appears that loving is the virtue of friends. So, when it happens that people love in accordance with merit, they are 1159b lasting friends and their friendship lasts. It is in this way that unequals as well can best be friends, since they can thus be equalized.

Affection consists in equality and similarity, and especially the similarity of those who are similar in possessing virtue. For, being the sort to stand firm in themselves, they stand by one another, and neither ask for nor offer services of a shameful kind, but, one might say, they even prevent them. For it is characteristic of good people neither to make errors themselves nor to allow their friends to do so. But wicked people have no constancy, since they do not even remain similar to what they were; they become friends for a short time, because they enjoy each other's wickedness. People who are useful or pleasant, however, remain friends longer, that is, as long as they provide pleasure or benefit for each other.

The friendship that seems to occur most of all between contraries is that for utility; that, for example, between a poor person and a rich, or an ignorant person and a learned one, since each of us is eager for whatever it is he happens to lack, and so gives something in return. One might include here lover and beloved, noble and ugly. This is why lovers sometimes look ridiculous, expecting to be loved as much as they love; presumably they ought to expect this if they are worthy of love in the same way, but when nothing like this is true it is ridiculous.

Presumably, however, contrary seeks contrary not in itself, but incidentally, and desire is for what lies in between: what is good for the dry, for example, is not to become wet but to arrive at the intermediate state, and the same goes for the hot and the others. But let us put these matters to one side, since they are in fact rather irrelevant.

Chapter 9

As we said at the beginning, friendship and justice seem to be concerned with the same things and to be found in the same people. For there seems to be some kind of justice in every community, and some kind of friendship as well. At any rate, people address as friends their shipmates and fellow soldiers, and similarly those who are members of other kinds of community with them. And the extent of their community is the extent of their friendship, since it is also the extent of their justice. The proverb, 'What friends have they have in common', is correct, since friendship is based on community. But while brothers and comrades have everything in common, what the others whom we have mentioned have in common is more limited – more in some cases, less in others, since friendships too differ in degree.

1160a   What is just differs as well, since it is not the same for parents in relation to children as for one brother to another, and not the same for comrades as for fellow citizens, and similarly with the other kinds of friendship. So what counts as injustice towards each of these friends differs as well, and the injustice increases the closer the friends involved. It is more dreadful, for example, to defraud a comrade than a fellow citizen, to fail to aid a brother than a stranger, or to hit one's father than anyone else. The demands of justice also naturally increase with the friendship, since both involve the same people and are of equal extent.

All communities seem to be parts of the political community, since people journey together with something useful in mind, to supply something for life. And the political community seems originally to have come together and to continue for the sake of what is useful, since it is this that legislators aim at, and it is said that what is useful, in common, is just.

Other communities aim at particular advantages – sailors, for example, at what is useful in a voyage, with a view to making money or something like that, fellow soldiers at what is useful in war, whether their object is money, victory or a city; and similarly members of tribes and demes. Some communities – religious guilds and dining societies – seem to develop for pleasure, since they are for sacrifices and companionship. All these seem subordinate to the political community, because it aims not at what is immediately useful, but at what is useful for the whole of life.

When people arrange sacrifices and the joint festivities connected with them, they render honours to the gods as well as providing pleasurable relaxation for themselves. For the ancient sacrifices and joint festivities seem to occur after the gathering of the harvest as a sort of first-fruits, since it was at this time of year that people had most time for leisure.

All these communities, then, appear to be parts of the political community; and the particular kinds of friendship will correspond to the particular kinds of community.

Chapter 10

There are three species of polity, and an equal number of deviations from them – corruptions of them, so to speak. The three are kingship, aristocracy, and a third based on ownership of property (*timema*), which it seems proper to call timocratic, though most people usually call it a polity. The best of these is kingship, the worst timocracy.

The deviation from kingship is tyranny. Though both are monarchic, 1160b there is a very great difference between them: the tyrant looks to his own advantage, the king to that of his subjects. For a person is not a king unless he is self-sufficient and superior in all that is good; such a person needs nothing further, so he will look not to his own interests but to those of his subjects. A king who was not like this would be a king in name only. Tyranny is quite the contrary, since the tyrant pursues his own good. It is more obviously the worst of the three deviations, and the worst is the contrary of the best. Tyranny emerges from kingship because tyranny is a debasement of monarchy, and a king who is bad becomes a tyrant.

Oligarchy emerges from aristocracy through the vice of the rulers, who distribute what belongs to the city contrary to merit – to themselves, all or most of what is good, and offices always to the same people, regarding wealth as the most important factor. So it is a few bad people who rule, and the wicked instead of the best.

Democracy emerges from timocracy, since they have the same boundary. For timocracy too is meant to be rule by the majority, and everyone with property is equal. Democracy is the least bad, because it oversteps the form of a polity only by a little.

These, then, are the changes to which political systems are especially prone, since the transitions involved are the smallest and easiest.

One can also find in households resemblances to these political systems and, as it were, models of them. The community of a father and his sons has the form of a kingship, since the father cares for his children. This is why Homer also calls Zeus 'Father',[66] since kingship is meant to be paternal rule. Among the Persians, however, the rule of a father is tyrannical, since they use their sons as slaves. Also tyrannical is the rule of a master over his slaves, since it is the advantage of the master that is realized in it. This kind of rule, then, seems correct, but the Persian variety is off the mark, since different kinds of rule suit different subjects.

The community constituted by man and woman appears aristocratic, since the man rules in accordance with merit and in those areas in which a man should rule; but whatever befits a woman, he places in her hands. If, however, the man is in charge of everything, the relation changes into

1161a oligarchy; for he does this contrary to merit and not in so far as he is

---

[66] Homer, *Iliad* i.503 and *passim*.

superior. Sometimes, however, women rule, because they are heiresses; their rule is thus not in accordance with virtue, but due to wealth and power, as in oligarchies.

The community constituted by brothers is like a timocracy, since they are equal, except in so far as they differ in age; so if their ages vary greatly, the friendship is no longer fraternal.

Democracy is found most of all in households lacking a master, since everyone there is on an equal footing, and in those where the person in charge is weak and everyone can do as he likes.

Chapter 11

Friendship can be seen in each of these political systems, to the same extent as justice. That of a king towards his subjects consists in superior benefit; he treats his subjects well, since being a good person he cares for them with a view to their well-being. A shepherd does the same for his sheep, which is why Homer called Agamemnon 'shepherd of the peoples'.[67]

The friendship of a father is similar to this, though it differs in the magnitude of the benefits conferred. He is responsible for his children's existence, which seems to be the greatest of benefits, as well as for their nurture and education. These benefits are attributed to ancestors as well. And it is by nature that a father tends to rule his sons, ancestors their descendants, and a king his subjects. These friendships involve superiority, which is why parents are honoured as well. And what is just between people like this is not the same, but in accordance with merit, because the same is true of the friendship.

The friendship of man to woman is the same as that in an aristocracy, since it is in accordance with virtue – the superior receives more of what is good, and each receives what is appropriate. And the same goes for what is just.

The friendship of brothers is like that of companions, since they are equal and contemporary in age, and such people are generally alike in their feelings and characters. The friendship appropriate to timocracy is like this, since the citizens are meant to be equal and good; so rule is

---

[67] Homer, *Iliad* ii.243 and *passim*.

taken in turn, and on equal terms. The same goes, then, for their friendship.

But in the deviations, as justice hardly exists, the same goes for friendship, and it exists least in the worst deviation: in a tyranny, there is little or no friendship. For when ruler and ruled have nothing in common, since there is no justice, there is no friendship either. Take, 1161b for example, the relation of craftsman to tool, and soul to body. The latter in each pair is benefited by its user, but there is neither friendship nor justice towards soulless things. Nor is there any towards an ox, or even a slave, in so far as he is a slave; for master and slave have nothing in common, since a slave is a tool with a soul, while a tool is a slave without one. In so far as he is a slave, then, there cannot be friendship with him.

But there can be friendship in so far as he is a human being, since there does seem to be justice of some kind between any human and any other capable of community in law and agreement. So there can also be friendship, in as much as he is a human being. Thus in tyrannies as well friendships and justice hardly exist, but in democracies they exist to a greater extent, because the citizens are equal and so have much in common.

Chapter 12

Every friendship, then, is found in a community, as we have said. But one might put the friendship of relatives and that of companions in a separate category. Those of fellow-citizens, fellow-tribesmen, shipmates and the like are more like friendships in a community, because they appear to be based on a sort of agreement; one might put the friendship of host and guest into this class as well.

Friendship between relatives, while it seems to have many species, nevertheless always appears to be derived from paternal friendship: a parent is fond of his child as being a part of himself, and children are fond of a parent as being their originator.

A parent knows his offspring better than the offspring know that they are from the parent. And the parent feels his offspring are his own more than the offspring the parent, because that which comes from something else belongs to that from which it comes, as a tooth or a hair or whatever belongs to its owner; but the producer belongs not at all to the product, or to a lesser degree. Parental love is greater in duration as well, because a parent is fond of his children as soon as they are born, but it is only after some time, when they have acquired judgement or perception, that children are fond of the parent. This also clarifies why mothers love their children more.

A parent, then, loves his children as himself, since what has come from him is, as it were, another self, which is other through its separate existence; children love their parent as being that from which they spring. And brothers love each other since they spring from the same parents; their identical relation to their parents produces the same result for each, which is why people talk of the same blood, the same stock, and so on. They are therefore in a sense the same thing, though in different bodies. Both a common upbringing and similarity in age contribute greatly to friendship, since 'the same age makes a comrade', and people with the same character become companions. This is why the friendship of brothers is like that of companions. And cousins and 1162a other relatives are akin through their relation to brothers, since this amounts to their descending from the same parents. They come to be more closely or distantly related through their nearness to or distance from the original ancestor.

The friendship of children with parents, like that of human beings with gods, is as with something good and superior. The parent has conferred the greatest benefits, being responsible for their being and their nurture, and their education from birth. And this kind of friendship includes pleasure and utility as well, more so than that between people who are unrelated, in as much as their life is lived more in common.

The friendship of brothers has the same qualities as that between companions, especially good ones, and in general that between people who are similar to one another. This is to the extent that they are more akin to one another, and fond of one another from birth, and to the extent that they are more alike in character, being from the same parents and having been brought up together and educated similarly. And in their case the test of time has been longest and most reliable. The qualities of friendship among other relatives are also proportional to the closeness of the relationship.

The friendship of man and woman also seems natural. For human beings naturally tend to form couples more than to form cities, in as much as the household is antecedent to the city, and more necessary, and reproduction is more widely shared with animals.

With other animals, the community extends only to this point, but human beings live together not only for reproductive purposes but also to supply what they need for life. For from the start their characteristic activities are divided, those of the man being different from those of the woman. They supply one another's needs, therefore, by putting their own talents into the common pool. These reasons explain why this friendship seems to include both utility and pleasure. But it may also be friendship for virtue, if they are good, since each has his or her own virtue, and can find enjoyment in this. Children seem to be another bond, which is why childless people separate more quickly: children are a good which is common to both, and what is common holds things together.

How a man should live in relation to his wife, and in general how one friend should live in relation to another, appears to be the same question as how they can live justly. For the demands of justice on a friend towards a friend are not the same as those towards a stranger, nor those on a companion the same as those towards a fellow-student.

Chapter 13

There are three kinds of friendship, as we said at the beginning. And in each case some are friends on the basis of equality, others in accordance with superiority, because not only can equally good people become 1162b friends, but also a better and a worse; and similarly in friendships for pleasure and utility, since the benefits conferred by each can be equal or different. Equals, then, must create equality in loving and other things, in accordance with their equality, while unequals must give in return what is proportionate to the relation of superiority.

Complaints and recriminations arise only, or at least mostly, in friendship for utility. And this is not surprising, since those who are friends for virtue are eager to benefit each other (this being characteristic of virtue and friendship), and there are no complaints or disagreements between people competing with each other in this way. For no one objects to another's loving and benefiting him; if he has good taste, he will respond by benefiting the other. And if the superior gets what he is aiming at, he will not complain against his friend, since each desires what is good.

Nor are complaints generally found in friendships for pleasure, since both at the same time get what they desire, if they enjoy spending time together; and one would look ridiculous if one were to complain that one's friend is not entertaining, when it is open to one not to spend one's days with him.

But friendship for utility is the sort to cause complaint. For they are using each other for their own advantage, and so always require more, thinking that they have less than they ought, and they complain because they are not getting as much as they require and deserve. And benefactors cannot supply as much as the recipients require.

Just as there are two kinds of justice, one unwritten and the other prescribed by law, so there seem to be two kinds of friendship based on utility, one related to character, the other to law. Complaints arise especially when people dissolve relationships in a spirit different from that in which they entered into them.

The type related to law is that on fixed terms. The purely commercial kind involves hand-to-hand exchange, while the more generous kind allows for time to pay, but is based on an agreement of the terms of exchange. In the more generous kind, while the obligation is clear and indisputable, the credit granted contains an element of friendship. This is why some cities do not allow legal actions in these cases, but think that people who have made a contract on trust ought to be content with the outcome.

The type related to character is not on fixed terms, but the gift or whatever is offered as to a friend. One nevertheless expects to get back as much or more, on the assumption that one has made not a gift but a loan. And if a person's situation when the relation is dissolved differs from that when he entered into it, he will complain. This happens because all or most people, though they wish for what is noble, rationally choose what will advantage them; and while it is noble to confer a benefit on another without any reciprocation in mind, it is 1163a receiving benefits that advantages one.

So we ought, if we can, to pay back the equivalent of what we have received, if our friend was acting voluntarily. (We should not make another our friend if he is acting involuntarily, but accept that we were mistaken at the beginning and that we received a benefit from a person from whom we should not have received it; since it was not from a friend nor from someone who did it for its own sake, we must dissolve

161

the relation as if we had received the benefit on fixed terms.) We would agree to make repayment if we could, and the giver would not have expected repayment from someone who could not pay; so we should repay if we can. We should consider at the beginning who it is that is conferring the benefit on us and on what terms, so that we can consent to receiving it on these terms, or decline it.

It is disputable whether we ought to measure a service by its advantage to the receiver and make our repayment with regard to that, or measure it by the beneficence of the giver. A recipient plays it down, arguing that the sort of thing he accepted from his benefactors cost them little, and could have been obtained from other people. The benefactors claim that, on the contrary, it was the greatest thing they could offer, that it could not be obtained from others, and was given in times of danger or other such difficulties.

Since the friendship is based on utility, then surely the measure is the advantage to the recipient? It is he who requires the service, and the other party helps him on the assumption that he will get back the same as he put in. So the service done is as great as the advantage to the receiver, and he ought therefore to return as much as he has gained, or even more, because that would be nobler.

In friendships based on virtue, however, there are no complaints. Rather, the rational choice of the benefactor seems to be the measure, since the authoritative element in virtue and character lies in rational choice.

Chapter 14

There are also quarrels in friendships based on superiority, since each expects to get more, and when this happens the friendship is dissolved. For the superior person thinks it is appropriate for him to have more on the ground that it is appropriate for more to be allocated to a good person. But the more useful person thinks the same; it is wrong, such people say, for a useless person to have an equal share, since it becomes a public service and not a friendship if what one gets out is not in accordance with the worth of what one puts in. They think that, as in a commercial partnership where those who contribute more profit more, so should it be in friendship.

But the person in need, the inferior party, makes the contrary claim, thinking it is characteristic of a good friend to help those in need. What, they say, is the use of being the friend of a good or powerful person, if you are not going to enjoy some benefit from it?

It seems, in fact, that the expectation of each is right, and that each 1163b should get more out of the friendship, but not more of the same thing. The superior person should get more honour, and the person in need more gain, since honour is the reward of virtue and beneficence, while gain is what ministers to need.

It appears to be the same in polities as well. The person who contributes nothing to the community is not honoured, since what is common is given to the person who benefits the community, and honour is something common. For it is impossible to take money from communal funds and to be honoured at the same time, because no one puts up with the smaller share in everything. So the person who loses financially is assigned honour in return, while the person who will accept payments is assigned money; for, as we have said, assigning benefits in accordance with merit equalizes and preserves friendship.

This, then, is the way in which unequals should associate. The person who is benefited with money or virtue ought to give honour in return, giving back what he can. For friendship seeks what can be done, not what accords with merit, because that is not possible in every case, such as honour to the gods or one's parents. No one could ever make a return corresponding to their worth, but the person who serves them as best he can is thought to be good.

This is why it seems a son may not disown his father, though a father may disown his son. For a debtor ought to make repayment, and since nothing that the son does will be worth as much as he has received, he is always in debt. But creditors may release debtors from their obligations, and so therefore may a father. At the same time, however, it seems unlikely that anyone would ever reject a son who was not excessively wicked; leaving aside their natural friendship, it is quite human not to spurn a source of assistance. But the son, if he is wicked, will try to avoid helping his father, or do it with reluctance; for the masses wish to receive benefits, but they avoid doing them, on the ground that they are unprofitable.

Let us end our discussion of these questions here.

Book IX

Chapter 1

In all friendships between dissimilar people, as we have said, it is proportion that produces equality and preserves the friendship; for example, in political friendship the shoemaker receives in return for his shoes what they are worth, and so do the weaver and the rest. In these cases, a common measure is provided in the form of money, and so everything is referred to this and measured by it.

1164a

But in erotic friendship the lover sometimes complains that his profound love is not requited (perhaps because he has no quality worthy of love), while the beloved often complains that the lover formerly promised him everything and now does nothing.

Things like this happen when the lover loves the beloved for pleasure, while the beloved loves the lover for utility, and these objects are no longer obtained by both of them. For if these are the reasons for the friendship, it is dissolved when they do not get what they were aiming at in their love; each was fond not of the other himself, but of his qualities, and since these do not last, such friendships do not last either. But friendship of character, since it exists for its own sake, does last, as we have said.

People quarrel when what they get is different from what they want, because not getting what one aims at is like getting nothing at all. Consider, for example, the person who promised a lyre-player that the better he sang the more he would receive, but, when the lyre-player asked him in the morning for what he had promised, said that he had given the lyre-player pleasure for pleasure. If this was what each had

164

wished, then that would have been enough. But if one wished for enjoyment, the other gain, and one has what he wants, while the other does not, things are not well with their partnership. It is what a person happens to require that he is anxious to get, and it is for this that he will give what he has.

But which one is to decide the worth of the service, the one who offers it, or the one who has benefited? The one who offers seems to leave it to the other person, as people say Protagoras used to do. For when he had given a lesson on anything, he used to ask the student to estimate the value of what he had learned, and took this as his fee. But in matters like this some people prefer the principle, 'A fixed fee for a man'.[68]

But those who, because of their extravagant promises, take the money first and then do none of the things they said they would do are, as one might expect, subject to complaints, since they are not fulfilling their agreement. The sophists, presumably, are compelled to do this because no one would pay for what they know; so they take the fee for something but do not deliver it and are, unsurprisingly, subject to complaints.

But where there is no contract for the service, people who offer it for the sake of the other person, as we have said, cannot be complained about, since this is the nature of friendship based on virtue; and the 1164b return should be made in accordance with rational choice, since it is rational choice that characterizes a friend and virtue. And this seems to be what those who have been accompanied on a course in philosophy ought to do; for philosophy's worth could not be measured in financial terms, nor could any honour match the service. But perhaps it is enough, as in the case of the gods or our parents, to give what we can.

When the gift is not like this, but made on a certain condition, the return in particular that should be made is presumably one that seems fair to both parties. If this is not possible, it would seem not only necessary but just that the person who received the benefit should assess the value. For if the one gets in return as much benefit as he conferred on the other, or as much as the other would have paid for his pleasure, he will have received what his original service was worth.

Indeed this is what appears to happen in market transactions. In some cities there are laws prohibiting legal action for breach of voluntary

---

[68] Hesiod, *Works and Days* 370.

contract, on the ground that one ought to dissolve a relationship with someone one has trusted in the same way that one entered into it; this is because the law considers that it is more just that the person to whom something is given should make the assessment than the person who gives it to him. For most things are not valued equally by those who have them and those who want them, since each group considers of great value what it possesses and what it offers; yet the return is made on the basis of the assessment by the recipient. But presumably the recipient should value a thing not at what it seems worth to him once he has got it, but at what he valued it at before he got it.

Chapter 2

Other puzzling questions include the following. Should someone always defer to his father and obey him in everything, or should he trust a doctor when he is ill, and appoint as a general someone skilled in war? Similarly, should someone help a friend rather than a good person, and show gratitude to a benefactor rather than offer a service to a companion, if he cannot do both?

It is, of course, no easy matter to make precise decisions in cases like this, because they allow all sorts of variations in respect of importance and unimportance, of what is noble, and of what is necessary. But it is quite clear that we should not give everything to the same person. In general, we should return a benefit instead of doing a favour for our companions, just as we should repay a debt instead of giving the money to a companion. But perhaps even this is not always so. For example, if you have been ransomed from kidnappers, should you ransom in return the person who freed you, whoever he is? Or if he has not been 1165a kidnapped, but asks for his money back, should you repay him, or ransom your own father instead? It seems that you should ransom your father even in preference to yourself.

As we have said, then, in general debts should be paid, but if a gift is overriding in its nobility or necessity, we should incline in favour of these considerations. Sometimes it is not even fair to return the equivalent of what one has received, when one person knows he is benefiting somebody good, while the repayment would be to somebody the other believes to be wicked. For sometimes you should not even lend in return to someone who has lent to you: he expected repayment when he lent to you as someone good, whereas you have no hope of it from someone bad. If this is really so, then, the demand is not fair; and even if it is not so, but you think it is, it would not seem at all odd for you to act like this. As we have often said, then, discussions of actions and feelings are as precise as their subject-matter.

That we should not make the same return to everyone, nor give everything to our fathers, as we do not sacrifice everything to Zeus, is pretty clear. And since we ought to give different things to parents, brothers, companions and benefactors, we should assign to each what is appropriate and fitting. This is what people actually seem to do: they invite their relatives to weddings, since they share the same family and hence its affairs; and they think that relatives especially ought to meet at funerals for the same reason.

It would seem that parents above all ought to be supported, since we think we owe it to them, and that it is nobler to support those who are responsible for our being than to support ourselves in this way. And we should render honour to our parents, as to the gods, but not every sort of honour. For we should not render the same honour to our father and our mother, nor should we render them the honour due to a wise person or a general, but that due to a father, and similarly that due to a mother.

To any older person, as well, we should render the honour appropriate to his age, by standing up, giving up our seat and so on. With companions and brothers we should be plain-speaking and share everything. To relatives, fellow-tribesmen and fellow-citizens and the rest we should always try to render what is appropriate, and compare the claims of each in the light of closeness of relation, virtue and usefulness. The comparison is easier when they are of the same class, and more of a job when they are different; and yet we should not for this reason shrink from the task, but decide the issue as best we can.

Chapter 3

Another puzzle that arises is whether or not to break off friendships with those who do not remain the same. Presumably there is nothing 1165b odd in breaking off friendships based on utility or pleasure when our friends no longer have these qualities. For it was the qualities we loved, and when they disappear, not loving is reasonable.

Still, we might complain if a person were to like us for utility or pleasure, but pretend that it was for our character. For, as we said at the start, most differences arise between friends when they are not friends in the way they think. So, if we are entirely mistaken in thinking that we are being loved for our character, and our friend is doing nothing to imply this, we have only ourselves to blame. But if we have been taken in by his pretence, we can justly complain against the deceiver – more justly even than we can against those who counterfeit coinage, in as much as the wrongdoing concerns something more honourable.

But if we accept another person as good, and he turns out to be an obvious villain, should we continue to love him? Or is that not impossible, if not everything is worthy of love, but only what is good? What is bad is not worthy of love nor should it be loved; we should not love what is bad, nor act like someone shameful, and we have already said that like is friendly to like.

Should it then be dissolved immediately? Or is this required not in all cases, but only when they are incurably wicked? If they could be reformed, we should save their character more than their property, in so far as character is better and more a part of friendship. But someone who does dissolve such a friendship would not seem to be doing anything odd, because he did not become the friend of a person like this. So if his friend has altered, and he cannot redeem him, he gives up.

But if one friend remained the same while the other became better and far excelled him in virtue, should the superior one treat the other as a friend? Surely he cannot? This becomes especially obvious when the gap between them is a large one, such as it is, for example, in friendships beginning in childhood. For if one still thinks as a child, while the other became the most superior kind of person, how could they be friends when they neither approve of the same things, nor find the same things enjoyable or painful? Not even with regard to each other will this be so, and without that they could not be friends, since it would not be possible for them to live together. But we have spoken about this already.

Then should the better person regard the other just as if he had never become his friend? Or should he not remember the close relationship they had? Just as we think that we ought to favour our friends over strangers, so also we should assign some consideration to past friends because of the former friendship, as long as it was not dissolved because of their excessive wickedness.

Chapter 4

The origin of relations of friendship towards our neighbours, and of the 1166a
characteristics by which we distinguish the various kinds of friendship,
seems to be in our relations to ourselves.

For some people define a friend as someone who wishes and does
what is good, or what appears to be good, for the sake of his friend; or
someone who wishes his friend to be and to live for his own sake – this
is the attitude of mothers towards their children, or of friends who have
come into conflict. Others define a friend as someone who spends time
with another and chooses the same things as he does; or someone who
shares in the sorrows and joys of his friend – and this quality too is
found in mothers in particular. It is by one or other of these characteristics that friendship is defined as well.

Each of these characteristics is found in the good person's relation to
himself, and in other people in so far as they think of themselves as good
– as we have said, virtue and the good person seem to be the standard in
each case. He is at one with himself, and desires the same things in his
soul considered as a whole. Therefore he wishes for himself what is
good and what appears to be good, and does it, since it is characteristic
of a good person to strive for what is good; and he does it for his own
sake, since he does it for the intellectual element, which is what each
person seems to be.

And he wishes himself to live and be preserved, and especially the
element with which he thinks. For being is a good to the good person,
and each person wishes for what is good for himself; and no one chooses
to have everything if he has first to become someone else (since as things
are god possesses the good), but only if he remains whatever he is. And
each person would seem to be the intellectual part, or primarily this.

And such a person wishes to spend time with himself, since he finds it
pleasant to do so. For his memories of his past actions delight him and
his hopes for the future are good, and so both are pleasant. And he has
in his intellect a wealth of subjects for contemplation.

And he, more than others, shares his own griefs and joys with himself,
since the same thing is always painful, the same thing pleasant, and not
one thing at one time, another at another. This, one might say, is
because he has nothing to regret.

So, because each of these characteristics belongs to the good person in relation to himself, and he stands in the same relation to his friend as to himself (his friend being another self), friendship too seems to be one of these characteristics, and those who have them to be friends.

Whether there is friendship towards oneself or not is a question we 1166b can put to one side for the present. From what we have said, however, and because the extreme of friendship is close to friendship of oneself, there would seem to be friendship in so far as someone is regarded as a plural entity.

It appears, however, that the characteristics we have mentioned belong even to the masses, bad as they are. Should we say, then, that they share in them only in so far as they are content with themselves and suppose themselves to be good? For no one who is altogether bad and wicked has them, or even appears to.

Indeed, even bad people scarcely have them, since they are in internal conflict, and have an appetite for one thing but wish for another; they are like incontinent people, since they choose harmful pleasures in preference to what seems good to them. There are others whose cowardice or laziness makes them shrink from doing what they believe to be best for themselves. And those who have committed many dreadful crimes and are despised for their wickedness run away from their lives and destroy themselves. And wicked people seek others with whom to spend their days, and they avoid themselves. For when they are by themselves they remember many disturbing actions and foresee others like them, whereas when they are with others they forget. Because they have no qualities worthy of love, they feel no relation of friendship to themselves. Nor, therefore, do people like this share their joys and griefs with themselves. For their soul is in a state of civil strife, and one element in it, because of its wickedness, grieves in abstaining from certain things, while the other element is pleased; the one draws them this way, the other that, as if tearing them apart. If a person cannot be pained and pleased at the same time, nevertheless after a short time he is pained because he was pleased, and he wishes these things had not become pleasant for him; for bad people are full of regret.

The bad person, then, appears not to be disposed in a friendly way even to himself, because he has nothing worthy of love. If to be like this is the height of wretchedness, we ought to avoid wickedness with all our might and try to be good; for this is how one can have a relation of friendship with oneself, and become a friend to another.

Chapter 5

Goodwill seems to be a characteristic of friendship, but still it is not friendship. For it can arise even towards people we do not know, and without their being aware of it, but friendship cannot. We have said this already. Nor is it even affection, since it does not involve either intensity of feeling or desire, both of which accompany affection. And affection involves intimacy, while goodwill can spring up suddenly, as it does 1167a towards competitors at the games. For people develop goodwill towards them and share in their wishes, but would not cooperate with them in any action: as we said, their goodwill comes into existence suddenly and their fondness is shallow.

Goodwill, then, seems to be the first principle of friendship, as pleasure through sight is first principle of love. For no one loves another if he has not been pleased beforehand by his appearance. But finding enjoyment in the form of the other does not mean that one loves him; this happens only when one longs for him in his absence and wants him to be there. So too, though people cannot be friends if they have not already developed goodwill for each other, those who have goodwill are nevertheless not friends; they merely wish what is good on those towards whom they have goodwill, and would not cooperate with them in any action or go to any trouble on their behalf.

By extending the scope of the word, then, one might describe goodwill as latent friendship, which becomes friendship as intimacy develops over time. It does not, however, become friendship for utility or pleasure, since goodwill does not arise for these reasons. For the recipient of a benefit does what is just in returning goodwill for what he has received, but someone who wishes for another's well-being in the hope of some advantage through him seems to have goodwill not to the other person, but rather to himself. In the same way, a person is not a friend to another if he looks after him with some reward in mind.

Generally speaking, however, goodwill develops because of some virtue and excellence, when one person appears noble or courageous or some such thing to another, as we suggested happens in the case of competitors at the games.

Chapter 6

Concord also appears to be a characteristic of friendship. For this reason, it is not agreement in belief, since this can occur even among people unknown to one another. Nor are people described as being in concord when they agree about just anything, for example, the heavens (since concord here has nothing to do with friendship), but a city is said to be in concord when people agree about what is beneficial, rationally choose the same things, and carry out common resolutions.

Things to be done, then, are what concord is concerned with, and of these only those that are important and are such that both parties or all the citizens can get what they want. A city, for example, is in concord when all the citizens think that public offices ought to be elective, or that they ought to make an alliance with Sparta, or that Pittacus[69] ought to govern, when he himself is willing.

But when each person, like those in *The Phoenissae*,[70] wants the same thing all for himself, then there is civil strife. For being in concord does not consist merely in each person's having the same thing in mind, whatever it may be, but in their having it in mind for the same person, 1167b as, for example, when the people and those of the better class both want the best individuals to govern; in this way it turns out that both sides get what they are aiming at.

Concord, then, seems to be political friendship, as indeed it is said to be, since it is concerned with what benefits people and what affects their lives. Concord like this is found among good people, since they are in concord with themselves and with each other, being as it were of the same mind (their wishes are constant, and do not flow this way and that, like currents in the sea); and they wish for what is just and beneficial, and aim at these in common as well. But bad people cannot be in concord, except to a small extent, just as they can be friends only to a small extent; for they try to get more than their share of advantages, while falling short in difficult jobs and public services. And since each wishes this for himself, he keeps a sharp eye on his neighbour and holds him back, because if people do not look out for the common interest, it is destroyed. So what happens is that they are in civil strife, pressing one another to do what is just while not wishing to do it themselves.

---

[69] *c.* 650–570 BCE. Statesman in Mytilene.
[70] Euripides, *Phoenissae* 590f.

Chapter 7

Benefactors seem to love their beneficiaries more than the beneficiaries love them, and this is discussed as if it were a paradox. It appears to most people that this happens because the beneficiaries are debtors, the benefactors creditors. Thus, just as in the case of loans debtors wish their creditors did not exist, while the creditors actually take thought for the safety of the debtors, so benefactors wish their beneficiaries to exist, since they expect gratitude in return, while the beneficiaries are not anxious to make such a return.

Epicharmus would argue, perhaps, that most people say this because they are 'looking on the bad side',[71] but it seems to be a human point of view; the masses do have poor memories, and aim more at being well treated than treating others well. But the cause would seem to be more of a natural one, and the case of creditors is not even similar. For they do not hold their debtors in affection, but wish for their safety just so that they can be repaid; whereas benefactors love and like their beneficiaries, even if they are of no use to them now and will not be in future.

The same happens with practitioners of skills; each likes his own product more than it would like him if it came alive. This happens 1168a especially perhaps with poets, since they have an excessive liking for their own poems, and are fond of them as if they were their own children. This, then, is what the case of benefactors is like, since what has been well treated is their product, and they therefore like them more than the product likes its producer.

The reason for this is that being is to all people something worthy of choice and love, and we exist by virtue of actuality (that is, by living and acting); and the product is, as it were, the producer in actuality, so he is fond of his product, because he is fond of his own existence. And this is natural, since what he is in capacity, his product reveals in actuality. At the same time, for the benefactor, what relates to his action is noble, so that he finds enjoyment in the person who is its object; for the beneficiary, however, there is nothing noble in the agent, but at most some advantage, and this is less pleasant and less worthy of love.

What is pleasant is the actuality of the present, hope for the future, and memory of the past; but what is most pleasant is what accompanies

---

[71] Epicharmus, fr. 146 Kaibel. Sicilian comic writer, who flourished during the first quarter of the fifth century. Various philosophical works were attributed to him by the ancients.

the actuality, and similarly it is the most worthy of love. For the producer, then, his product remains (since what is noble is lasting), but for the object of the action, the utility passes away. And the memory of noble things is pleasant, while that of useful things is not generally pleasant, or less so. The contrary, however, seems to be true of expectation. Also, affection is like production, while being loved is like being an object of action; and love and friendly qualities follow for those who play the greater part in action. Again, everyone is more fond of what has cost them effort; for example, those who have made their money are more fond of it than those who have inherited it. And while being well treated seems to require no effort, treating another well is hard work. This is also why mothers love their children more, since bringing them into the world requires more effort from the mothers, and they know better that the children are their own. It would seem that this is a feature of benefactors as well.

Chapter 8

There is also a puzzle about whether a person should love himself or someone else most of all; for people criticize those who like themselves most, and call them by the derogatory term 'self-lovers'. Indeed, it does seem that the bad person does everything for his own sake, the more so the more wicked he is; and so people reproach him for doing nothing of his own accord, for example. The good person, however, acts for the sake of what is noble, and the more so the better he is; and he acts for the sake of his friend, neglecting his own interest.

1168b   But the facts are not in harmony with these arguments, nor is this surprising. For people say that we ought to love most the one who is most a friend, and the one who is most a friend to another is he who wishes goods on the other for the other's sake, even if no one is to know it. But these characteristics are found most of all in a person's relation to himself, and so are all the others by which a friend is defined; for, as we have said, all the features of friendship towards others extend from this relation. All the proverbs agree on this as well; for example, 'A single soul',[72] and 'Friends hold things in common', and 'Equality is friendship', and 'The knee is nearer than the shin'.[73] All these apply most of

---

[72] Euripides, *Orestes* 1046.   [73] Theocritus, xvi.18.

all to a person's relation to himself, because he is most of all a friend to himself and so ought also to love himself most of all.

It is quite natural that there is a puzzle about which view we should follow, since both are plausible; presumably, then, we should separate arguments like this from one another and determine how far and in what way those on each side are true.

Perhaps things would be clear if we were to grasp what each side means by 'self-love'. Those who use it as a term of reproach describe as self-lovers those who assign themselves the larger share of money, honours and bodily pleasures. For it is these that the masses desire and take trouble over as if they were the greatest goods; and this is why they are objects of competition.

People who want more than their share of them are gratifying their appetites and their feelings in general, and the non-rational part of their soul. And since the masses are like this, the word has taken its meaning from the most common self-love. And because such self-love is bad, those who exhibit it are justly reproached. It is evidently those who assign things like this to themselves that the masses usually describe as self-lovers; for if someone always takes trouble that he of all people does what is just or temperate or whatever else is in accordance with the virtues, and in general always makes what is noble his own, no one will call him a self-lover or blame him.

But a person like this seems to be more of a self-lover. At any rate he assigns to himself what is noblest and best above all, and gratifies the most authoritative element within himself, obeying it in everything. And just as a city or any other organized body seems to be above all the most author-itative element within it, the same is true of a human being; and therefore someone who likes this part and gratifies it is most of all a self-lover.

Also, a person is described as self-controlled or incontinent according to whether his intellect is or is not in control, on the ground that this element constitutes each person. And it is acts involving reason that 1169a seem to be most of all our own and voluntary. It is clear, then, that this, or this most of all, is what each person is, and that the good person likes this most of all.

So he of all people is most a self-lover, but in a different way from the person who is reproached, being as unlike him as living according to reason is unlike living according to feelings, and the desire for what is noble unlike the desire for what seems advantageous.

Everyone approves of and praises those who take special trouble to act nobly. And if everyone strives for what is noble and strains to do the noblest actions, everything will be as it should be for the common interest, and individually each will have the greatest goods, since such is virtue.

So the good person should be a self-lover, since he will help himself as well as benefit others by doing noble acts, but the wicked person should not, because he will harm both himself and those around him by following his evil feelings. There is, then, a clash for the wicked person between what he ought to do and what he does; whereas what the good person does is the same as what he ought to do, since intellect always chooses what is best for itself, and the good person obeys his intellect.

It is true also of the good person that he does a great deal for his friends and his country, and will die for them if he must; he will sacrifice money, honours, and in general the goods for which people compete, procuring for himself what is noble. He would prefer a short period of intense pleasure to a long period of mild pleasure, a year of living nobly to many indifferent years, and a single noble and great action to many trivial ones. Presumably, this is what happens with those who die for others; it is indeed a great and noble thing that they choose for themselves. They will also sacrifice money on the condition that their friends gain more; while the friend gets money, he gets what is noble, and therefore assigns himself the greater good. Honours and public offices he deals with in the same way; he will sacrifice all of them for his friend, since for him this is noble and praiseworthy. It is quite reasonable, then, that he is thought to be good, since he prefers what is noble to everything. It is even possible to sacrifice actions for his friend, and it may be nobler to be responsible for his friend's acting than to act himself. In all praiseworthy actions, then, the good person is seen to
1169b assign himself the larger share of what is noble.

So, as we have said, we ought to be self-lovers. But in the way that the masses are, we should not.

Chapter 9

There is also a dispute about whether a happy person will need friends or not. People say that those who are blessed and self-sufficient have no need of friends, since they already have the things that are good, and, being self-sufficient, need nothing further. But a friend, since he is another self, provides what a person cannot provide by himself; hence the saying, 'When fortune is generous, what need of friends?'.[74]

But it seems odd, when we assign to the happy person all good things, not to give him friends, who seem to constitute the greatest of external goods. Again, if it is more characteristic of a friend to treat another well than to be treated well, and characteristic of the good person and of virtue to benefit people, and if it is nobler to treat friends well than strangers, the good person will need people whom he can treat well. This is why people wonder whether there is greater need of friends when our fortunes are good than when they are bad, since it is assumed that not only do we need people to benefit us when our fortunes are bad, but people whom we can benefit when our fortunes are good.

Surely it is also odd to make the blessed person solitary, since no one would choose to have all good things and yet be by himself. For a human is a social being and his nature is to live in the company of others. So this will be the case with the happy person as well, because he possesses the natural goods, and it is clearly better to spend his days with friends and good people than with strangers or anybody he happens to bump into. So the happy person does need friends.

What, then, do those who hold the first view mean, and in what way is it true? Perhaps the reason for it is that the masses think friends to be those who are useful. The blessed person will indeed have no need of such people, since he already has what is good. And he will have no need, or little need, of friends for pleasure (because his life is pleasant, it has no need of imported pleasure). Since he has no need of these sorts of friends, he seems not to need friends at all.

But this is presumably not true. As we said at the beginning, happiness is a kind of activity, and it is obvious that an activity comes into being and is not there for someone, like a possession. If being happy consists in living and engaging in activity, and the activity of the good person is good and pleasant in itself, as we said at the beginning; and if what is our own is pleasant; and if we are better able to contemplate our neighbours than ourselves, and their actions than our own; and if the good person finds pleasure in the actions of good people 1170a who are his friends (since they have both the qualities that are pleasant

---

[74] Euripides, *Orestes* 667.

by nature); then the blessed person will need friends like this, since he rationally chooses to contemplate actions that are good and his own, and the actions of a good person who is his friend are like this.

Again, people think that the happy person ought to live pleasantly. On his own, life would be difficult, since it is not easy by oneself continuously to engage in activity; but with others and in relation to them it is easier. So his activity will be more continuous, and will be pleasant in itself, which is what ought to happen in the case of a blessed person; the good person, in so far as he is good, enjoys actions that are in accordance with virtue, but is appalled by those done from vice, as the musician finds pleasure in noble tunes, but is pained by bad ones. Also, as Theognis points out,[75] a sort of training in virtue emerges from good people's living in each other's company.

But if we consider things more from the point of view of nature, a virtuous friend would seem worthy of choice by nature for a good person, since, as we have said, what is good by nature is for the good person good and pleasant in itself. People define animal life by the capacity for perception, and human life by the capacity for perception or thought. But the capacity is relative to its activity, and what really matters lies in the activity; so living in the real sense seems to be perceiving or thinking. And living is one of the things that are good and pleasant in themselves, since it is determinate, and the determinate is characteristic of the nature of the good. What is good by nature is also good for the good person, which is why life seems to be pleasant for everyone. But we must not consider here the case of a wicked and corrupt life, or of a life of pain; a life like this is indeterminate, as are its qualities. (In what follows, the issue of pain will be clarified.) But if life itself is good and pleasant (and it seems to be so from the fact that everyone desires it, especially those who are good and blessed, because their life is the most worthy of choice, and their being the most blessed); and if someone who sees perceives that he sees, and one who hears that he hears, and one who walks that he walks, and in the case of other activities there is similarly something that perceives that one is engaged in them, so that, if we perceive, we perceive that we perceive, and if we think, we perceive that we think; and if to perceive that we perceive or think is to perceive that we exist (since we saw that to exist is to perceive

---

[75] Theognis, 35.

or think); and if perceiving that we are alive is pleasant in itself (since 1170b
life is by nature a good, and perceiving some good thing as present in us
is pleasant); and if life is worthy of rational choice, and especially so for
good people, because to them being is good and pleasant (since they are
pleased when they perceive in themselves what is in itself good); and if
the good person is related to his friend as he is related to himself
(because his friend is another self); then, as his own being is worthy of
choice for each person, so that of his friend is worth choosing in the
same way, or almost the same way.

Someone's being we saw to be worth choosing because he perceives
that he is good, and perception like this is pleasant in itself. He ought
therefore at the same time to perceive the being of his friend, and this
will come about in their living together and exchanging words and
thoughts; this is what living together would seem to mean in the case of
people, and not, as in the case of cattle, grazing in the same place.

So if being is worth choosing in itself for the blessed person, since it is
by its nature good and pleasant, and if the being of his friend is pretty
much the same, a friend will also be worthy of choice. Whatever is
worthy of choice for him he ought to have, or else he will be lacking in
that respect. Anyone who is to be happy, then, will need virtuous
friends.

Chapter 10

Should we, then, make as many friends as possible? Or is it like
hospitality, of which it has been said, aptly it seems, that one should
have 'neither many guests, nor none'?[76] Will this be the proper thing in
friendship as well, neither to be without friends nor to have an excessive
number of them?

With friends for utility, this suggestion seems quite right, since
returning favours to many people is laborious, and life is too short to do
it. So more friends than suffice for one's own life are superfluous, and a
hindrance to noble living; there is therefore no need of them. In the case
of friends for pleasure, too, a few are enough, as a little seasoning in
food is enough.

As regards good people, however, should we have as many as possible

---

[76] Hesiod, *Works and Days* 715.

as friends, or is there some limit to their number, as there is to the number that can constitute a city? For ten people will not make a city, but a hundred thousand would no longer be a city; presumably, however, the right amount is not a single number, but any number

1171a within a certain range. So for friends too there is some limit to their number, and presumably this is the largest number in the company of whom one can live, because that seemed to be the most characteristic element in friendship. And it is obvious that one cannot live in the company of many people and share oneself between them.

Again, they too ought to be friends with one another, if they are all to spend their days together, and this is a difficult task among a large number of people. It also becomes hard to share personally in the joys and sorrows of many, because it is likely to turn out that one shares the pleasure of one and the distress of another at the same time. Presumably, then, it is as well not to seek as many friends as possible, but as many as are sufficient for living in each other's company – in fact it does not even seem possible to be a close friend to many. This is why it also seems impossible to be in love with more than one person, since love tends to be a sort of excess of friendship, and it is felt towards a single person; so close friendship, too, is only with a few.

This seems to be what happens in practice, because friendships of companionship are not formed between large numbers of people, and the celebrated cases are spoken of as between two people. Those, however, who have many friends and treat everybody they meet as if they were close to them seem to be friends of nobody, except in the sense that fellow-citizens are friends. These people are called obsequious. In the way fellow citizens are friends, indeed, one can be a friend to many and yet not obsequious, but a genuinely good person; but one cannot have many friends for their virtue and for their own sake. We must be content to find even a few friends like this.

Chapter 11

Is the need for friends greater in good fortune or in ill fortune? For they are sought after in both, since in ill fortune people need help, while in good fortune people need others to live with, and to benefit, because they wish to treat others well. Friendship is in fact more necessary in ill fortune, and so it is useful friends that are called for in that instance.

But it is nobler in good fortune, so we also seek good people for friends, since it is more worthy of choice to confer benefits on such people and to spend time with them.

The very presence of friends is also pleasant, both in good and ill fortune, since pain's burden is lightened when friends share one's distress. So one might be puzzled about whether they, as it were, share the load, or whether it is not this, but their presence, through its pleasantness, and the awareness of their sharing the distress, which decrease the pain. Whether these are the reasons for our loads' being lightened, or whether there are others, we can put to one side; what we have described at any rate does seem to happen.

Their presence, however, appears to consist in a mixture of things. The sight of one's friends is pleasant in itself, especially if one is in ill fortune, 1171b and it helps in relieving our pain, because a friend tends to console us both by the sight of him and by what he says, if he is tactful, knowing our character and what pleases and pains us. But being aware of his pain at our own ill fortune is painful, since everyone tries to avoid causing pain to his friends. This is why someone of a manly nature will take care that his friends do not share his own pain. Unless he is exceptionally insensitive to pain, he cannot bear their becoming pained; and in general he does not allow people to lament with him because he is not himself given to lamentation. But womankind and effeminate men do enjoy people grieving with them, and love them as friends who share their distress. But in all things, of course, one ought to imitate the better type.

The presence of friends in good fortune, however, involves passing the time pleasantly, and the thought of their pleasure in the good things we have. For this reason it seems that we ought readily to call upon our friends to share our fortune when it is good, since doing good is noble, but hesitate to do so when it is bad. For we should share troubles as little as possible, which gives rise to the saying, 'Enough is my own misfortune'. We should summon friends most of all when they are likely to benefit us greatly at little trouble to themselves.

Conversely it is presumably proper to go readily to those in misfortune without being asked; for it is characteristic of a friend to confer benefits, especially on those who are in need and have not asked for them, since this is more noble and more pleasant for both. When the fortunes of our friends are good, we should join readily in what they do, since they need friends for this as well, but be circumspect in receiving benefits, since eagerness to be benefited is not a noble thing. Presumably, though, we should avoid any rejection's giving rise to a reputation for unpleasantness, since this does happen sometimes.

The presence of friends, then, seems worth choosing in all circumstances.

Chapter 12

So, as what the lover likes most is the sight of his beloved, and this is the perception he chooses over the others, assuming that it is on this that love depends most for its being and its source, is it not the same with friends, so that what they find most worthy of choice is living together? For friendship is community, and as we are in relation to ourselves, so we are in relation to a friend. And, since the perception of our own being is worthy of choice, so is that of the being of a friend. This perception's activity arises in our living together, so that, as one would expect, this is what we aim at. And whatever being consists in for each, or whatever the end for which each chooses to live, it is this that they wish to pursue in the company of their friends. So some drink together, some dice together, others join in athletic games and hunt together, or philosophize together, each type spending their days together in that which they like most in life; for since they wish to live with their friends, they do these things and share in them as much as they can.

1172a

The friendship of bad people therefore turns out to be an evil. For, because of their lack of stability, they share in bad pursuits, and turn evil through becoming like one another. But the friendship of good people is good, and increases through their association. They seem to become even better through their activity and their improving each other, because each takes impressions from the other of what meets with his approval, which gives rise to the saying, 'From noble people nobility. . .'.

So much, then, for our account of friendship. Next we must discuss pleasure.

Book X

Chapter 1

After this our next task is presumably to discuss pleasure, because pleasure seems to be especially closely associated with beings like us. This is why people educate the young by steering them in the right direction with pleasure and pain. Also, enjoying and hating the right things seem the most important factors in virtue of character, because pleasure and pain run through the whole of life; and they have weighty significance for virtue and the happy life, since people rationally choose what is pleasant, and avoid what is painful. It would seem, then, that these are the last things that should be ignored, especially since there is much dispute about them: some say that pleasure is the good, while others say on the contrary that it is thoroughly bad.

Some of those who say it is bad presumably say this because they are convinced that this is how things are. Others, however, say it because they believe that it is better with a view to how we live to represent pleasure as a bad thing, even if it is not. For they think that the masses are inclined towards it and are slaves to their pleasures, and that we ought therefore to lead them in the opposite direction, since in this way they might arrive at the mean point. But surely this view is incorrect. For in matters to do with feelings and actions, arguments are less reliable than the facts; so when they conflict with the facts of perception, they are scorned, and undermine the truth as well. For if a person who 1172b criticizes pleasure is once seen aiming at it, the reason for his inclining towards it is thought to be that he regards all pleasure as worth pursuing, because it is not characteristic of the masses to draw distinctions. True arguments, then, seem to be the most useful, not only in the acquisition of knowledge, but in how we live. For since they are in harmony with the facts, they are believed, and for that reason they spur those who understand them to live in accordance with them.

Enough of such matters, then; let us consider the views that have been expressed about pleasure.

Chapter 2

Eudoxus thought pleasure was the good because he saw that all things, whether rational or not, aim at it. And in everything, he says, what is worthy of choice is good, and what is most worthy of choice is best; thus the fact that everything is borne towards the same thing shows that this is what is best for all, since each thing finds its own good, as it finds its own food; and that which is good for all things and at which all aim is the good.

His arguments were accepted more because of the virtue of his character than on their own account. For since he seemed remarkably temperate, it seemed that he was not saying these things because he was a friend of pleasure, but that this was really how things were. He thought that the matter was just as clear if one considered it from the opposite point of view. Pain, he thought, is in itself something to be avoided by all, and therefore, similarly, its contrary is something to be chosen by all. What is the most worth choosing is what we choose neither because of nor for the sake of something else. And everyone agrees that pleasure is like this, since no one asks for justification of anyone's being pleased, on the assumption that pleasure is worthy of choice in itself. He said too that pleasure, when it is added to any other good, such as acting in a just or temperate manner, makes the other good more worthy of choice; and that the good is increased by the addition of itself.

This last argument, at least, seems to represent it as one good among others, and no more a good than any other, because any good thing is more worthy of choice when another good is added to it than it is on its own. Indeed, it is with an argument like this that Plato destroys the claim of pleasure to be the good:[77] the life of pleasure is more worthy of

---

[77] Plato, *Philebus* 60c–61a.

choice with the addition of intelligence than without it, and if the mixture is better, pleasure is not the good, because the good cannot become more worthy of choice by anything's being added to it. And clearly nothing else can be the good either, if it becomes more worthy of choice with the addition of anything that is good in itself. What, then, is there that is like this, and that we share in? This is what we are looking for.

People who object that what all things aim at is not good are talking nonsense: whatever seems to all to be the case, we say is the case. And 1173a the person who attacks this belief will not generally have anything more convincing to say. If it were creatures without intellect that desired pleasures, there might be something in what they said; but if intelligent beings do so as well, what sense can be made of it? Presumably even in the lower animals there is some element better than themselves that aims at their proper good.

Nor does the argument about the contrary of pleasure seem plausible. They say that if pain is an evil, it does not follow that pleasure is a good, because evil is also opposed to evil, and both are opposed to what is neither good nor evil. This is fair enough, but is not true in the case we are discussing. For if both were evils, they ought both to be things to be avoided, and if neither is an evil, neither ought to be something to be avoided, or they should be so to the same extent. But people manifestly avoid the one as an evil, and choose the other as a good; so this is the way they are opposed to one another.

Chapter 3

Again, if pleasure is not a quality, this does not prevent its being a good, because the activities of virtue are not qualities either; nor is happiness.

But they say that the good is determinate, whereas pleasure is indeterminate, since it admits of degrees. If they make this judgement on the basis of the experience of pleasure, the same will apply in the cases of justice and the other virtues. In respect of these, people are plainly said to have a certain character, and to act in accordance with the virtues, to a greater or lesser degree, since people can be more just or more courageous, and one can act in a just or temperate way to a greater or lesser degree.

But if their judgement is based on the pleasures, surely they are not giving us the real reason, if some pleasures are in fact unmixed and others mixed? And why should pleasure not be like health, which is determinate despite admitting of degrees? For it does not consist in the same proportion in everyone, nor is it even always the same one proportion in the same person, but even when it is fading it remains up to a point, and differs in degree. So the same may go for pleasure as well.

And they assume the good to be complete, and processes and comings-to-be to be incomplete, and try to represent pleasure as a process and a coming-to-be. But it would seem that they are wrong, and that pleasure is not a process, since quickness and slowness seem to be proper to every process, if not in itself – as, for example, with the cosmos – then in relation to something else. But neither of these is true 1173b of pleasure. For though one can become pleased quickly, as one can become angry quickly, one cannot be pleased quickly, not even in relation to another person; we can, however, walk, grow and so on quickly. So, while one can change quickly or slowly into a state of pleasure, one cannot quickly engage in the activity in accordance with it, that is, be pleased quickly.

And how could it be a coming-to-be? For, it seems, not any chance thing comes to be from any other chance thing, but things are resolved into that from which they came to be; and where pleasure is the coming to be of something, pain would be the destruction of it.

They say as well that pain is a deficiency in our natural being, and that pleasure is replenishment. But these experiences are bodily; so if pleasure is replenishment of our natural being, that in which the replenishment takes place will experience pleasure. It will therefore be the body that does so. But this does not seem to be true. The replenishment, then, is not pleasure, though one would be pleased when the replenishment was taking place, as one would be pained if one were being cut. This belief seems to have arisen from consideration of the pains and pleasures connected with eating: because we have developed a need and experienced pain beforehand, we take pleasure in the replenishment. But this does not happen in the case of all pleasures: those of learning are painless, as are, among those involved in perception, the pleasures of smell, and many sounds, sights, memories and hopes as well. Of what, then, will they be the comings-to-be? For no deficiency of anything has arisen, of which there might come to be a replenishment.

Against those who bring up disgraceful pleasures, we could argue that these are not pleasant. For if they are pleasant to people in a bad condition, we should not think that they are also pleasant, except to these people, just as we should not think that things that are healthy, sweet or bitter to sick people are such, except to them, or that things that appear white to those with diseased eyes are such, except to them.

Or we might argue in the following way: that the pleasures are worthy of choice, but not when they come from these sources, as wealth, for example, is worth choosing, but not at the price of being a traitor, or health, but not at the price of eating anything whatsoever. Or perhaps pleasures differ in species; those from noble sources are different from those from bad ones, and we cannot experience the pleasure of the just person without being just, nor that of the musical person without being musical, and similarly in the other cases.

The difference between a friend and a flatterer seems to make it plain that pleasure is not good, or that pleasures differ in species. For in associating with us the friend seems to have his eye on the good, the flatterer on what is pleasant; and the flatterer is criticized, while the friend is praised, on the ground that he is associating with us for 1174a different reasons.

And no one would choose to live the whole of his life with the mind of a child, even if he were to take the utmost pleasure in what pleases children, or choose to enjoy doing some terribly disgraceful deed, even if he would never suffer any pain as a consequence.

And there are many things we should be concerned to have even if they brought no pleasure with them, such as seeing, remembering, knowing, possessing the virtues. Even if pleasures necessarily accompany these, it makes no difference, since we should choose them even if no pleasure arose from them.

It seems to be clear, then, that pleasure is not the good, that not every pleasure is worthy of choice, and that some pleasures are worthy of choice in themselves, differing from others in species or in their sources.

Enough said, then, about pleasure and pain.

Chapter 4

What pleasure is, or what sort of thing it is, will become clearer if we take up the question again from the beginning.

Seeing seems at any moment to be complete, because it does not lack anything that will come to be later and complete its form. And pleasure seems to be like this as well, since it is a whole, and at no time can one find a pleasure such that, if it comes to be for a longer time, its form will become complete.

For this reason it is not a process either, since every process – building, for example – takes time and has an end, and is complete when it has produced what it aims at; it is complete, therefore, in the whole time it takes, or at the final moment. And each process is incomplete during those processes that constitute its parts – the time it takes, in other words – and these parts differ in form from the whole and from each other. For there is a difference between placing stones together and fluting a column, and these are both different from the production of the temple. The production of the temple is complete, since it needs nothing further to achieve what was proposed, while that of the foundation and the triglyph is incomplete, since each is the production of a part. They differ in form, then, and one cannot find at any particular moment a process complete in form, but, if at all, only in the whole time. The same goes for walking and the other processes. For if locomotion is a process from one place to another, there are differences of form here as well – flying, walking, jumping, and so on. And not only this, but even in walking itself there are differences: the starting-point and the finishing-point are not the same in the whole racecourse as they are in a part of it, or in one part as in another; nor is traversing the length of this line the same as traversing the length of that, since one does not merely travel along a line, but a line in a certain place, and this line is in a different place from that.

1174b We have discussed process in detail in another work, but it does seem that it is not complete at every moment, and that the many movements are incomplete and different in form, since the points from where they begin and where they end give them their form. But the form of pleasure is complete at any given moment, so it is clear that it is different from a process, and that pleasure is something whole and complete. This would seem true also from the fact that a process must take time, whereas being pleased does not, since what takes place at the present moment is a kind of whole.

It is also clear from these considerations that it is wrong to say that there is a process or a coming-to-be of pleasure. For not everything can be so described, but only what has parts and is not a whole; for there is no coming-to-be of seeing, or a point, or a unit, and none of these is either a process or a coming-to-be. Thus, since it is a whole, there is no coming-to-be of pleasure either.

Every sense engages in activity in relation to its object, and its activity is complete when it is in good condition in relation to the noblest of its objects. For this seems in particular to be the nature of complete activity, and we can assume it to be irrelevant whether one says that it is the sense that engages in activity or the subject in which it exists. In the case of each sense, then, the best activity will be that of the subject in the best condition in relation to the best of that sense's objects.

And this activity will be the most complete and the most pleasant. For there is a pleasure corresponding to every sense, just as there is to thought and contemplation; and it is most pleasant when it is most complete, and most complete when the subject is in good condition and it occurs in relation to the best of its objects. Pleasure completes the activity, but not in the same way as the object of the sense and the sense complete it when they are both good, just as health and the doctor are not responsible in the same way for one's being healthy. For it is obvious that a pleasure comes about corresponding to each of the senses, since we speak of sights and sounds as pleasant; and it is obvious too that it comes about most of all whenever the sense is at its best and engaged in activity in relation to the best sort of object. When both object and subject of perception are at their best, there will always be pleasure, since what will produce it and what will experience it are both present. Pleasure completes the activity not as the inherent state does, but as a sort of supervenient end, like the bloom on the faces of young men. So long, then, as the objects of intellect or perception, and the faculties of judgement or contemplation, are as they should be, there will be 1175a pleasure in the activity. For when that which experiences and that which produces the experience remain similar, and are in the same relation to one another, the same thing naturally comes about.

How is it, then, that no one is continuously pleased? Is it that one grows weary? For nothing human is capable of continuous activity, and so no continuous pleasure comes about, since pleasure follows upon the activity. And some things delight us when they are new, but less later, for the same reason. For at first our thought is stimulated and engages vigorously in activity in relation to them, as happens with people's sense of sight when they are looking closely at something; but afterwards our activity is not like this and we lose interest, and for this reason the pleasure is dimmed as well.

Because everyone aims at life, we might think that everyone desires pleasure. Life is a kind of activity, and each person engages in activity in relation to those objects and with those faculties that he likes best; the musician, for example, engages in activity with his hearing in relation to songs, the student with his thought in relation to what he studies, and so on in each case. Pleasure completes the activities, and therefore also life, which they desire. It is reasonable, then, for them to aim at pleasure as well, since for each person it completes life, and life is something worth choosing.

But whether we choose life for the sake of pleasure or pleasure for the sake of life is a question we may dismiss for the present. For they appear to be bound closely together and not to admit of separation, since pleasure does not occur without activity, and it completes every activity as well.

Chapter 5

For this reason, pleasures also seem to differ in species, because we assume that things of different species are completed by different things. This is apparently what happens with natural and artificial objects, such as animals, trees, a picture, a statue, a house, or a tool. Similarly, we assume that activities that differ in species are also completed by things differing in species. The activities of thought differ in species from those of the senses, and both differ among themselves; so therefore do the pleasures that complete them.

This is evident also from the fact that each of the pleasures is closely related to the activity it completes. For the pleasure proper to an activity enhances it, because those who engage in activity with pleasure show better and more accurate judgement. It is people who enjoy geometry, for example, who become geometricians and understand each aspect of it better, and similarly lovers of music, building and so on improve in their own proper sphere by finding enjoyment in it. And the pleasures 1175b enhance the activities, and what enhances an activity is proper to it; and what are proper to things different in species are themselves different in species.

This is even more evident from the fact that activities are hindered by pleasures arising from different activities. Lovers of the flute are incapable of paying attention to a discussion once they overhear someone playing the flute, since they find more enjoyment in flute-playing than in their present activity; so the pleasure connected with the flute ruins the activity of discussion. This same thing happens in other cases as well, when a person engages in activity in two spheres at the same time; the more pleasant activity pushes aside the other, the more so if the difference in pleasure is a large one, even to the point where the other activity ceases. This is why, when we enjoy something a great deal, we do not really do anything else, and when we are only mildly pleased by something, we do other things; people who eat sweets in the theatre, for example, do it most when the acting is bad.

And since activities are made more rigorous, longer lasting and better by their proper pleasure, and impaired by foreign pleasures, it is clear that the two kinds of pleasure are very different. For foreign pleasures do almost what the pains proper to an activity do; the pains proper to activities ruin them, so that if, for example, someone finds writing or calculating unpleasant and painful, he does not write or calculate, since the activity is painful. So an activity is affected in contrary ways by the pleasures and pains proper to it, those occurring in relation to the activity in itself. And, as we have said, foreign pleasures produce much the same result as pain, since they ruin the activity, though not in the same way.

Since activities differ in their goodness and badness, and some are worthy of choice, some to be avoided, others neither, the same goes for pleasures, each activity's having its own proper pleasure. Thus the pleasure proper to a virtuous activity is good, and that proper to a wicked one bad, because appetites for noble objects are to be praised, those for disgraceful things blamed. And the pleasures in activities are more proper to them than the desires for them, since the desires are distinct both in time and in nature, while the pleasures are closely related to the activities, and are so difficult to distinguish that there is a question whether the activity and the pleasure are the same. Nevertheless, pleasure does not seem to be thought or perception, since that would be odd. But because they are not found separately they appear to some people to be the same.

As activities differ, then, so do pleasures. Sight differs from touch in 1176a purity, as do hearing and smell from taste, and so their pleasures also differ in the same way. The pleasures of thought differ in turn from these, and within each class some differ from others.

Each animal seems to have its own proper pleasure, as it has its own characteristic activity, since its proper pleasure will be that in line with the activity it engages in. This will be evident if we consider each kind as well. A horse, a dog and a human being have different pleasures; and, as Heraclitus says, a donkey would choose sweepings over gold, since donkeys find food more pleasant than gold.[78] So the pleasures of animals that differ in species themselves differ in species, and it is plausible that those of a single species do not differ.

But, in the case of human beings at any rate, they do vary a great deal, since the same things delight some people and pain others, and while to some they are painful and hateful, to others they are pleasant and worthy of love. This happens too with sweet things. For the same things do not seem sweet to a feverish as to a healthy person, or hot to a sick as to a fit person; and the same thing happens in other cases. But in all such things, it seems that what is so is what appears so to the good person. If this view is right, as it seems to be, and virtue – that is, the good person in so far as he is good – is the measure of each thing, then pleasures will be what appear so to him, and pleasant things will be what he enjoys. And if things that he finds disagreeable appear pleasant to someone, that is not surprising, since there are many ways for people to become ruined and perverted. The things are not pleasant, except to these people, with this disposition.

Clearly, then, we should say that those that everyone agrees to be disgraceful are not pleasures, except to people who have been ruined. But of those that seem good, what kind of pleasure, or what particular pleasure, should we say is the pleasure characteristic of a human being? Or, since the pleasures follow upon the activities, will it not be clear from the activities? So whether the complete and blessed person has one activity or several, the pleasures that complete these will be said to be the pleasures really characteristic of a human being, and the rest will be so in a secondary and less real sense, as are the activities.

---

[78] Heraclitus 22 B 9 DK.

Chapter 6

Now that we have discussed the virtues, friendships and pleasures, it remains for us to offer an outline account of happiness, since we assume it to be the end in human affairs. Our argument will be more concise if we first sum up what has been said already.

We said, then, that it is not a state, since if it were it might be possessed by someone asleep all his life, living a vegetable existence, or someone suffering the greatest misfortunes. So if this is implausible, we 1176b should put it rather in the class of activities, as we said above. And some activities are necessary, that is, worth choosing for the sake of something else, while others are worthy of choice in themselves; clearly, happiness must be classed as one of those worthy of choice in themselves and not as one of those worth choosing for the sake of something else. For happiness lacks nothing, but is self-sufficient; and an activity is worthy of choice in itself when nothing is sought from it beyond the activity. Actions in accordance with virtue seem like this, since doing noble and good actions is worthy of choice in itself.

But pleasurable amusements also seem to be in this class; for people do not choose them for the sake of other things, since they are more harmed than benefited by them, through failing to take care of their bodies and their property. And most of those called happy have recourse to pastimes like this, which is why those who are adroit in them are highly esteemed at the courts of tyrants; they offer themselves as pleasant purveyors of what the tyrants are after, and the tyrants want people like this. And so these amusements seem to be connected with happiness, because those in positions of power spend their leisure time on them.

But presumably people like this prove nothing, since virtue and intellect, from which come good activities, do not depend on positions of power. And if these people, never having tasted pure and gracious pleasure, have recourse to bodily pleasures, that is no reason to believe these pleasures to be more worthy of choice, since children also believe that what they give honour to is best. So it is to be expected that, just as different things appear honourable to children and adults, so it will be with good people and bad.

As we have often said, then, what is honourable and pleasant is what is so for the good person. And for each person the activity that accords with his own proper state is the most worthy of choice, and therefore for the good person it is that which accords with virtue.

Happiness, then, does not consist in amusement, because it would be absurd if our end were amusement, and we laboured and suffered all of our lives for the sake of amusing ourselves. For we choose virtually everything for the sake of something else, except happiness, since it is the end; but serious work and exertion for the sake of amusement is manifestly foolish and extremely childish. Rather, as Anacharsis[79] puts it, what seems correct is amusing ourselves so that we can engage in some serious work, since amusement is like relaxation, and we need 1177a relaxation because we cannot continuously exert ourselves. Relaxation, then, is not an end, since it occurs for the sake of activity.

And the happy life seems to be one in accordance with virtue, and this implies a level of seriousness, and is not spent in amusement. And we say that serious things are better than funny or amusing ones, and that in every case the activity of the better person, or the better part of a person, is more serious, more virtuous; and the activity of what is better is superior, and for this very reason more conducive to happiness. And absolutely anyone, a slave no less than the best of people, can enjoy the bodily pleasures; but no one attributes a share in happiness to a slave, unless he also attributes to him a share in the life we live. For happiness does not consist in occupations like this, but in activities in accordance with virtue, as we have also said before.

Chapter 7

If happiness is activity in accordance with virtue, it is reasonable to expect that it is in accordance with the highest virtue, and this will be the virtue of the best element. Whether this best element is intellect or something else we think naturally rules and guides us and has insight into matters noble and divine, and whether it is divine or just the most divine element within us, its activity, in accordance with its own proper virtue, will be complete happiness.

That this activity is that of contemplation we have already said. This would seem to agree both with our earlier discussion and with the truth. For this is the highest activity, intellect being the highest element in us,

[79] Primarily legendary Scythian prince, said to have travelled in Greece in the sixth century and become famous for his wisdom.

and its objects are the highest objects of knowledge. And it is also the most continuous, since we can contemplate more continuously than we can do anything. And we think that happiness must have pleasure mixed in with it; and the most pleasant of activities in accordance with virtue is agreed to be that in accordance with wisdom. At any rate, philosophy seems to involve pleasures remarkable for their purity and stability, and it is reasonable to expect that those who have knowledge will pass their time more pleasantly than those who are still in search of it. And the self-sufficiency that is spoken of will belong to the activity of contempla-tion most of all. For though a wise person, a just person, and anyone with any other virtue, all require the necessities of life, nevertheless, when they are adequately provided with such things, the just person will need people as associates in and objects of his just actions, and the same is true of the temperate person, the courageous person and each of the others; but the wise person can contemplate even when he is by himself, the more so the wiser he is. Maybe he can do it better with collaborators, but he is nevertheless the most self-sufficient.   1177b

Again, contemplation alone seems to be liked for its own sake, since nothing results from it apart from the fact that one has contemplated, whereas from the practical virtues, to a greater or lesser extent, we gain something beyond the action. Again, happiness seems to depend on leisure, because we work to have leisure, and wage war to live in peace. The activity of the practical virtues occurs in politics or war, and actions in these spheres seem to involve exertion. This seems entirely so as regards those in war, since no one chooses to make war, or even starts a war, for the sake of making war; for if someone turned his friends into enemies to bring about battles and killings he would seem utterly murderous. But the activity of a politician also involves exertion, and, apart from the business of politics itself, it is designed to secure power and honours, or at least happiness for himself and the citizens, which is different from politics and which we clearly pursue as something different.

So, among actions performed in accordance with virtue, those in politics and war are distinguished by their nobility and extent, but they involve exertion, aim at some end, and are not worthy of choice for their own sake. The activity of intellect, on the other hand, in so far as it involves contemplation, seems superior in its seriousness, to aim at no end beyond itself, and to have its own proper pleasure, which augments the activity; it seems also to possess self-sufficiency, time for leisure, and freedom from fatigue, as far as these are humanly possible. And clearly this activity also involves whatever else is attributed to the blessed person. Thus it will be complete happiness for a human being – if it consumes a complete span of life, because there is nothing incomplete in matters of happiness.

Such a life is superior to one that is simply human, because someone lives thus, not in so far as he is a human being, but in so far as there is some divine element within him. And the activity of this divine element is as much superior to that in accordance with the other kind of virtue as the element is superior to the compound. If the intellect, then, is something divine compared with the human being, the life in accordance with it will also be divine compared with human life. But we ought not to listen to those who exhort us, because we are human, to think of human things, or because we are mortal, think of mortal things. We ought rather to take on immortality as much as possible, and do all that we can to live in accordance with the highest element within us; for

1178a even if its bulk is small, in its power and value it far exceeds everything.

It would seem, too, to constitute each person, since it is his authoritative and better element; it would be odd, then, if he were to choose not his own life, but something else's.

And what we said above will apply here as well: what is proper to each thing is by nature best and pleasantest for it; for a human being, therefore, the life in accordance with intellect is best and pleasantest, since this, more than anything else, constitutes humanity. So this life will also be the happiest.

Chapter 8

The life in accordance with the other kind of virtue is happy in a secondary way, since the activities in accordance with it are human. For we do just actions, courageous actions, and the other actions in accordance with the virtues, in relation to each other, observing what is proper to each in contracts, services and actions of all kinds, and in feelings as well; and all of these are manifestly human. Some feelings seem in fact to have their origin in the body, and virtue of character in many ways to be closely bound up with the feelings.

Practical wisdom, too, is tied up with virtue of character, and this with practical wisdom, since the first principles of practical wisdom are in accordance with the virtues of character, and correctness in the virtues of character is in accordance with practical wisdom. And since they are also united with the feelings, the virtues of character must be concerned with the compound. Because the virtues of the compound are human, so are the life and happiness in accordance with them. The virtue of intellect, however, is separate. Let us leave it at that, since a detailed account would be beyond the scope of our project.

It would seem also to require external means to a small extent, or to a smaller extent than virtue of character. Let us accept that they both require the necessities of life, and to an equal extent, since even though the politician expends more effort on matters of the body and suchlike, any difference here would be a small one; nevertheless, in what they need for their activities, there will be a big difference. For the generous person will need money for doing generous actions; and the just person will need it for repaying debts, since wishes are uncertain, and even those who are not just pretend that they wish to act justly. And the courageous person will need power, and the temperate person opportunity, if they are to accomplish any of the actions that accord with their virtue. For how else will he, or any of the others, make manifest what he is?

It is debated as well whether it is the rational choice or the actions that are more really characteristic of virtue, on the assumption that it 1178b depends on both. Its being complete would clearly involve both, but for actions many things are needed, and the greater and nobler the actions, the greater the number of things needed. But a person who is contemplating needs none of these, for that activity at any rate; indeed, one might say that they are even obstacles, to contemplation at least. But in so far as he is a human being and lives together with a number of others, he chooses to do actions in accordance with virtue; he will therefore need such things for the living of a human life.

That complete happiness consists in some contemplative activity is also apparent from the following. We assume the gods to be supremely blessed and happy; but what sorts of actions should we attribute to them? Just actions? But will they not obviously be ridiculous if they make contracts, return deposits and so on? Courageous acts, then, enduring what is fearful and facing dangers because it is noble to do so? Or generous acts? To whom will they give? And it will be absurd if they have money or anything like it. And what would their temperate acts consist in? Is such praise not cheap, since they have no bad appetites? If we were to run through them all, anything to do with actions would appear petty and unworthy of the gods.

Nevertheless, everyone assumes that they are at least alive and therefore engage in activity, since we do not take them to sleep like Endymion.[80] So if we remove from a living being the possibility of action, and furthermore the very possibility of producing anything, what is left apart from contemplation? So the god's activity, which is superior in blessedness, will be contemplative; and therefore the human activity most akin to this is the most conducive to happiness.

There is an indication of this in the fact that the other animals have no share in happiness, being completely deprived of the activity in question. For while the life of the gods is entirely blessed, and that of human beings is so to the extent that it contains something like this sort of activity, none of the other animals is happy, because they have no share at all in contemplation. Happiness, then, extends as far as contemplation, and the more contemplation there is in one's life, the happier one is, not incidentally, but in virtue of the contemplation, since this is honourable in itself. Happiness, therefore, will be some form of contemplation.

But because the happy person is human, he will also need external prosperity; for human nature is not self-sufficient for contemplation, but the body must be healthy and provided with food and other care. Nevertheless, we should not think that someone who is going to be happy will need many substantial things, just because one cannot be blessed without external goods. For neither self-sufficiency nor action depends on excess, and we can do noble actions without ruling over land and sea, because we can act in accordance with virtue even from modest resources. This can be seen quite clearly, since private individuals seem to do good actions no less – indeed more – than those in positions of power. And it is enough to have moderate resources, since the life of a person whose activity conforms with virtue will be happy. Solon, too, was presumably right in his portrayal of happy people, when he said that they had been modestly furnished with external goods, but had

1179a

---

[80] Loved by Selene, goddess of the moon, Endymion was made immortal, and sleeps in a cave on Mt Latmus in Caria.

done what he regarded as the noblest actions and had lived temperately. For people can do what they ought even when their possessions are modest. Anaxagoras also seems to have assumed the happy person to be neither rich nor powerful, since he said that he would not be surprised if the happy person appeared an absurd sort of person to the masses;[81] for since they perceive only externals, it is by these that they judge. The beliefs of the wise, then, seem to harmonize with our arguments.

But while such things do carry some conviction, the truth in practical issues is judged from the facts of our life, these being what really matter. We must therefore examine what has been said in the light of the facts of our life, and if it agrees with the facts, then we should accept it, while if it conflicts, we must assume it to be no more than theory.

The person whose activity is in accordance with intellect and who cultivates it seems to be in the best condition and dearest to the gods. For if the gods feel any concern for human affairs, as they seem to, it would be reasonable for them to find enjoyment in what is best and most closely related to them – namely, intellect – and to reward those who like and honour this most, on the assumption that these people care for what is loved by the gods, and act rightly and nobly. And it is quite clear that all of these qualities belong most of all to the wise person; he, therefore, is dearest to the gods. And it is likely that this same person is also the happiest; so in this way too the wise person will be more happy than anyone else.

Chapter 9

We have now said enough in outline about the above questions and the virtues, and about friendship and pleasure as well, so should we think that our project has been achieved? Or is it not true that, as we say, in practical studies the end consists not in contemplating and knowing 1179b about each point, but rather in acting upon them? So knowing about virtue is not enough, but we must also try to attain and exercise it, or become good by any other available route.

If arguments were sufficient by themselves to make people good, then they would have won many great rewards, and justly so, as Theognis says,[82] – in other words, it would have been right to award them. But as

---

[81] Anaxagoras 59 A 30 DK.   [82] Theognis, 432–4.

things are, though they appear to have the power to influence and encourage those young people who possess generosity of spirit, and perhaps to make susceptible to virtue a character that is well bred and truly loves what is noble, they seem unable to influence the masses in the direction of what is noble and good. For the masses naturally obey fear, not shame, and abstain from shameful acts because of the punishments associated with them, not because they are disgraceful. For, living by their feelings as they do, they pursue their own personal pleasures and the means to them, and avoid the opposed pains; and they do not have even an idea of what is noble and truly pleasant, since they have never tasted it. What argument, then, could reform people like this? For displacing by argument what has been long entrenched in people's characters is difficult if not impossible. And presumably we should be content if, when we have everything that seems required for becoming good, we attain some share of virtue.

Some think we become good by nature, some by habit, and others by teaching. Nature's contribution is clearly not in our power, but it can be found in those who are truly fortunate as the result of some divine dispensation. Argument and teaching, presumably, are not powerful in every case, but the soul of the student must be prepared beforehand in its habits, with a view to its enjoying and hating in a noble way, like soil that is to nourish seed. For if someone were to live by his feelings he would not listen to an argument to dissuade him, nor could he even understand it. How can we persuade a person in a state like this to change his ways? And, in general, feelings seem to yield not to argument but to force. There must, therefore, somehow be a pre-existing character with some affinity for virtue through its fondness for what is noble and dislike of what is disgraceful.

But if one has not been reared under the right laws it is difficult to obtain from one's earliest years the correct upbringing for virtue, because the masses, especially the young, do not find it pleasant to live temperately and with endurance. For this reason, their upbringing and pursuits should be regulated by laws, because they will not find them 1180a painful once they have become accustomed to them.

Perhaps it is not enough, however, that when they are young they get the right upbringing and care; rather, because they must continue to practise and develop their habits when they are grown up, we shall need laws for this as well, and generally for the whole of life. For the masses heed necessity rather than argument, punishments rather than what is noble.

This, some people think, is why legislators ought to urge people to virtue and encourage them to act for the sake of what is noble – on the assumption that those who have been trained well in their habits will respond – but ought also to impose punishments and penalties on those who disobey or whose nature is more deficient, and completely banish the incorrigible. For, they think, the good person, since he lives with a view to what is noble, will listen to reason, while the bad person, since he desires pleasure, is chastened by pain, like a beast of burden; this is also why they say the pains inflicted should be those most opposed to the pleasures they like.

As we have said, then, the person who is to be good must be nobly brought up and habituated, and then spend his life engaged in good pursuits and do nothing bad whether involuntarily or voluntarily. And this would happen when people lived in accordance with a kind of intellect and a correct system with power over them.

Now the command of a father has no strength or compulsive power, nor in general does that of a single person, unless he is a king or something like that; but law does have compulsive power, and it is reason proceeding from a kind of practical wisdom and from intellect. And people hate a human being who stands in opposition to their impulses, even if he is right to do so; but there is no oppressiveness in the law's prescribing what is good.

But it is in the city of Sparta alone, or almost alone, that the legislator seems to have been careful about people's upbringing and pursuits. In most cities, such matters have been neglected, and each person lives as he wishes, 'laying down the law for children and wife', like a Cyclops.[83] The best thing, then, is for there to be correct public concern with such things. But if they are neglected in the public sphere, it would seem appropriate for each person to help his own children and friends on the way to virtue, and for them to be able to do this, or at least rationally choose to do so. From what we have said, however, it would seem that he will be better able to do this if he has the chance of legislating, because care at the public level is evidently demonstrated through laws, and good care through good laws. And whether they are written or 1180b

---

[83] Homer, *Odyssey* ix.114f.

unwritten, whether they are to educate one or many, seems not to matter, any more than it matters in the case of music, gymnastics and other pursuits. For just as in cities laws and people's characters are powerful, so in households are the words and character of fathers, all the more because of the relation of kinship and the benefits he confers; for from the start the children are naturally fond of him and inclined to obey.

Again, education on an individual basis is superior to education in common, as in the case of medical care. For though in general rest and abstinence from food are beneficial for a person in a fever, presumably they may not be for a particular person; and a boxer, presumably, will not prescribe the same style of fighting for all his pupils. It would seem, then, that particular cases are treated with greater subtlety if there is attention to individuals, since each person is more likely to obtain what suits him.

But the best at providing individual attention will be the doctor, the gymnastic instructor or anyone else who has the universal knowledge of what is good for everyone or for specific people, since the sciences are said to be, and indeed are, concerned with what is common. Nevertheless, there is perhaps nothing to prevent someone's taking care of an individual person well, even lacking any scientific knowledge, if he has considered precisely, in the light of experience, what happens in each case, just as some people seem to be their own best doctors, though incapable of helping anyone else. None the less, presumably it does seem that if a person does wish to become practised in a skill or in something theoretical, he must go to the universal, and come to know it as well as he can; for, as we have said, it is with this that the sciences are concerned.

Then perhaps as well a person who wishes to improve people, whether many or few, through his concern for them should try to develop a capacity for legislating, if it is through laws that we will become good. For producing a noble disposition in just anyone, whoever is put before one, is not a task that just anyone can perform; if it is anyone's task, it is that of the person who knows, just as in the case of medicine and the other sciences that require some kind of care and practical wisdom.

Should we not move on, then, to consider where or how one might acquire a capacity for legislation? Is it, as in other cases, from politicians? For we did think that it was part of political science. Or is there not an apparent difference between political science and the other sciences and capacities? For in the others, we find the same people – doctors and painters for example – both imparting their capacities to others, and exercising them too. The sophists, however, profess to teach politics, though none of them practises it; that is done by the politicians, 1181a and they seem to act with some kind of capacity and experience rather than with thought. For we do not find them writing or speaking about such matters, though it would presumably be nobler than speaking in legal cases or the assembly; nor do we find that they have made their sons or any other of their friends into politicians. And yet one would have expected them to do so if they were able, since there is nothing better than such a capacity that they could have bequeathed to their cities, or could rationally choose to have for themselves, or therefore for those dearest to them. Nevertheless, experience has much to contribute, for otherwise people would not have become politicians through familiarity with politics. So it seems that those who seek to know about political science also need experience.

But those of the sophists who profess to teach appear very far from actually doing so, being completely ignorant about what kind of thing it is and what its sphere of concern is. Otherwise, they would not have classed it with rhetoric or even as inferior to it, nor would they have thought it easy to legislate by collecting those laws of which people think well. For they think it is possible to pick out the best laws, as if the very act of picking out did not call for judgement and as if correct judgement were not the most important factor, as in music. For it is people experienced in any area who judge its products correctly, and understand by what means and how they are accomplished, and what is in harmony with what; the inexperienced must be content if it does not escape them whether the product has been well or badly made, as in painting. Laws seem to be the products of political science; how, there- 1181b fore, could one develop a capacity for legislation, or judge which are best, from laws alone? For neither do doctors appear to acquire their skill from books.

And yet doctors try to describe not only the treatments, but also how particular groups could be cured and ought to be treated, distinguishing the various states. This seems beneficial to those with experience, but useless to the ignorant. So presumably collections of laws and political systems might be very useful to people who can study them and judge which are noble, or the contrary, and which suit particular circumstances. But those who go through them without being in this state will not be able to judge well, unless by instinct, though they may perhaps become more discriminating in such matters.

Since, then, our predecessors have left the question of legislation unexamined, it is presumably better that we study it, and the question of political systems in general, so that our philosophy of humanity might be as complete as possible. First, then, if any part of what has been said by those before us is plausible, let us try to go through it. Then, in the light of the political systems we have collected, let us try to consider what sorts of things preserve and destroy cities and each type of political system, and what causes some cities to be well run, and others badly run. For when these issues have been considered, we shall perhaps be more likely to see which political system is best, how each must be arranged, and what laws and habits it should employ. Let us, then, discuss these matters from the beginning.

Glossary

Many of the English words used in this translation, as in any translation of Aristotle, have connotations not found in the Greek, and fail to bring out aspects of the Greek term they translate. Here I list some of these Greek terms, along with the English translation I have used. Note that the alternative translations suit some contexts better than others.

archē first principle. Alternative translations: 'source'; 'beginning'; 'moving principle'; 'origin'; 'cause'. Used in a wide range of technical and non-technical senses (see index, s.v.). Note that I have made use of the alternative translations in non-technical cases.

aretē virtue. Alternative translation: 'excellence'. Covers non-moral as well as moral characteristics, as in, e.g., 'This book has many virtues.' Aristotle usually has in mind either moral excellences of character or intellectual excellences when using the term. It is related to the notion of 'characteristic activity' (*ergon*): the virtue of something consists in its capacity to perform well its characteristic activity (the virtue of an eye, for example, is to see well). Analogously, a vice (*kakia*) may be seen as a defect or flaw.

boulēsis wish. Alternative translation: 'rational desire'. One of the forms of desire (*orexis*). It is based on a rational belief in some good worth attaining by action.

dei one should *or* it is right *or* one ought. Alternative translations: 'one must'; 'one has a duty'. This term also is not purely moral, but it does cover many cases of what we would call moral duty. In answer to the question, 'What is our duty?', Aristotle would answer, 'To do and feel the right things, at the right times, and so on, i.e., to be virtuous.' The same word is also translated 'it is necessary' or 'one needs'.

energeia activity. Alternative translation: 'actualization'. The realization or exercise of a 'capacity' (*dunamis*), and in particular of a 'state' (*hexis*). It is also used in opposition to 'process' (*kinēsis*) and 'coming-to-be' (*genesis*). Note that 'characteristic activity' translates the Greek *ergon*.

epistemē knowledge *or* science *or* scientific knowledge. Note that Aristotle uses the same word to cover all three of these notions. Knowledge is opposed to belief (*doxa*). The sciences include the skills (*technai*), while scientific knowledge is opposed to skill (*technē*). Note that the word 'science' is not to be taken in the modern sense in which it covers physics, chemistry, etc., as opposed to history, English literature, etc.

epithumia appetite. Alternative translation: 'bodily desire'. Another form of desire, based on a non-rational awareness of an available pleasure.

eudaimonia happiness. Alternative translations: 'flourishing'; 'well-being'. A broad term, roughly equivalent to 'whatever makes a human life good for the person living it'. Happiness must not be understood to be a contented state of mind, as in, 'I feel happy today.' The Greek *eu* means 'well', and *daimōn* 'fortune', which accounts partly for Aristotle's occasional readiness to use the word 'blessedness' (*makariotēs*) instead of 'happiness' and for the discussion of the relation between happiness and fortune at the end of book I.

hekousios, hekōn voluntary. Alternative translations: 'intentional'; 'willing'. Note that to be voluntary, an act need only meet the conditions for voluntariness in III.1. It may, as in the case of a captain's throwing his cargo overboard, be done 'unwillingly'. Further, children and animals may perform voluntary actions.

ison equal *or* fair. The same Greek word can be translated in either way. This is especially important to remember at the beginning of book V.

kalos noble. Alternative translations: 'fine'; 'beautiful'; 'good'. Opposed to 'shameful' or 'disgraceful' (*aischros*). An aesthetic notion, used in the *Ethics* in particular to refer to the good aimed at by the virtuous person.

logos reason. Alternative translations: 'reasoning'; 'rationality'; 'rational principle'. Often used to refer to the capacity for rational thought. 'Correct reason' (*orthos logos*) may refer either to that capacity as exercised correctly ('correct reasoning'), or to the result of its correct exercise ('correct rational principle'). *Logos* is a common word, its other meanings including 'argument', 'account', 'word', 'discussion', and 'ratio'.

lupēros painful. Alternative translation: 'distressing'. Covers all mental as well as bodily suffering and distress. Opposed to 'pleasant' (*hēdus*).

pathos feeling *or* way of being affected. Alternative translation: 'passion'. Opposed to 'actions' (*praxeis*), connotes passivity as against activity, experiencing rather than doing.

philia friendship. Alternative translation: 'relationship'; 'personal relationship'. The verb *philein* is translated as 'to love'. A broader notion than friendship as we understand it, *philia* includes not only familial relations of non-humans as well as humans, but business partnerships and the natural kinship felt by one human being with another.

praxis action. Alternative translations: 'doing'; 'conduct'. Used to cover action in general, rational action, or action which is an end in itself (as opposed to 'production' (*poiēsis*)).

prohairesis rational choice. Alternative translation: 'choice'; 'intention'. A choice of some particular action, resulting from a wish and deliberation (possibly carried out beforehand).

psuchē soul. Alternative translation: 'life force'; 'living function'. Not to be understood as (solely) any kind of 'spirit': plants and animals have souls, in that they are alive through performing successfully certain characteristic activities, such as taking in nutrition. See Aristotle's *On the Soul* (*De Anima*).

teleios complete. Alternative translations: 'final'; 'perfect'. Like many of Aristotle's terms, this is often used with a technical philosophical sense in connection with ends or goals: the more an end is pursued for its own sake and not for the sake of other ends, the more complete it is.

thumos spirit. Alternative translation: 'anger'; 'emotion'. A further form of non-rational desire, for some apparent good.

to kalon the noble *or* what is noble. Alternative translation: 'nobility'. Note that these phrases translate the same Greek phrase (which may also mean 'a noble thing', or 'the noble thing'). The same goes for 'the just' and 'what is just', 'the good' and 'what is good', 'the lawful' and 'what is lawful', etc., except of course where 'the F' refers to those people with the property F.

Index

Cambridge texts in the history of philosophy

Titles published in the series thus far

Arnauld and Nicole *Logic or the Art of Thinking* (edited by Jill Vance Buroker)

Aristotle *Nicomachean Ethics* (edited by Roger Crisp)

Bacon *The New Organon* (edited by Lisa Jardine and Michael Silverthorne)

Boyle *A Free Enquiry into the Vulgarly Received Notion of Nature* (edited by Edward B. Davis and Michael Hunter)

Bruno *Cause, Principle and Unity* and *Essays on Magic* (edited by Richard Blackwell and Robert de Lucca with an introduction by Alfonso Ingegno)

Clarke *A Demonstration of the Being and Attributes of God and Other Writings* (edited by Ezio Vailati)

Conway *The Principles of the Most Ancient and Modern Philosophy* (edited by Allison P. Coudert and Taylor Corse)

Cudworth *A Treatise Concerning Eternal and Immutable Morality* with *A Treatise of Freewill* (edited by Sarah Hutton)

Descartes *Meditations on First Philosophy*, with selections from the *Objections and Replies* (edited by John Cottingham)

Descartes *The World and Other Writings* (edited by Stephen Gaukroger)

Hobbes and Bramhall on Liberty and Necessity (edited by Vere Chappell)

Humbolt *On Language* (edited by Michael Losonsky, translated by Peter Heath)

Kant *Critique of Practical Reason* (edited by Mary Gregor with an introduction by Andrews Reath)

Kant *Groundwork of the Metaphysics of Morals* (edited by Mary Gregor with an introduction by Christine M. Korsgaard)

Kant *The Metaphysics of Morals* (edited by Mary Gregor with an introduction by Roger Sullivan)

Kant *Prolegomena to any Further Metaphysics* (edited by Gary Hatfield)

Kant *Religion within the Boundaries of Mere Reason and Other Writings* (edited by Allen Wood and George di Giovanni with an introduction by Robert Merrihew Adams)

La Mettrie *Machine Man and Other Writings* (edited by Ann Thomson)

Leibniz *New Essays on Human Understanding* (edited by Peter Remnant and Jonathan Bennett)

Malebranche *Dialogues on Metaphysics and on Religion* (edited by Nicholas Jolley and David Scott)